How Will We Live Tomorrow?

*48 States * 2 Wheels * 1000s of Possibilities*

Paul E. Fallon

Fallon Associates * Cambridge, MA

Published in the United States by Fallon Associates
Cambridge, MA

Library of Congress Cataloging-in-Publication Data
Name: Fallon, Paul E., author.
Title: How Will We Live Tomorrow?
Description: First edition | Cambridge, MA: Fallon Associates
Identifiers:
Library of Congress: 2017917862 (hardcover)
ISBN 978-0-9996002-0-7 (hardcover)

Book Design: Paul E. Fallon
Logo Design: Chris Marston, Stonefish Graphics

5 4 3 2 1   21 20 19 18 17

First edition

*For every person
who opens his door to a stranger
and welcomes him in*

Acknowledgments

Thanks to Paul Beaulieu, my longtime housemate and friend, who keeps the home front steady while I wander.

Thanks to Chris Marston of Stonefish Graphics for his excellent maps and logo.

Thanks to Lindy Ruddiman for making iPhone photos pop into coffee table book quality.

Thanks to Mary Bagg, my valued editor, equal parts pleasant and precise.

Special thanks to thousands of people who offered their thoughts on tomorrow. Hundreds shared their lives and ideas during conversation, scores more who shared their home, their bread, and their vision of what we will become. Although I changed a few names as requested, I remain truthful to your voices, your stories. They are the energy that fueled every mile.

PART ONE
ISSUES

I wish there was a way
to get to less fossil fuel
and use more wind.
But I like my air conditioning.
I've lived the old way,
but I don't want to go back to that.

Vicky Mortenson, horsewoman, La Porte, CO

7

You are journeying into what most of us would consider the known and finding the unknown.
—Lieutenant Dave Wohlgemuth, police officer, Racine, WI

Wellington, OH—May 30, 2015, 11:30 a.m.

My stomach grumbles as I pedal beneath the broad shade trees that line East Herrick Avenue approaching Wellington, Ohio. Maybe there's a German deli in this town, with pretzel-bread sandwiches. Black Forest ham with spicy mustard on a heavy roll with a caramel sheen sounds perfect right about now. The thought alone keeps my legs pumping after 40 morning miles.

Pfffft. My rear wheel drags. My bike, a Surly Long Haul Trucker, sways to the right. Air whistles out of the tire, masking the murmur of the overhead leaves. A curse forms on my lips; it dissipates into a sigh. I've got nothing to complain about. My first flat, 1,400 miles out, on a pleasant morning just outside a town: this is a minor irritation. I swing off my saddle. I trace my fingers over the rubber. No obvious penetrations, though the leak is too quick to keep riding. I could flip Surly over and repair the flat under a tree. But clouds are gathering and it's never a good idea to repair a bike on an empty stomach. I walk Surly into town.

First place I come upon is a Subway. As a rule, I don't eat fast food. Not for noble reasons: a guy pedaling 50-plus miles a day can eat whatever he wants. I avoid fast food because it could easily become a habit that keeps me from exploring local joints. But today, on foot, with nothing else in sight, I make an exception. Besides, Subway's a notch above most food; there are a few actual vegetables among the processed meat and chips.

Subways are everywhere. Unlike franchises whose signature buildings rise out of asphalt, a Subway can occupy a vacant storefront or nest in the corner of a gas station. In many towns, the former café is now a Subway. That makes me sad. A foot-long Sweet Onion Chicken Teriyaki assembled by a distracted high school student weighing chicken strips and laying them across exactly four precut triangles of shiny cheese can blunt my hunger. But it doesn't satisfy same as an actual chicken breast on a toasted bun with mozzarella melting over its contours, all delivered by a gum-clacking waitress whose order pad is holstered to her hip. Or a pretzel-bread sandwich.

Still, a hungry man with a flat tire on the edge of an unknown town is glad to see that Subway sign. I prop Surly outside, tote my panniers to a booth, order a foot-long and say yes to all the toppings the counter girl offers.

As Belinda hands me my tray and receipt, I tell her of my journey and ask, "How will we live tomorrow?"

"Gosh, I have no idea," she giggles.

I jot her words in my spiral pad. This is what I do: ride my bike; ask people how will we live tomorrow; and record every response without regard to its gravity. Been doing it for almost a month now. It doesn't feel like vacation anymore, though it's not exactly a job.

A thunderstorm rolls through, followed by another. When the sun comes out I upside my bike and repair the flat. The manager, Mike, comes out and offers me cookies. "They're broken, I can't sell them." People are always giving me things.

I thank Mike and ask him, "How will we live tomorrow?"

"Live life to the fullest." He replies with an immediacy that indicates he's given the question some thought.

Mike disappears to the back. I pack up my stuff. As I stack my tray, Mike returns. "I want to explain my answer." I pause, look him straight, and pay attention. I like when my question percolates.

The manager steps close. The crease in his permanent-press sleeve is sharp. Worry lines cut across his forehead. "My son died five years ago; he was 25. He had cancer. After he was diagnosed his motto became 'Live life to the fullest.' And he did. He moved to Chicago, went to cooking school, and even ran a marathon. He fought cancer for three and a half years. When he died, I adopted his motto as my own."

Mike's face softens when I offer condolences for his son. I thank him a second time, with greater appreciation.

Americans favor the pleasant and predictable over the uncharted and unique. That's why Subways have replaced cafés all over our country. Mike's earnest expression and personal revelation are discordant with the eatery's garish colors and over-bright lights; this is not an interior conducive to confession. I wonder what prompts this solid citizen with his narrow tie and plastic nametag to share confidences with a broken-down cyclist.

Mike Sartor understands that I respect his story, and the man wants a chance to share his pain. His heavy yet undefeated countenance, his confidences, bestow value on my endeavor. Value that I vaguely intuited during months of planning and my first weeks of riding, but never fully grasped until I hear Mike's story. My cycling, my question, my journey—this is not just the frivolous undertaking of an over-privileged man with time on his hands. An interested stranger with sympathetic ears has something to offer others, simply by being present, asking, and listening.

When I turned 60 I was doing okay, making a decent living and doing more and more commissions.
But I was not doing what I wanted.
By the time you're 60, you want to feel like you've figured life out.
And of course I haven't.
　　　　—Mark Davis, artist, Boston, MA

Cambridge, MA—March 14, 2015, 3:00 p.m.

Backpedal ten weeks. I'm a 60-year-old father of two; my children, Abby and Andy, are in their 20s, out of college, well launched. They have little need of me. Their mother and I divorced 20 years ago; I've been single ever since.

I'm an architect, though I always modify that descriptor by adding, "I design hospitals." Some people are impressed that I devoted effort to such a complex building type. Others snort, "I didn't know architects designed hospitals; they are such a maze."

A serendipitous email prompted me to volunteer to design a clinic in Haiti. I visited the Magic Island and fell under its scorching charm in the summer of 2009. Five months later, the earthquake hit. As an architect with personal connections to the tragedy, I needed to step up beyond writing a check. I offered to design an orphanage, then a school, in Grand Goave, 10 miles from the earthquake's epicenter. I commuted back and forth, Cambridge to Haiti, every few months. Assisted with cleanup, assessed sites, drew up plans.

During that same period I made my first bicycle tour: Denver to Boston—3,000 miles in seven weeks—a 70-mile-per-day test of crankshaft and speed. The most fun I ever had, though I never quite figured out how to communicate the exhilaration of hard saddle days and cheap motel nights. People nodded wary heads against my gushing babble; they dropped glazed eyes. By the time I returned home and wheeled my trusty Surly into the basement on Labor Day weekend, my calendar listed a long string of workdays ahead. But my mind penciled in more cycle touring.

Haiti intervened. Our projects would never succeed without ongoing onsite supervision, so I left my job and lived in Grand Goave part-time. The satisfaction of fundamental construction eclipsed the abstract rewards of complex hospital design. When my Haiti projects were finished, so too was my interest in American-style healthcare. I retired. I wrote a memoir of Haiti, a fine book that few bought and even fewer read.

I have enough money; I don't live large. But I wasn't inclined to become a philanthropic disaster chaser. Haiti made me wary of philanthropy, the hierarchy rooted in "I have" and "you need." The prevailing attitudes that people with money are superior—in every way—to people without. The assumption that Haitians will be grateful for what we choose to give, but we have nothing to gain from them.

The Magic Island made me thirsty to explore my own country with a fresh perspective. I love the United States so much and understand it so little.

Why does so much affluence yield so little satisfaction?

I decide to return to my bicycle, to traverse a broader canvas. I will ride for a year, and visit each of the 48 contiguous states. I have no interest in being a tourist. I want to witness our land and engage our people with eyes so wide open they dilate expectations.

Union, ME—May 9, 2015, 7:00 a.m.

On the morning of the fourth day, I wake to sun spotlighting my face. I'm in a sleeping bag on a sofa in the center of a yurt in the middle of the woods in a remote village in Maine. Voices circle me, the reverberation of last night's discussion: 13 back-to-the-landers considering tomorrow.

The voices recede. The air is cold, the sunlight pleasant. My legs ache. I stretch my calves and flex my feet. Surly may be slow moving, but she's already taken me far; three states in three days, thanks to New England's tiny proportions.

Yesterday, however, I overdid it. Morning began with a conversation at SMRT Architects about how the maker movement will shape tomorrow. Fueled by two cups of coffee and three potato donuts from Portland's renowned Holy Donut, I pedaled to Yarmouth. After a conversation with DeLorme engineers about advances in GPS tracking that guide backwoodsmen where Google Maps fear to tread, I stood in humble awe at the base of the world's largest globe rotating within their three-story lobby. I saddled on, battled headwinds all afternoon, and by dusk I was lost on a confusion of narrow roads. Perhaps, I should have adopted DeLorme's navigation system. I arrived in Union in the dark. The potluckers were already deep into second helpings of vegan casserole.

Rose Swan and Jeremy Clough are friends of a friend who invited me to stay with them. Rose is a family constellation therapist. I don't really know what that is, but Rose is sweet and earnest and strikingly beautiful: the translucent physical beauty that radiates from a peaceful soul.

Though I'd never been inside a yurt, its appeal was clear the moment I stepped from the raw wind into the warm circle. No corners to draw shadow; a simpler, truer life beneath a cone. But even a yurt sparks friction. The kitchen counter, the desk—right-angled, hard-edged artifacts of a rectilinear world—compromise the harmony implied by a round dwelling on a spherical planet.

We talked of human energy zones, electronic-induced brain reformation, finite resources, Facebook, Little Debbie snack cakes, Waldorf education, ancient Greeks, the schism between people and the land, La Grange suppers, screening calls to voicemail, conscious living. I sat among the circle, scribbling every idea that bounced off the perimeter and landed in our center. We decried dystopian chaos and mapped utopian visions. We examined subjects I anticipated: technology, environment, inequality, education, religion. Yet one aspect of tomorrow I had not considered bubbled up time and again: the further we projected into the future, the deeper we referenced our past.

Rose's words matched her dazzling beauty. "People have forgotten where we have been. History helps us understand our place in the fabric of existence. If we have a context, today, of where we are from, we will be prepared for tomorrow. We shape tomorrow by standing in truth today. Myths and stories give us context. They root our place in this world."

Cambridge, MA—April 22, 2015, 7:00 p.m.

Americans are not a rooted people. We are an uprooted people. Almost all of us came from somewhere else. The roots we share are tangled up by ideas rather than soil. My exploration of our national psyche must be more than a physical tour; it must address the underlying ideas, the ideals that bind us. I want to engage with my fellow citizens. So I decide to ask a question.

Asking the same question of everyone I meet for a year resonates well with me, a man of habit who thrives on structure. But what shall I ask?

I balance my penchant for order with lateral thinking. Long ago I learned that once I identify a problem or condition, not to sit at my desk and press for an answer. Take a yoga class, garden, paint a room, ride my bike, exert my body, and in due time, my mind will reveal solutions.

My first clue to what question I want to ask rises out of self-assessment. I am a healthy middle-aged man who no longer needs to work. I have no direct obligations and too much house. A man of privilege. When my grandfather was my age, he had terminal cancer and died soon thereafter. When my father was my age, he still had 10 years of work ahead but he died soon thereafter. Although I might perish tomorrow, there's a good chance I will remain fully capable for 10, 20, even 30 more years. I represent an emerging demographic: graduated from the workforce yet still healthy. How will I spend my time? I consider focusing on other middle-aged people, exploring how we transition from work and children to living post nuclear family, post obligation.

I brainstorm this idea among friends, each of whom projects his personal fantasy on my venture. "Explore regional food." "Visit every major-league stadium." "Pedal the highest road in every state." My friends' ideas reveal more about their true interests than my own, but they underscore the scope of my undertaking. Asking middle-aged people blessed with time and resources how they live taps a very small portion of our nation. Open the question up; make it broad; make it a question that can be asked of anyone. Ask a question as big as the adventure.

"How will we live tomorrow?" It takes months to pare my query to five simple words. Purposefully open-ended, trite perhaps, or maybe profound.

How is a logistical word. Our country's why and what, our reasons for being a nation, are embedded in the Constitution, our laws, and our economic and social patterns. Our system is up and running. We can comply, legislate, protest, or riot against the system. But until we revolt, we cannot revisit our fundamentals. We tweak our why and what by how we act.

Will is a declarative word. If I ask people, "How should we live tomorrow?" I let everyone off the hook. We all know we should live in peace and harmony. But in a culture where intentions often fall short of deeds, peace and harmony are in rather short supply.

We is the key word. It's not I; it's not you; it's not they. We is the only pronoun that fuses the individual and the collective. It acknowledges that the only viable future on a planet with seven billion people must consider the needs of many as well as singular. It's a word a lot of Americans gag on, as history and geography have blessed us with more opportunities for individual expression than any other country on earth. But it's a word we must embrace as our population continues to grow, in number and kind, within fixed geographic limits.

Live is my optimistic word. I like to think we are going to live, as individuals, as a nation, as a species, for a long, long time. I can't argue with those who think our demise is imminent; there's plenty of evidence for that. But I'm not interested in how we will die. Dystopian sci-fi movies have cornered the market on speculating our end.

Tomorrow is the word that invites interpretation. When is tomorrow? It is 24 hours away; it is the distant future. This is the word that makes my question both practical and ephemeral. It invites specific answers as well as fantastic speculation. It acknowledges the facts of today and understands that we move forward from our present reality.

No one knows how we will live tomorrow; humans cannot determine the future. But neither are we hapless victims of it. We have the capacity to create a vision of tomorrow, and if we work toward that vision, we can be agents of our destiny.

That's easy. I live tomorrow for my twin two-year-olds.
Since they've been born I've been so much better.
I quit smoking. I don't drink as much.
I am doing the right thing for them.
—Audie, McDonald's employee, Corning, NY

Chippewa, PA—May 28, 2015, 1:00 p.m.

I don't think of myself as homeless. Homeless implies no other options. I live on the road by choice and can credit-card a motel on those rare nights a local host doesn't invite me into her home. I do, however, share one thing in common with people who lack a designated place. My body needs to occupy space 24/7, and oftentimes, I just need a place to park it.

My travel objective, 50 to 60 miles a day, equals five to six hours in the saddle. I can't show up at my host's house at two in the afternoon; people have lives to lead. So, I develop the habit of a mid-day break, time to rest my legs and log the musings in my head. Within a few weeks, I identify preferred places to loiter. I either go to America's Living Room, a public library; or America's Family Room, McDonald's. Both welcome passing strangers, offer free Wi-Fi, and allow me to linger, as long as I don't fall asleep. Libraries demand nothing but a quiet demeanor. McDonald's expects me to purchase something: a 59-cent ice cream, a cup of coffee, or a diet coke. Refills are free.

McDonald's is the Wikipedia of fast food: everyone goes there and no one admits it. I prefer it to Starbucks, where patrons are glued to their devices. People at McDonald's engage; they catch my eye and bend my ear. Lawyers meet clients, poets debate meter, farmers bemoan rainfall. Businessmen, single moms, senior citizens, teenage girls, backpackers, software consultants, bikers, ministers, homeless men; we are all at McDonald's.

A man and his wife slide into the booth next to mine. He removes two hamburgers and two bags of fries from their brown sack, unwraps his wife's sandwich, smooths the paper on the table, and fans her fries around the bun. He pokes a straw through the lid of her drink. Does the same for himself. Bows his head a moment, then takes a bite. Only then does his wife raise food to her lips.

"Hey, how are you?" The man calls to me over his wife's shoulder. I smile in return. "Come, have lunch with us. I like your shirt." I carry my drink to their table. "Let me buy you something." I refuse. (True confession: I love many things about McDonald's, but I don't actually eat their food.) "Names Ed, Ed Morton. This is my wife Crystal." Crystal shifts over. I sit next to her.

Ed's a talker; 40 years as a stock clerk for US Air in Pittsburgh fills a man with stories. Foul weather, lost luggage. Crystal is mute. She nibbles on her hamburger. Ed talks with his mouth full.

When they finish their food, Ed collects the leftover paper and announces it's time to go. We stand and shake hands. He grabs me with two palms and holds tight; gestures for Crystal to take my other hand. "Let us pray." He announces, above the din of the noon rush. "Lord, bless this pilgrim on his journey. Keep him safe under Your watch. Let him find the light he seeks in You, O Lord. Amen."

Ed drops my hand and pushes a pamphlet into my to my chest, *The Seven Words of the Cross.* "God Bless you." He nods to me, to Crystal, and they leave.

I look about the restaurant. Others look my way, acknowledging that they witnessed our prayer circle. There's no privacy at McDonald's. I take my seat, bewildered but thankful.

I am a little yellow speck on the face of this broad continent, a slow moving morsel in the shadow of speedy behemoths; grateful for all blessings.

If I could pull it off, I'd like to go to the moon. That's my thing—we need to DO more.
—Sister Gordon, retired science teacher, Saint Joseph Provincial House, Latham, NY

Cambridge, MA—April 9, 2015, 3:00 p.m.

There are thousands of paths that string together 48 states. How do I decide which to follow? I start with pushpins and ribbon and a Sierra Club map of the United States.

White is for families and friends: 4 siblings and 12 nieces and nephews spread over 8 states. High school and college friends flung even farther afield. How did Steve wind up in Ashland, Oregon, and Leanne in Slaton, Texas?

Clear pins reflect my quirky idea of tourist attractions. Heavy on architecture: Calatrava's museum addition in Milwaukee; the Getty in LA; Crystal Bridges in Arkansas. I also want to visit buildings from my own career: hospitals in Augusta, Maine; Lebanon, New Hampshire; and Kalamazoo, Michigan. How is my very first project, housing for people with cerebral palsy in Norman, Oklahoma, holding up after 35 years?

I attach pins to places that reflect our nation's pulse, past and present: utopian communities, immigrant strongholds, industrial might, technological innovation. I am keen to visit Silicon Valley whiz kids and Santa Fe artists but even more interested in places where the American dream strikes a dissonant chord.

I want to go to Ferguson, Missouri.

I puncture the map in upwards of a hundred places, and then weave blue ribbon between them. A yearlong flow unspools, respectful of weather: north in summer; south when it's cold. I stand back to appreciate the whole. There are odd gaps. Not a single national park; few pins in the South. I don't know much about that part of the country, yet.

The map gives shape to my pilgrimage, but not constraints. Pushpins and ribbon are malleable. It's so easy to turn a bicycle in a new direction when opportunity beckons.

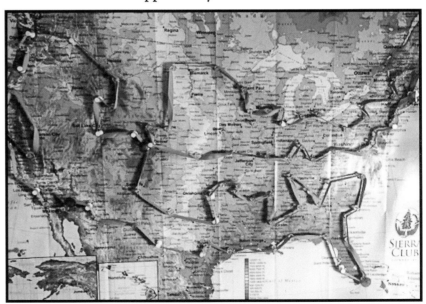

19

Dearborn is a choice. You come to Dearborn to work hard and have the opportunity to move out. Everybody is stepping up; nobody is stepping down. The waves of migration last a long time, a generation maybe two, but they are not permanent.
    —Bob Basse, Dearborn native, Denver, CO

Dearborn, MI—June 1, 2015, 5:00 p.m.

Pedaling along Diversey Avenue near Middlepointe Street on a late June afternoon is like riding through the opening credits of a John Hughes movie: solid brick houses with trim lawns and mature trees, mothers sitting on front porches, children playing ball in the yard, toddlers riding tricycles along wide sidewalks: a bucolic vision of security and prosperity. Except, unlike a John Hughes movie, the women wear hijab; the children have dark skin.

History books herald Dearborn as the birthplace of modern manufacturing: Henry Ford perfected assembly-line production here. But Dearborn's manufacturing heart is not what attracted me to this place. I'm interested in the city's more recent moniker: Muslim Capital of America.

"Good Afternoon. I am Housalla Elmoussa. Call me Bob."

Bob straddles a bike one of his children abandoned on the lawn. He came to Dearborn from Lebanon in 1989, lived with his older brother, an earlier émigré, and worked as a mechanic in a Lebanese-owned auto shop. In 2000 Bob purchased his own house on the same street. Later, he bought an investment property. Now, Bob's a nurse at the children's hospital; his wife teaches second grade, currently on leave to care for their newborn child.

The immigrant saga in the United States is predictable. Foreigners arrive. They are spurned. They do menial work. They gain a foothold. Relatives and friends follow. Their population swells. The establishment - immigrants of an earlier time - moves up and out. More recent immigrants rise through the ranks. They become the establishment. Newer immigrants arrive, from even less desirable corners of the earth. They take menial jobs, and nip at the heels one rung up the ladder.

The trajectory of assimilation is always the same, what varies is time. If you speak English and have white skin, it may only take a few years. Immigrants with economic gumption might move up in a generation; witness the Koreans in Fullerton, California, and Indians in Fremont. The darker your skin is, or the murkier your motives seem, the longer it takes to get your chunk of the American Dream. Too many African Americans are still on the fringe.

Early assembly lines in Dearborn were full of German workers, replaced by Poles. Lebanese immigrants first arrived in the 1950s. Over two generations they cemented their place in this city, creating Arab shopping districts, building mosques. Every diner in Dearborn serves hummus.

What's fascinating to this architect, and fuels my John Hughes analogy, is how Muslims have enlivened the city's east side, a tight fabric of one- and two-family homes with small apartment buildings anchoring corners. While most Americans since World War II turn our homes inward, shifting living spaces to the back and thrusting blank garage doors to the street, Dearborn's Lebanese add spacious front porches to their homes. People sit together and talk, call out to neighbors, invite them to join.

"ISIS has nothing to do with Islam, any more than the Ku Klux Klan has to do with Christianity." Bob doesn't mention sharia law or jihad; neither do any other Arab Americans I meet. Bob's primary concerns, like most of us, reveal a narrower focus. "An Iraqi bought the house next to me. He doesn't keep his place nice. He had a broken window and stuck a towel in it; he doesn't cut his grass. He doesn't realize that it's important to keep the place up. I'm thinking of moving out of Dearborn. My insurance is so high because of where I live. My brother in Livonia pays less than half of what I do here. I want more space for my family. And there's the Iraqi. He makes me want to move."

I visit the Dearborn Administrative Center, an unremarkable office building in the shadow of Ford's World Headquarters, to talk with Mary Laundroche, Dearborn's director of public information. I figure she's got a tricky job, given that her city's major minority is often demonized. She doesn't see it that way. Within minutes Mary states, "We don't think of ourselves as the Muslim Capital of America."

Since I'm in the business of listening rather than correcting, I don't argue with Ms. Laundroche. Besides, it's unfair to single out the first official who even agrees to talk with me. Still, Ms. Laundroche's message obscures more than it clarifies. It's unfortunate that Dearborn's Director of Public Information won't acknowledge how the world sees her city; especially when we could benefit from the positive images of Muslim community that I observe here.

As I leave the low-slung building, set apart by parking lots and lawns, I feel, for the first time on my journey, the fissure between our government and our people. When Dearborn abandoned it's historic, monumental City Hall to inhabit an Administrative Center in an office park, it abandoned government as a noble enterprise, as the standard bearer of our aspirations. It diminished government to a transactional entity: a place to pay your water bill. When the director of communication delivers a message rather than engage in conversation, she triggers more skepticism than reassurance. Everywhere I go, people envision business, technology, individual initiative, community, and faith as pathways to an improved tomorrow, but no one cites government, in any form, as an agent for positive action.

People are people.
There is too much arguing and too many labels.
We're all just people.
　　　　—Jack D. Jolie, musician, Bridgton, ME

Postville, IA—June 14, 2015, 11:00 a.m.

Before I leave home I query my various representatives, from city councilor to governor to US senator: *How will we live tomorrow?* None respond. The Cambridge City Council delivers an embossed resolution supporting my endeavor, physical proof that our elected officials tinker in form over content. Every elected official I meet during my first 12,000 miles ducks the question, from Kshama Sawant, Seattle's socialist city council member, to Steve Pougnet, mayor of Palm Springs, California.

I arrive in Postville on Flag Day, a somnolent Sunday seven months before the Iowa caucuses. The presidential campaign is fully unfurled, though you wouldn't know it from my conversations about tomorrow. We worry about our families, our environment, and technology's grip on society; we celebrate our families, our ingenuity, and technology's liberation. Our religious bent colors whether we welcome, fear, or scoff at the End Times. We invoke both Lady Gaga and Mahatma Gandhi as harbingers of our future. Though I try not to direct conversation, and am often surprised what people reveal to an itinerant cyclist, there is one thing we never discuss: politics. Perhaps our politics are too personal, too tender, to share with a stranger. But I interpret the tangential complaints and shaken heads that accompany event the slightest reference to our elected officials as a sign that our political system is so broken as to be incapable, even irrelevant, in shaping tomorrow.

The welcome sign along US 18 claims Postville is "Hometown to the World," a grandiose boast, to be sure, that piques my curiosity. I meander through the quiet downtown late morning, surprised to find an open grocery. A small sign in the window indicates that Glatt's is closed on Saturday, open Sunday. Inside, Shirley Glatt

offers me a tight smile and a bottle of soda. Four young children peer at me from beneath her skirt. The boys are barely beginning to sport long, curling sideburns. Mrs. Glatt explains that Postville is home to Agriprocessors, the world's largest kosher meat packing plant. Two thousand melting-pot souls call the place home: Orthodox Jews, Ukrainians, Somalis, Mexicans, Germans, Russians, and Hispanics. Each plays a particular part in Postville's leading enterprise; hence the town's motto.

As she speaks, Postville's notoriety rises out of my foggy memory. In 2008, Immigration and Customs Enforcement raided the Agriprocessor plant. Whether the Justice Department was uncovering workplace abuse, targeting powerless illegals, or baiting Jews depends on your ethnic perspective. According to Mrs. Glatt, the town enjoyed harmony, balance, and summer picnics before the raid, and nothing but clouds of distrust and fear since. Illegal immigrants were deported; an Orthodox Jew imprisoned; the money guys escaped unscathed.

I spend the hot afternoon inside Taste of Mexico, a spacious cantina with steamy tamales. Since I'm in the state that delivers the first quadrennial opinion of who should be our Commander in Chief, I pull out my laptop and visit the websites of the 19 candidates seeking the job, as of that date. I ask each of them, "How will we live tomorrow?," in salutary prose that celebrates a political system so grand it invites broad participation. I don't expect many responses; presidential wannabes don't have much to gain by responding to the author of an obscure blog. But my question is noble, worthy of our future leaders' consideration, so I solicit their thoughts anyway.

23

Mexican laborers troop in for lunch, laughing, chatting—a looser bunch than Mrs. Glatt and her children. Not because they've forgotten their deported countrymen, they simply don't dwell on what they cannot control.

Back on my bike, I ride through the landscape of political imagery: 40 miles of expansive fields, muscular barns, and picturesque towns with broad front porches. I wave to folks enjoying the sweet afternoon. They wave in return. Iowans are friendly. They're also accustomed to glad-handers from beyond state lines twisting a message in exchange for a vote. How else to explain ethanol subsidies masquerading as free enterprise?

I'm not looking for their vote. I want something more complex. Fresh ideas about where we're going. Little wonder no politician will respond.

Fargo, ND—June 21, 2015, 6:00 a.m.

Touring bicycles are designed to carry as many as six containers: two rear rack panniers, two front wheel panniers, a rear rack pack (often a tent or a sleeping bag), and a front pouch for food, drink, and maps. Riders strap lights, odometers, and smart phones to their handlebars. I've seen them haul guitars, fishing poles, pets, and extra bags of shoes. Some pull trailers that weigh a hundred pounds or more. Tiny House proportions.

I keep things light, a year's worth of stuff in two bright yellow bags. My right pannier is for dry goods: one pair of long paints, a pair of shorts, two black T-shirts, one collared shirt, two bike jerseys and a pair of bike shorts, five pair of wool socks—socks get dingy quick—three pair of nylon underwear, and a pair of scrubs; my laptop, writing pad, chargers, mouse, and a paperback book that I swap out at a curbside book exchange after it's read.

My wet pannier includes sleeping bag, repair tools, first aid kit, toiletries, insulated jacket, rain parka, extra gloves, and snack food: energy bars, dried fruit, beef jerky, trail mix. I hang two water bottles on my bike.

Bike, lock, and bags weigh 72 pounds; light for a tourist. But I cannot prepare a hot meal, and when I sleep outside I either spread out under the stars or find cover from rain.

Downtown Fargo is a busy place. I wait at a railroad crossing for 8, maybe 10 minutes as grit black oil car after oil car rattles past on their way west to Dickinson, to Williston, to the oil and gas fields that have turned North Dakota, for the moment, into the second largest energy supplier state in our nation.

Fargo's population recently tipped 100,000: a big city in these parts. The old railroad station has been turned into an upscale bicycle emporium. I stock up on lube and tubes; the next bike shop is over 1,000 miles away.

I treat myself to a night out at the RedHawks minor league ball game on the longest day of the year. It's still light when I check into the Super 8 motel on the west access road of I-29. Next morning, first light stretches across the Plains from my fourth-floor window. The horizon is a thin straight line of nothing.

Everything changes at Fargo.

For 2,500 miles I have never been more than 20 miles between towns. Today, I'm pedaling 90 miles to Cooperstown, with no verified services along my route. I put three more bottles of water in my wet pack; 100 ounces ought to hydrate me the distance.

Super 8's breakfast buffet is carb-delight. I consume two flip waffles, a bowl of oatmeal, a bagel, and two cellophane Danish; wash it all down with tepid orange juice and three cups of coffee. I chat with oil riggers. Thanks to the fracking boom, this the most expensive motel of my trip, though still under 100 bucks.

When I can eat no more, I stuff two extra Danish in my bag and pedal out. A mile west of the interstate, it's just me and blue sky and waving grass and a west headwind pressing hard against my face.

I get up in the morning and put one foot in front of the other.
—Joanne Larsen, city emergency manager, Orem, UT

Florence, OR—September 12, 2015, 10:00 a.m.

One thing is consistent from Maine, across the Dakotas, all the way to Washington State: whatever weather greets you in the morning is as good as it's going to get. A drizzly dawn rarely turns bright. Sunny skies may continue through evening, though more often scattered clouds swell into afternoon thunderstorms. I wake with the dawn and strike out for my destination before the weather turns.

Morning activity is also good for my psyche. Ever since I was a child, first light is my dark time. My brain wakes numb; looming dread gnaws in my belly. For long stretches of my life—during college and the years I was an inadequate husband—daybreak's anxiety clouded my entire day. Eventually I learned that nothing gives depression the slip better than action, so I forced my carcass out of bed to take a run or hit the gym. The quicker I got moving; the sooner my mood improved.

Atmospheric conditions change along the Pacific Coast. The gloomy morning sky is soft cashmere; it entices a body to curl up and roll over. The shroud doesn't lift until 10 or 11; then the sun shines steady until dark. Unlike the East, the day's countenance improves with time.

Morning fog dampens my get-up-and-go. My schedule shifts. I write in the morning, linger with hosts; push exertion to later in the day. I succumb to the West Coast's rhythm, dawdling against my habit of morning frenzy. I fear that familiar, despicable void; that stern voice demanding purpose, will rise up in me. But it does not. Perhaps this journey is loosening a half-century of equating value with action. Or maybe everyone gets laid back coming on to California.

27

The world is in big trouble. Politically, this country is a mess.
We're in a black hole with droughts, wildfires,
and sexual craziness.
The world is in a dark place.
  —Kristin Black, devout Christian, Leavenworth, WA

Crescent City, CA—September 15, 2015, 3:00 p.m.

California—home to one in nine Americans, supplier of fresh fruit, high-tech gadgets, and Hollywood fantasies to the rest of us. The day I enter the Golden State, the morning haze never lifts. Tepid fog mingles with the acrid breeze of fires beyond the ridge.

I've enjoyed 133 days of benign weather—a gift I dare not mention for fear of jinxing. But day after day of dry, sunny skies, so ideal for cycling, curses the landscape. Forest fires rage in Montana and Washington, closing highways, summoning National Guard. They sweep through Northern California as well.

But I bring hope; a forecast of rain. Isn't "hope" what California means? Isn't the terminus of our great continent the place we all come for a fresh start?

The forecast proves true. I wake to rain for the first time on my journey and linger in my Crescent City cabin until noon. When the downpour turns to drizzle I pedal to Jedediah Smith State Park and hike among the redwoods, the tallest organisms on earth. Sentinels on their bluff overlooking the sea. The air is heavy with moisture, the ferns dense underfoot; the trunks spiral dizzy to the sky. The incredible trees don't make me feel small. On the contrary, my chest swells. I rode 7,000 miles to stand beside these giants.

Two generations ago the aquifer was 30 feet deep. Now it is 300 feet deep.
We need more dams and more water storage.
If we turn the valley into a desert we'll have to get our food from South America.
  —Anita, Walmart shopper, Madera, CA

Fresno, CA—October 3, 2015, noon

When I announce my 48-state tour, my 24-year-old son Andy, a graduate student in coastal geology, gives me Marc Reisner's *Cadillac Desert*, and advises, "This is the one book you have to read before you visit the West."

I ride past my first Bureau of Reclamation project in North Dakota, a surreal landscape of sculpted, tan contours squiggling out of a flat sheet of solemn water, deep cobalt.

In Utah I trek up and up along US 40. Near the apex I reach Strawberry Reservoir. This inverted relationship between water and land prompts my first theory of regional dichotomy: In the East, gravity governs water; it collects in rivers and valleys. In the West, man governs water; it hovers at high elevations.

I visit Washington's Grand Coulee Dam on a day too thick with wild fire smoke for a prudent cyclist to breath, and then follow the Columbia River, dam to dam to dam, for several days. The Columbia is no longer a river; it's a string of lakes.

Still, none of these interactions with our most fundamental substance of life prepares me for California's cauldron of money, politics, and drought: the epicenter of the water wars.

All roads converge on Interstate 5 at the Siskiyou Summit; cyclists join motorhomes, bikers, and semi's descending south into California. I'm happy to exit at the Klamath River Highway, a thrilling series of turns tight against rugged hills and across elegant WPA-era bridges spanning the river below. My first view of Mount Shasta is a distant cone, framed between symmetrical slopes. For 60 miles I track ever closer to this singular mountain and arrive at my host's after shadows fall. Mike Sojka collects an offering from the tap, filtered through ancient volcanic rock. He hands the glass of crystalline liquid to me, with an equally clear warning. "This water will never be piped south."

Dried mud and shallow grass suggest a time when Eagle Lake's shore lapped up against California Highway 139. But when I roll along the water's edge on a warm September day, the shore is half a mile or more beyond the shoulder.

I pedal Yosemite National Park on the 125th anniversary of its founding. Speeches and bunting. El Capitan rises proud and tall. But Bridalveil Fall is a tearful trickle.

Fresno is the first place I visit with a Southern California vibe: convertibles weave along wide boulevards; ranch homes sprawl across their lots like sun-drenched lizards; palms tower overhead; fruit trees burst with ripe pops of color; all strung together by verdant stretches of lawn. The patio pools make a cyclist want to quit pumping, take a dip, and drape over a chaise lounge. I spin through the streets of California's fifth-largest city, marveling at the lifestyle genius who invented this climate cocktail: three parts desert, two parts irrigation, and one part air conditioning.

The *Fresno Bee* reports that the city faces fines for failing to achieve Governor Brown's conservation targets. Enraged, clench-jawed citizens object that lawn watering has been cut back to twice a week. They violate the restrictions in protest. I wind along Van Ness Boulevard past a series of Ivy League college–named streets, inhaling the citrus breeze, spritzed by sprinklers overshooting their lawns.

31

The Central Valley is an irritable place. Dust dries my mouth. Road tar clings to my calves. Pickups roar past me on narrow roads. Angry dogs dart out of fields. Mostly Chihuahuas, fearless Napoleons too tiny to even nip my heels, harboring the elemental frustration of feeling permanently maligned and misunderstood. After all, dogs reflect their owners. "It's uncomfortable in this desert, so we need to keep our lawns and foliage."

More than half of the wells in East Porterville have failed. Most residents have no running water, yet I cycle past flood-irrigated orchards, a simplistic system that wastes more than half the water delivered.

Billboards pillar Nancy Pelosi, Jerry Brown, and Barack Obama. Some beseech God for help.

In Madera, a local complains, "We grow the crops for everyone here. They ought to give us the water we need." As if people, rather than nature, control snowmelt in the Sierras.

An immigrant in Merced laughs at the entire situation. "People here have no idea what a drought is. Drought is when you turn on the tap and no water appears. In India, it happens several times a year."

A guy in Modesto explains that his water "ration" of 7,000 cubic feet per winter month is adequate, but the 26,000 cubic feet for seven summer months is insufficient. "Lawns can't grow here without water. And the cost keeps going up. I pay $40 a month for water now." Since people prefer to sound off about perceived wrongs rather than listen to rational correction, I refrain from telling this man that I pay more than twice that for water in Cambridge, a city that gets 48 inches of rain per year compared to Modesto's mere 12.

An evening with Jeannette and Jerry Neuberger in Lodi provides welcome respite. Not from the inescapable topic of water. Rather, from the angry, emotional cloud that obscures reasoned discourse throughout the Central Valley.

The Neubergers own a 1920s-era bungalow a few blocks from downtown. A quarter-acre lot, at most. Yet between the solar panels on their roof and their greenhouse backyard, they are net electricity producers who grow a fair amount of food. Their sustainability efforts may be tiny compared to the mammoth political, economic, and climate issues that determine the region's woes, but doing something is always more empowering than complaining.

Jeannette and Jerry explain the history of 1972's Central Valley Project Improvement Act and the State Water Project. They acknowledge the political shortcomings that continue water flow into Kern County's desert, despite provisions to only open the spigot when there's surplus. They're flummoxed by agreements that provide water at $200 per acre-foot that can be resold for $6,000 per acre-foot. They're frustrated by how the water interests line politician's pockets to continue unsustainable policies. They understand that "there will be no solution to this water problem until we stop farming the desert." Yet, they don't let these realities immobilize them.

I tell Jerry I'm headed to Napa. He explains that cyclists cannot navigate California Route 12, and then acknowledges there is no other route. He proves correct on both counts.

Escaping the Central Valley proves to be the most treacherous ride of my trip: two-lanes of heavy traffic without a shoulder. Route 12 must have a history of danger: bright yellow stanchions along the centerline prevent drivers from wandering into the opposing lane. They also prevent vehicles from granting me three-foot clearance. I stop often to let traffic pass; I walk my bike through several miles of shoulder too soft to ride. When I reach Fairfield

I figure I'm out of trouble, but the detour for a new intersection at I-80 and I-680 has no provision for bicycles. I white-knuckle a half-mile stretch of interstate, no doubt illegally, before I finally climb Lincoln Highway to reach Napa's promised land.

As I approach the Bay Area, attitudes about water make an about-face. Every host keeps a bucket in her shower to collect the extra water. A Berkeley economist demonstrates his piping system to divert washing-machine-grey water to his backyard fruit trees. From San Francisco to Santa Cruz to Santa Maria to Santa Ynez, conservation is fashionable; a virtuous way of life.

Route 154 passes Cachuma Lake, Santa Barbara's reservoir, before mounting San Marcos Pass and descending to the sea. The water level is so low the dam creating the basin is fully exposed. One flexible pipe siphons what little water remains to the city below. But Santa Barbara's water projections are tilting up as it prepares to stop relying on the mountains for water and quench its thirst from the sea.w

Back in the 1980s, during California's last severe drought, the citizens of Santa Barbara approved and constructed a desalinization plant. By the time the design/build facility opened in 1992, conservation measures had slashed the city's water use by 60%, from 16,500 acre-feet per year to less than 10,000. Rains returned; water was plentiful once again. So, the city beta-tested the $35 million plant for three months, resold key components to Jeddah, Saudi Arabia, and for 20 years performed a minimum amount of maintenance.

By 2011, Santa Barbara's water usage had climbed to over 13,000 acre-feet and another, more severe, drought threatened capacity. The city created a long-term water plan with ambitious conservation targets and proposed reactivating the desalinization plant. They would start with generating 3,125 acre-feet of desalinated water per resident per year, with phased expansion to 7,500 acre-feet or 10,000 acre-feet. By 2015 conservation measures dropped water use below 11,000 acre-feet and the plant will reopen early next year. Santa Barbara will be one of the few California cities with surplus water.

What do the water wars tell us? They illustrate the full spectrum of human response to any challenge. I witness fear, as a fundamental element of life grows scarce. I witness doubt, as the foundation of a region sinks. I witness rage that nature denies us the water we demand—water we feel entitled to. I witness ingenuity in the face of adversity. I witness people putting their faith in technology and in their God, though never in politicians.

The more I journey through the land of the water wars, the more I realize that as long as we consider it a war—with winners and losers—we cannot reach equilibrium.

In less than a hundred years we created Fresno, an oasis in the desert. We watered it so lavishly it sustains a half-million people, alien grass and trellised roses. The city is a blip in geologic time. Yet for the families who live there, Fresno is their permanent reality.

We are no longer nomads, inclined to move on because conditions have changed. And so we dig in, drain what little ground water remains, pipe more water from farther away, truck it in if necessary. Expend increasing energy to prop up a system that was never balanced in the first place. Fresno is an oasis that will become a mirage. We can tinker with the timing, but eventually it will evaporate.

I can make plans but I can't determine the outcome.
I can say the Cubs will win the World Series, but I can't know the outcome.
—Frank Bolin, before the Cubs won the World Series, Chicago, IL

Chicago, IL—June 7, 2015, 6:00 p.m.

This rambling cyclist, damp from a morning downpour, spins all day beneath oppressive clouds that obscure a drying sun. He arrives moist and dank at a sleek apartment tower within Chicago's Loop. Its crisp, taut profile lines render his soggy body even more pathetic. Certainly, he has the wrong address.

I double-check my smartphone. The address confirms. I lock my bike to a stanchion: it might be a bike rack, or maybe it's art. My tennis shoes squeak across the marble lobby. The doorman is more professional than I deserve, he doesn't even flinch at my mud-caked shins and grimy shirt. "Good evening, Mr. Fallon. Ms. Brennan is expecting you."

Within minutes an exuberant blonde of indeterminate age, with broad shoulders and a confident stride, bursts out the lobby door. "Welcome to Chicago! You must be Paul!" Bonnie ushers me to the bike storage room where Surly will spend the night amidst her urban cousins. We humans elevator to the seventh floor. Bonnie introduces me to her boyfriend Frank, offers me a glass of ice water, points to the guest bath—the blue towels are mine—and guides me to the den, where the sleeper sofa is already pulled out, freshly sheeted, and tucked in. I strip off my clinging spandex, shower the silt away, and slip into T-shirt and shorts.

When I emerge to the living room, Bonnie is standing on her balcony, chatting with a neighbor below. "I have a visiting cyclist staying with me. … Sure, we'll join you. ... What can I bring?" The three of us gather wine, crackers, and cheese, pad the corridor to the stairway, and descend one floor.

Ginny's apartment is identical to Bonnie's, except that, being directly above the parking podium, Ginny has a spacious deck. We spread the appetizers on the bar-height table. Ginny's boyfriend Joe grills kielbasa. He offers me a Goose Island Summertime Kölsch. We straddle stools and make a toast as the sun sets over the gabled roofs of the townhouses to the west. Within a half hour, tops, I have morphed from grimy stranger to a guy with a brew, a view, and four new friends.

Welcome to the world of warmshowers.org, a website that connects long-distance cyclists with overnight hosts. Not all accommodations are as commodious as Bonnie's. Some hosts offer a backyard tent site, a utility-room floor just long enough for my sleeping bag, or a loveseat that necessitates draping my knees over the arms. Yet other digs are even more luxurious: private suites with 800-threadcount linen, embossed guest books, and snack baskets filled with Clif bars. I stay in a few guest cottages with fully stocked kitchens. Many hosts are as outgoing as Bonnie, though recalcitrant mountain men usher me in with a few words and go about their business. All warmshowers hosts provide fresh water, a warm shower, and a place to sleep; most serve dinner; some even offer laundry facilities, bike repairs, and breakfast. What do I bring in exchange for this hospitality? Stories of the road.

No money changes hands. The only currency is that critical internet asset: the peer review. I am conscientious about reviewing my hosts, which is easy since the vast majority of them are extraordinary people. Occasionally my host and I don't resonate. Perhaps we miscommunicated, and he wants me to sleep outside even though I noted that I prefer a roof; perhaps she arrives home an hour later than we agreed. These trifles are annoying, but my

mother's words ring clear, "If you can't say something nice, don't say anything," so I refrain from penning a review. If anything untoward or dangerous ever occurred, I would report it, but it never does. The only thing remotely questionable about warmshowers is the soft-porn twist in the website's name. Warmshowers is the sharing economy, without the pesky economy part.

Bonnie and I form a fast bond, sharing stories of pumping over Vail Pass; our dinner group enjoys speculating on my question. The following morning, Bonnie and Frank take me on a personal bike tour of Chicago's Pilsen neighborhood topped by lunch at Nuevo Leon. Turns out, Bonnie is older than I figured: the far side of 70. She is not the first, or last, person a decade or more my senior whose vitality offers me a walloping upbeat perspective on what my own tomorrow might hold. A lot of cyclists prove that 60, maybe even 70, is the new 40.

The further I pedal west, the more warmshowers hosts I seek. In desolate areas I can go a week without finding one. Other times I snag hosts for three or four nights in a row. By the time I reach California I've stayed with almost 50 families. I appreciate their hospitality and perspective on tomorrow. However, these gracious people create one drawback to the arching vision of my journey. Although my odyssey is unscientific in every respect—I talk with whoever will give me their time—I strive to meet a wide cross-section of Americans. Unfortunately the cycling community, and warmshowers hosts, trend affluent and white. I never meet a warmshowers host of color. I never even meet one who is poor.

Until I meet Jim Andrews.

I think about what Lloyd Pendleton said.
The extremely rich, their main concern is connection.
For the middle class it's possessions.
For the extremely poor it's relationships.
　　—Kelli Bowers, Palmer Court Housing, Salt Lake City, UT

Ceres, CA—October 6, 2015, 6:00 p.m.

Cycling through the Central Valley is easy; the place is flat. But the constant rants about water parch my spirit. I arrive in Ceres tired and hot. I wind through streets of ill-kept houses, abandoned vehicles, and loose dogs. At the sight of my host's house, my spirit flatlines.

Poverty in America is revealed by excess as often as scarcity. Broken wheelbarrows, abandoned refrigerators, and crippled lawn chairs litter Jim Andrews's yard. Can this be home to a warm-showers host who advertised being a single father with two sons who like to play board games? I consider pedaling on just as a pit bull runs out to inspect me and an obese man with a huge grey beard follows.

"Are you Paul?"

My opportunity to cut and run dashed, I dismount, muster a smile, and roll Surly down the driveway, skirting scrap metal and threadbare tires stockpiled against some unforeseen need. I lock her to the electric meter out back and follow Jim through a lean-to addition, past a rusty washing machine, into a windowless galley kitchen illuminated by a single bulb. He leads me to a table with three chairs set plumb center in a small room whose walls are filled with shelves bulging bric-a-brac, books, and dusty boxes. Not a single inch of bare wall. There are five, maybe six doors, all shut. The space is dark and hot. The dog sniffs me. Jim points to the best chair where I stay seated all evening. There is no place to move.

Jim's son Benjy sleeps in the alcove directly in front of me. The door behind opens to Jim's room, where my host shifted stacks of clothes to create a nest for my sleeping bag. Other doors flank the kitchen; Jim subleases one room to a Vietnamese immigrant, another to a woman with a two-year-old daughter.

The air is so close I smell Jim's perspiration. He opens the front door to let in a breeze. "We have no air conditioning. We have an evaporative cooler but it costs too much to run." The late-day sun streaks through the portal, highlighting our shabbiness.

Jim's a talker, happy to bend a new set of ears. He grew up in Oregon, poor, wanting to be a missionary in Cambodia. He only got so far as marrying a refugee. Half a world away and two sons later the Khmer Rouge still haunts her feeble, so Jim raised their boys. Benjy recently graduated from high school. The young man wants to be a cook. After a lot of noise from the kitchen he serves up something like fajitas, drenched in so much Tabasco it singes my nasal cavities.

Jim recently earned his college degree after 28 years of night school. He's a substitute teacher, but he can't venture far; he had to sell his car and can only get around by bike. Jim checks his phone all evening, hoping for a call to report to a local school tomorrow. A call means 90 dollars. That's a lot.

The more Jim talks, the less I notice the heat, the smells, the dim light. "I don't complain about being poor. What bothers me is when people look down on me. I look back at my life; I messed up so much. But I still have hope. I should be dead. My health is terrible: bad back, no pigment in my skin, hernia. I am dealing with depression. I have my sons, my mom, my belief in God. We all have problems but I take one day at a time and I have hope."

We turn in early. It's awkward to sleep curled up among another man's clothes. I dream of the road—wide space and fresh air.

In the morning, Jim makes hot cereal. He holds out a loaf of sweet bread, a local specialty purchased in my honor. I don't want to accept this extravagance, but recall other food offered in other homes, Haitian homes, where withholding hospitality is greater shame than mere hunger. Jim slices the bread and makes cheese sandwiches for my lunch.

Before I leave we take photos with our bikes. Jim never got that call. He has no place to go, no money to earn. He inspects my gear, asks questions about my shoes, my parka. He and Benjy would like to tour some summer. When they can afford it. When Jim's stamina grows beyond 20 miles a day.

Jim takes my hand as I mount to go. "Not many cyclists stay with us. We'd like to host more. Please give us a good review so others will choose us."

I am ashamed. In last night's dusk I wanted to move on: what a loss that would have been. I write Jim a good review, but it falls short of expressing everything that the most generous host—pro-portionately—of my entire trip gives to me. Never again do I let piles of junk or ratty clothes cloud the opportunity to converse with another human.

*The answer must lie in our resolve to persevere and do what is right,
no matter how challenging the obstacles must be.
Oftentimes that's a lonely place to be.*
　　　　　—Harry Mears, oceanographer, Seabrook, NH

Dartmouth, NH—May 13, 2015, 6:00 p.m.

When someone suggests I meet the coordinator of the local bike coalition, I smile politely but don't pursue it. I do, however, jump at the chance to meet an oil/gas executive, farmer, or mechanic. I strive to meet as broad a spectrum of our nation as possible, but travelling by bicycle, staying with people who open their homes to strangers, automatically skews my rendezvous to folks on the fringe of our car-centric, privacy-focused society.

Regardless whether I meet cattle rancher or raw vegan, my job is to listen and report with as little judgment as possible. Although I fact-check content I compose, I don't correct direct quotes: perceptive facts often illustrate beliefs more accurately than objective ones. When the permaculture farmer proclaims that we must overthrow corporate food, I don't press him on how to scale local produce to feed seven billion people. When an executive claims, "McDonald's will evolve and change as we need, and always involve the community," I don't point out the local businesses that shutter when McDonald's comes to town.

Everyone's actions are benevolent from his or her own perspective. My task is to embrace the stories I receive without cross-examination and discover the overlaps, the sweet spots of commonality.

Within a few months I discover that the less I have in common with someone—ethnicity, age, gender, race, education—the easier I can accept their story. I lack the perspective required to cast doubt. But when I meet someone of my own ilk, at least on the surface, judgment swells. This may constitute a failure of intent. Or it might just prove that middle-aged white men are a cantankerous and disingenuous lot.

We are indulging personal preferences to society's limits. That's why you see so little commonality. Income disparity is growing. We're building government deficits that will haunt our grandchildren and great-grandchildren.
—Dana Timaeus, candidate for judge, Beaumont, TX

Houston, TX—February 17, 2016, 8:00 p.m.

"I spent a great deal of my youth seeking truth. Around age 19 I was interested in the difference between hope and faith. I erased my hard drive and looked for my first truth: 'There are no absolutes.' Unfortunately, that's an absolute."

Michael Finley grew up in Houston's fifth ward, the poor side of town. "In 1967 I realized my grammar was holding me back from being taken seriously. Houston had transfer systems to avoid busing. I went to another school and honed my debating skills." Michael went on to Stephen F. Austin State University in Nacogdoches, joined the debate team, and became student body president. "We spent one whole year on a single question, which we had to debate from each side. Argumentation and debate are the two primary ways of decision. What you learn is the world is all grey."

Michael's rhetorical skills are still impressive. The evening we spend together, he weaves his personal success and business acumen into a cohesive narrative that articulates where we are as a nation and where we ought to go. Since I am predisposed to listen, and he's prone to pontificate, our conversation falls short of the balance required for true debate.

Michael's been an entrepreneur his entire life. He's owned several companies, large and small, first in architectural woodwork, then exploration of helium, tungsten, and oil. These days, Michael runs a lean operation with a home in Galveston and an "office" in Houston: a two-story condo in a loft building overlooking Minute Maid Stadium and the city skyline. The view reflects Michael's economic perspective. "Houston is a dynamic city, a city of opportunity. We've always been part of Texas and the South but we've never had the racial or divisive problems that happen in other areas. Houston is a place to work. We are all about economic opportunities."

Yet as Michael discusses his own business, he focuses on perceived restraints rather than opportunities. "I've worked for myself my whole life and I've been screwed by both political parties. We are just over-regulated, but we regulate what's politically expedient or has a secondary benefit. Take energy. We have a list that says, 'Do this' and 'Don't do that'. I think we're a responsible industry. If I hit a bird, I get a fine of $10,000. Windmills get exempt from killing birds.

"We won't make CNG cars but we create ethanol, which takes six gallons of water per gallon to produce. Not to mention that ethanol disrupts the price of corn worldwide. All because the politicians won't touch Iowa."

Since I know little about regulatory fines or ethanol subsidies, I don't dispute Michael's claims, though I imagine a wind energy or ethanol executive could stake similar claims of regulatory advantage bestowed upon the oil and gas industry.

Michael articulates positions I've heard from others, but with greater conviction. "A free market system is the best system because it allows for the nature of man. I haven't seen a more efficient system. ... Big government is a velvet glove on a 10-ton arm. It has no sensitivity. ... At a federal level, we need a standing army; we need to have things like the highway system. The Federal government should only do what it can do. It should decentralize as much as possible."

Michael's desire for limited Federal intervention is not unique. The problem is, beyond maintaining a standing army, few people I speak with agree on what activities the government should oversee and which it should decentralize.

This dichotomy colors Michael's opinion about the direction of public education—"There's no accountability"—and the loss of other institutions. "We're tearing down things but not replacing them with anything else. We're pulling apart the Catholic Church, corporal punishment, discipline of all sorts. But what have we replaced them with? Fear and divisiveness." From Michael's perspective, everything is clear through an economic lens. "The issue is socioeconomic, not race. Race is used as a divisive correlation."

Michael's opinions are a gift. He gives me so much to ponder as I cycle east from Houston toward the Deep South. Humans seek to preserve what works well and dismiss, or dismantle, what doesn't serve our personal interest. Michael's a self-described, self-made man who rose from a meager background to affluence and influence. I admire his tenacity, grit, and ability. But as a man of similar age—and skin color—who has managed to climb a few socioeconomic rungs myself, I'm skeptical of anyone who believes he's made it based on his own abilities.

People of status pretend the world is a meritocracy; people without status know better. Every successful person receives assisting hands, seen and unseen, along the way. And for white males, privilege comes so early and so strong we do not consider it extraordinary. It is our norm. We embrace it as our right.

A person who's never experienced racial prejudice cannot know whether socioeconomic distinctions trump race. A man who's benefited from the structure imposed by the Catholic Church, corporal punishment, and other forms of discipline doesn't consider how these inequitable institutions hold others down. A man who possesses the rights to extract resources three states away from his home ought to be more favorably disposed to a Federal system that allows him to remove something from our earth and sell it for personal gain. But when you're a white male, accustomed to getting what you want, just because, our economic and cultural systems bestow reality, not privilege. Having to discuss, let alone defend, our advantage is an intrusion, a threat.

One irony of my journey across this land is how often middle-aged white men, the disproportionate beneficiaries of our society, feel mistreated by the very country that enables our success. The innate privilege that comes with being born white and male is so profound; it's invisible to those of us born into the club.

You can't live tomorrow. You can only live today.
Tomorrow is mind-made.
It was invented when we made time.
  —Brian D'Apice, Bicycle Around America, Sultan, WA

Denver, CO—July 17, 2015, 7:00 a.m.

Michael Finley is not the only disgruntled middle-aged white man I meet. There's the vitriolic ice cream vendor in Dixon, Montana; the immigrant-bashing Fourth of July patriot in Chadron, Nebraska; and the obese attorney loitering at *La Loma de Chivo* collective in Marathon Texas—a self-described touring cyclist who pedals less than 100 miles in a year. These men's bleak worldviews, a mash-up of entitlement and persecution, singe my ears. I listen until I can no longer endure their pontifications: so righteous, so angry, my own psyche flees to a dark place. I am embarrassed, ashamed, that to the outside world, I look like them.

But then morning comes and I remount Surly and get back on the road. My legs spin; my irritations dissolve; endorphins obliterate the blues. My spirits rise and inevitably, I encounter someone who restores my faith in humanity.

At the Bear Creek Lake Park reservoir, 10 miles outside of Denver, a day cyclist comes astride. I hand him my card, ask my question, explain I'm bound for Copper Mountain. Colorado is ripe with fitness cyclists. We chat a few minutes, but I know this guy is a 25-mile-per-hour stallion spinning titanium on a day trip to the mountains and back. He won't hang with a plodding mule like me, weighed down by Ortlieb panniers and steel. After a few moments, Mark Weiler rides on ahead.

I continue apace, basking in the morning sun on the gentle foothills, trying not to let the magnitude of what rises behind them cloud the moment. Copper Mountain is 99 miles from Denver by bike; a distance I've covered before in one day. But never with two miles of vertical rise.

My parents hail from metropolitan New York, less than 20 miles from where their parents, grandparents, and great-grandparents disembarked the ship from Ireland. I grew up along the Jersey shore. In 1971, my dad moved our family to Oklahoma, and ever since our family's epicenter has shifted west. My brothers and sister spread to Colorado and Utah. I alone returned east. I typically visit Denver once a year, often to ride the Courage Classic bicycle fundraiser for the Colorado Children's Hospital with an assortment of brothers and in-laws. This year I am integrating the Courage Classic into my 48-state adventure. I wanted two days to climb from Denver to the fundraiser's start at Copper, but family fun whittled that down to one. Everyone else is driving to the mountains this afternoon. I could tie Surly to a car, but when you're riding your bike cross-country, sagging over the Continental Divide feels like a cheat.

A few minutes later, Mark Weiler loops back.

"Mr. Paul E. Fallon, are you actually cycling to 48 states?" Yes, I reply.

"And you ask everyone your question?" Yes, again.

"And you are riding all the way to Copper Mountain today?" Again, I affirm.

"Well, Mr. Paul E. Fallon, you are the person God sent to me today. I do not know how I will live tomorrow, but today I will stay with you."

Mark's an odd duck for sure. But I figure if this guy wants to dawdle with me for a few miles, scripture quoting will pass the time. Bible verses notwithstanding, my gaydar detects a live one. He sure is handsome.

Gaydar is my most disjointed, if well honed, skill. Of all the attributes that contribute to being Paul E. Fallon, being gay is the most perplexing. Though I came of age during gay liberation, my Catholic upbringing decreed homosexuality a sin. I suffered vague unease among cocky, boyhood athletes, and accepted the fault of shame that ran through me without the courage to trace its root. I trundled through puberty. I focused on my head, ignored my body, married a nice woman, collected several degrees, and sired a pair of children. All the right things yielded hollow satisfaction. By the time my marriage ended in the 1990s, the world had shifted so much I could no longer ignore that what I'd always dismissed as "odd" was actually "gay": a three-letter shift that only took me 38 years to comprehend.

Twenty-plus years later, I'm a most ambivalent gay man. God gave me a hankering for firm forearms and a disquieting memory for show tunes, but I don't use product, I don't do brunch, and Cosmos give me a headache. I don't dish, though I have been known to spoon. I certainly don't have a boyfriend. The journey from straight man to gay guy is shorter than one might think when you're unconvincing in either role. None of which much matters as I happily trail Mark's pumping thighs up Route 93 out of Morrison.

As we approach Genesee on old US 40, Mark easy pedals, upright in his seat, outstretched arms exclaiming the glory of the Lord. "And when they heard this, they lifted their voices to God with one accord and said, "O Lord, it is You who MADE THE HEAVEN AND THE EARTH AND THE SEA, AND ALL THAT IS IN THEM" (Acts 4:24). Me and my sturdy Surly and my panniers, we huff in his wake.

When Mark finally stops calling me Paul E. Fallon and begins to relate his life story in a conscious, albeit not chronological narrative, I realize that the man is serious about riding me the distance. Mark is a US Post Office mail carrier and Air Force veteran, mar-

ried to a women he adores. They have three sons. Mark is the 12th of 15 children born to alcoholic parents, raised Catholic. His father died at age 57 from liver disease and four of his siblings had early, tragic deaths related to alcohol and drugs. There's a parallel narrative about being tortured as an effeminate youth, joining the military to prove his masculinity, and then getting drummed out for homosexual behavior.

Gaydar never lies.

By the time we approach Idaho Springs, Mark's story descends into depression. He describes a TV-watching couch potato, dabbling in Buddhism and Pantheism, until God calls him to rise above his origins. Thus emerges the new Mark, a born-again Christian and Robert Bly devotee who's openly gay but even more devoted to his wife, the woman who saved him from so much sin. Mark cycles 250 miles a week, lifts weights, belongs to a men's group and a Bible-based church. He is a warrior on a bicycle; his training rides are his mission. "Today, my mission is you."

After four hours, our lopsided conversation slides into complete monologue: I am breathing too hard to form words. Mark's tale spins more elaborate with every rotation. "I have never had a day like this. You are my captive audience. I can tell you my entire life story."

We arrive in Georgetown after 1 p.m., later than I'd hoped, but I need a break and insist on buying us lunch. Between bites of buffalo chicken and salty fries I offer snippets of my own life, emphasizing our commonalities: I'm also gay; will always love my ex-wife; am fortunate to have children.

The bicycle path from Georgetown to Loveland Ski Resort is shady and fresh paved, but the constant pitch makes my thighs holler for relief. Cyclists stream down upon us at 40, 50 miles per hour. No other cyclists press in our direction; it's already late to mount the summit. When my thighs refuse to pump anymore the woods open up and there it is: Loveland Pass. Four giant switchbacks snake above the treeline.

I fall off my bike and sprawl on the grass, gulp a bottle of water and devour a PowerBar. Mark sits beside me, closer than he ought. I feel his heat. He stares into my eyes, talks not of his past, or our present, but the future.

"What's going to happen when we get old? When our looks fail and our energy gives out and we can't keep moving, moving, moving to stay in balance? Will the lives we've cobbled together—acknowledging who we are without actually being who we are—sustain us then?"

Mark fears growing old, losing his looks. He struggles how best to hand off his warrior nature to his sons. His words, his gaze, his forearms, his breath, dance upon my own. He burns himself into persistent memory.

I ache. Then rise. I climb back on my bike, lift my head to the mountain and begin to pedal. If I can maintain four miles per hour, we will reach the summit by six.

I cannot. Even before the first switchback, my odometer slips to 3.8, then 3.4. On the second rise, it dips to 2.9. Mark's racing bike can barely stay upright beside Surly's loaded crawl on the 8% grade. He literally loops circles around me. "If I have the gift of prophecy and can fathom all mysteries and all knowledge, and if I have a faith that can move mountains, but do not have love, I am nothing" (1 Corinthians 13:2).

Loveland Pass is a parade of strange bedfellows: hazardous cargo 18-wheelers and bicycles, vehicles at opposite ends of the transit spectrum prohibited from I-70's Eisenhower Tunnel. The road is narrow. We frustrate the trucks downshift as they approach; we inhale their exhaust as they pass. Yet truck drivers and cyclists are mutually respectful. The camaraderie of Interstate exile supersedes the irritation of coexistence.

Mark offers unflagging encouragement. "You are going to be the first man—ever—to climb Loveland Pass on a loaded bike in tennis shoes. Man, you are one weird cyclist."

We reach the summit at 6:30 p.m., the only cyclists at this late hour. I'm surprised how many truckers stop to take in the panorama, plus a few automobile tourists who took the long route specifically for this view. Mark and I take photos. We exchange a public hug; the only time we physically touch. The gesture carries no emotion compared to being lovers all day of shared stories, sweat, and achievement.

Mark turns around and heads back to Georgetown, where his wife will meet him and sag his bike home. It will only take him half an hour to descend.

I stream down 10 miles through Arapahoe Basin and Keystone to Dillon Reservoir. When I have to actually pedal again, my legs revolt. I splay across a grassy meadow and call my brother to let him know I'm on the far side of the Continental Divide. He wants to fetch me, but I refuse. I don't know how to make my quivering body propel 14 more miles through Frisco and up Officers Gulch, but having mounted Loveland under my own power, I'm not about to submit to assistance now.

It takes me almost three more hours to reach Copper Mountain. The setting sun gives way to guiding stars. My family is already passing the brownies when I arrive. They saved a bowl of spaghetti for me to carb up for tomorrow's Vail Pass. But I am too hungry to eat; too tired to sleep. Vail Pass is a minor hump compared to what I accomplished today. My brother riddles me with questions about my climb. My responses are scattered, unsatisfactory. My mind wanders above the endless upgrades. I see Mark's eyes, the depth of his gaze. I ponder the forms that god takes, confident in the existence of guardian angels.

Leavenworth, WA—August 22, 2015, 7:00 p.m.

It's been fifty years since I've thought about guardian angels, an altar boy down on my knees, gazing up at the strong shoulders of the priest who held the body of Christ high in his two hands. I adored the man who adored Our Lord.

Then they translated Latin to English, turned the priest to face the congregation, and stripped the Mass of mystery. Catholicism lost its magic and my adoration descended from spiritual ecstasy to sticky shame.

I've been a seeker ever since, intrigued by all forms of the Creator. Too much a man of reason, of science, to give myself over to any one creed, yet fascinated by every form of religious expression. This journey nourishes that seeking. I meet people of faith everywhere I travel and they all claim an inside track on tomorrow.

Unfortunately, that doesn't mean they're open to nuanced spiritual discussion. The freedom of religion embedded in our Constitution too often manifests itself as righteousness, obsession, or disdain. True believers are resolute in their absolute truth. Their one God is true and should not —cannot—be reconciled with another's one true God.

I meet Jews and Hindus, Buddhists, and Muslims, Baha'i, even atheists along my path. But the vast majority of religious people I meet are Christians; insistent in calling the United States a "Christian country." The United States is not a Christian country. It was consciously conceived contrary to that very idea. But in our age of information glut, repetition is reality. So many people chant "Christian country" so loud and so often that the idea is lodged as fact in many heads.

Occasionally I meet true believers open to the joust and parry of theological debate. People who don't try to win me over. I savor those conversations that expand mutual understanding and appreciation rather than press my conversion.

Leavenworth, Washington, is a Cascades mountain town that fancies itself an alpine village: a Tyrolean tourist attraction of beer steins, half timbers, and the world's largest collection of nutcrackers. Nothing about the place seems real, though the breathless beauty of pedaling up Icicle Canyon on a misty afternoon affirms the presence of something greater than mere man.

Sally Worthington is the grandmotherly wife of an evangelical minister; Kinna McMahon is a young college graduate. The two women share a common bond: Jesus as father, brother, teacher, nurturer. Theirs is a God of fireside chat rather than fire and brimstone. The strength of their belief is balanced with openness, their convictions strong enough to welcome and withstand debate.

During our deep night talk, I reveal my fundamental misgiving with Christianity, with any religion really. "I'm fine with people believing whatever they want. What I don't understand is the need to proselytize and convert. Why can't those who believe in Jesus, or Muhammad, be content in their God? Why must they impose it on others?"

Sally replies, "We believe that Jesus Christ is real, that he is fact. It's our duty to share our knowledge with others."

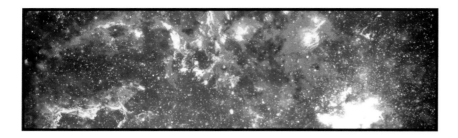

I appreciate Sally's positive spin on people I often consider insecure zealots. Yet I point out the problem with tying the words "believe" and "fact" in the same sentence. The fact of Jesus as Son of God requires belief. Lacking that, Jesus is simply a role model.

"You are a relativist." Kinna breaks in. "You think there are many possible answers. We know there is only one answer. At the End Times, our faith will prove true."

Kinna's got me pegged. We finish our evening in good fellowship; I am richer for meeting them and hope they feel the same. Yet I have trouble falling asleep. Kinna's surety, the conviction that comes with absolute truth, is a powerful bind, but such surety also breeds hatred, division, and war.

I believe there are many possible answers about the nature of god, the nature of man, the nature of everything. The more I pedal, the more possibilities I reveal; yet relativism is itself a pitted path. Every belief is not equally valid. A white supremacist does not apply the Golden Rule to all. Racial superiority and racial equality are not equivalent beliefs; they don't deserve the same protections.

There are absolute truths, and there are absolute lies. The people of faith I meet inhabit fully formed moral universes that guide their actions. Problem is, each person, each religion, each moral construct, defines a different universe. The intersection of these universes is growing ever smaller; the absolutes we all agree upon are shrinking. What are the absolute truths in a society based in pluralism? How do we define and agree upon what is good and what is evil? Each pilgrim I meet along my path clarifies, and obscures, my search.

I ask Adam Collier in Panama City, Florida, what makes the Bible, supposedly the word of God channeled through its various authors, different from any other creative endeavor. "Shakespeare may be inspired writing, but it doesn't have near the scope of the Bible. The Bible tells a great story and it outlines how we are supposed to live and it describes a future. If you believe in it, it includes everything you need to know."

Hayden Sewall, a Christian missionary in Fayetteville, Arkansas, tells me, "There are 83,000 different Christian denominations throughout the world, whose shared principles are few." He sees no need to reconcile them.

Nicolas Kazan in Reno, Nevada, wants to reconcile all religions, by abolishing them. "Religion is the means of subjugating the masses. The societies that have broken away, like Scandinavia, demonstrate that rational decisions create strong societies. The obsession with religion in this country is dragging us down."

But to Julie Hollar in Livingston, Montana, it is not religion that needs to be abolished, but secular government. "There is a political antichrist and a religious antichrist that is trying to make the world one. Obama is the key to this."

Every perspective has a counter-perspective. The most reasonable point of view I hear is from Frank Bolin, a retired cook and AA member in Chicago. "All faiths are legitimate. It's not rational. It's faith. There are prophets alive today, and visionaries alive today." It's no surprise his thoughts resonate in me: they are rooted in relativism.

My theological head spin may oscillate, but it isn't aimless. Religion in the United States is moving in a clear direction, away from grey, toward black and white. Mainline Protestants are a shrinking brood, personality pastors are on the rise, and one American religion is surging with explosive growth.

Christians need to be "children of Christ," blind believers.
Religion offers us a lot: socialization, comfort, economic strength;
it moderates negative behavior. But it does not correlate with reality.
I am looking for the comfort that my mind can rationalize.
—Kevin Lee, deep-sea photographer, Fullerton, CA

Grants Pass, OR—September 19, 2015, 7:00 p.m.

Brian Heron moves from place to place working himself out of a job. He's a peculiar expert; taking the helm at a struggling congregation and transitioning it into something stable, though that often means merging or closing a church. He recently spent six years with a congregation near Portland that successfully merged with a growing United Church of Christ and turned their remaining real estate into a homeless shelter and community garden. Now Brian's assigned to a shrinking church in Grant's Pass. Since more than half of all Presbyterians are over age 65, and 60% of Presbyterian churches will close in the next 10 years, Brian's role as a workout man is an important gig. "The mainstream religions are nuanced. People who align with ambiguity can do that without a church."

These days, people once described as liberal Christians back off the term "religion" altogether. "There's a shift taking place from religion to faith and spirituality. Take marriage. I haven't performed a wedding in a church since the 1990s. People don't want to be married within church walls; they want to be married outdoors or in a place meaningful to them."

Brian's ministry navigates the transition from an institution, a church, to spiritual fulfillment. The older people in his congregation come to church for the "truth;" others embrace ambiguity, if only to provide structure to the morass. "We're living out and embodying our ideals. It's the breakdown of authority. It used to be that you believed before understanding. Now, we have to understand to believe. We are moving to a post-religion, post-authoritarian time. We are taking over the means of our lives."

Brian has identified what he considers five essential beliefs within the Presbyterian Church. These are not commandments that dictate behavior. Rather, they outline commonalities that accommodate personal interpretation.

"First, God is sovereign. The idea of God is rooted in an omnipotent being. This connection is dropping away as God is interpreted as spiritual energy. In the 1960s, Death of God theories flourished as theologians, in response to the Holocaust, questioned an all-powerful, all loving God when actions proved otherwise. The language of the omnipotent God fell away in seminaries, but the trend never trickled down to congregations. We would be in a better, more honest, place today if we had followed the Death of God idea, but congregations didn't want to hear it.

"Second, we are Christo-centric. Different denominations stress different aspects of God. Pentecostals focus on the Holy Spirit. Unitarians are theists. Presbyterians know God through Jesus.

"Third, we believe the Bible is the ultimate criterion for hearing God's voice. Other writings can be inspired, but the Bible is the primary source.

"Fourth we are a priesthood of believers. This goes directly to the Reformation idea that we are all priests. What is happening now, with people developing their own faith perspectives, is really the logical evolution of Martin Luther's ideas.

"Finally, we are reformed and are always reforming. We don't believe that we have the 'right' interpretation, but will continue to search for deeper truth."

Brian Heron demonstrates a form of strength when he acknowledges that he doesn't have the "right" interpretation, but it is not the strength of conviction. Thus, in this era of religious certainty, Presbyterians are a diminishing breed.

In North Carolina I witness the physical reality of the 83,000 different Christian denominations Haydn Sewall describes. Established churches in town centers wallow, landmarks of discarded mainline doctrine, while new brick edifices, mounted with steeples and surrounded by asphalt, bloom on the outskirts of town. The new churches aren't tied to any organizing structure. Rather, they belong to a particular preacher and his following—almost always a "he." These churches are not built around a creed. They are built around a personality.

Look at our belief systems. Every human has their own, every family, every group. The ability to evaluate and question what we believe, and to logically consider what others believe, is not available to everyone.

—Louise Goldberg, songwriter, Oklahoma City, OK

Cambridge, NY—May 16, 2015, 11:00 a.m.

I take a detour my first morning in New York State to indulge in Saturday breakfast at Country Gal's Café. Enter with an empty belly and leave fully satisfied. I mount Surly and pedal along Main Street, past a man sitting on a gracious porch. We wave to one other; I notice a sign above his front steps, Twelve Tribes Community. I stop and we chat.

James has lived in this rambling 19th-century house for 22 years, the senior member of a community rooted in Acts 2:4: *All of them were filled with the Holy Spirit and began to speak in other tongues as the Spirit enabled them.*

James describes life in this small commune as a matter of the heart. "The community is a container that allows each of us to see the hurtful things within us, and work toward healing." 25 people—12 adults and 13 children—share the house, vehicles and other aspects of life. "But most important we share common struggles. I have four children. I can offer support to the new fathers. As a result, we develop faster here than in other Christian experiences. We share physical work, but the hard thing is working on spiritual problems. It's like a dance. Not ballet, a tap dance."

James nourishes my soul just as Country Gal fills my belly. I ride away in appreciation of those who live in a simple way.

Then I search for Twelve Tribes on the internet and come upon all sorts of allegations: child abuse, hate. The internet is a vast collection of unfiltered, unedited pronouncements, virtually impossible to verify. The sum of all these supposed truths reinforces the predilections of anyone who chooses to go deep but refuses to search broad. The World Wide Web assertions cloud my good will toward James and his community. They cast doubt on everything James professed.

Latham, NY—May 17, 2015, 11:00 a.m.

There is no doubt, no ambiguity, among the fastest growing religious group in America, the Mormons. I can tell within five minutes when I land in a Mormon household. There's a piano in the living room, instead of a TV, several polite and inquisitive children, devotional paintings on the wall, and a photo of the temple where my hosts' marriage was sealed. I drop the phrase "LDS"—that's what Mormons call each other—and we're tight.

Offering hospitality must be an extension of Mormon faith; I am invited to Mormon homes all over our country. Not just in Utah, but also New York, Illinois, Idaho, California, and Texas. The more time I spend with Mormons, the more I like them. Their theology baffles me, but arriving at a Mormon household is like stepping into a Frank Capra movie. We share an enjoyable evening of conversation, music, and games. Everyone is appreciated and goes to bed feeling loved.

When I spend Saturday night with a family of faith, they often invite me to their Sunday service, and I usually accept. The Mormon service in Latham, New York, is too chaotic for Frank Capra; it's as if Robert Altman made a G-rated family film. The sanctuary is full to overflowing. Clean-cut men wear starched white shirts. Modest women wear even more modest dresses. Noisy toddlers run everywhere. Lay people mount the pulpit; Mormons don't have ministers. Congregants stand up and share how Mormon teachings resolve their daily dilemmas. Dara Blanchette debates getting her ears pierced. Austin Peterson describes his struggle to lose weight. "When I go to Google with a question, I get a discussion board with a variety of answers and opinions. Having a prophet is like having a search engine run by God. The answers may not be popular, but they are definitive."

For a kid weaned on Roman Catholicism spoken in a dead language with 2,000-year-old readings, I'm astonished at how relevant all this joyful chaos appears.

After service I pedal on, toward the Catskills. I can appreciate why people become Mormons. I can understand why evangelicals are on the rise and mainline Protestants on the wane. Why even the number of atheists is growing while the term "agnostic" is losing favor. Ambiguity is too much work. People want ideologies that dole out complete answers. The more complex our world gets, the more we hunger for simple solutions.

Stone Cabin, AZ—November 12, 2015, 1:00 p.m.

The United States is one giant manifestation of Newton's third law: for every action there is an equal and opposite reaction. Our country is immense, yet I can traverse it on a bike. The 24-hour news cycle foments conflict in a land where freedom of speech without requirement of truth promotes exaggeration. New Jersey is dense packed; Wyoming is empty. Ordinary citizens face diminished economic opportunity while the one percent gets wealthier, by every measure, every day. People in the Midwest want to be liked, people in the Mountain States just want you to move on. Citizens' bellyache about our government, yet every immigrant I meet chooses our problems over the ones they left behind and angles to remain here permanently. Nevada is parched desert; Louisiana is swamp marsh.

I never know in advance whether a particular person will put an upbeat or dreary slant on tomorrow, but patterns emerge. Issues crop up in clumps. Oscillating attitudes sprout in contradictory succession. Mathematical analysis might reveal an equal share of positive and negative perspectives, but it would not capture the rumbling undercurrent that courses through our landscape: the dissonant frequency that ripples through billowing Nebraska grass and whistles up the shaft of West Texas oil wells; that rolls the California surf and clatters across Minnesota freight trains; that boils in Atlanta traffic.

Every issue I encounter—immigration, climate change, education—festers in vague unease until I can no longer ignore the pressure it exerts. Then its contours take shape. I begin to grasp its constituent sides (gathering multiple perspectives is the whole reason I pedal) until I luck upon the person or story that illustrates the conflict.

Our national dissonance simmers on the back burner of my mind for some time. Is it the natural result of spreading Newton's third law over an entire continent, or a bipolar disorder hard-wired into the American psyche? And then I meet Randy, whose story makes our confusion perfectly clear.

Randy owns a hamburger stand in the Arizona desert just north of the US Border Patrol checkpoint beyond Yuma. He's a Vietnam-era Marine, a beefy guy, proud of our military heritage. His son served in Iraq. While I eat an ice cream cone, Randy explains how he landed stateside from 'Nam in 1969, got harassed by a hippie protestor, slugged the guy in the Seattle airport, and was arrested before he even swallowed one gulp of American fresh air.

Randy stares across the Arizona desert as he fast-forwards 30 years to his daughter's wedding. His eyes moisten to a completely different scene. His words slow to the cadence of the steady march as he leads his precious baby to the altar.

Randy shakes his head, as if in disbelief that he gave his princess away. Then he holds his jaw firm, his voice turns resolute. He describes arriving at DFW airport, to meet his son returning from Iraq. The terminal is mobbed. Cheering citizens hoist banners to greet our uniformed heroes. Randy's son emerges from the crowd and strides straight toward his father. Randy opens his arms to embrace his oldest child, but his son pumps out his hand before they touch. He gives his father a crisp salute. "Thank you, Sir, for your service to our nation." Fat tears roll down Randy's cheeks. I lick ice cream melting in the desert sun. "My son gave me the homecoming I never received."

Randy is a tough guy. Randy is a tender man. Tender toughness is the essence of the American character; so elemental we reveal it within 15 minutes to an ice cream–craving cyclist. We want to police the world and be loved by it at the same time. We flip from strong to vulnerable and back on a dime and wonder why the rest of the world does not understand us.

I pedal away from the odd collection of metal buildings and trailers called Stone Cabin. I wonder at Randy's bravado, his longing, out here alone peddling road food to bikers and tourists released from the border patrol's questioning grip, 25 miles north of the Mexican border. What motivates a man to flip burgers under sweltering tin roofs beside the generator hum that keeps ice cream cold? If it's solitude he seeks, then what compels Randy to boast, and cry, to a visitor wearing a question?

I spin 35 miles north on US 95 to Quartzite. The road is mostly flat. I scoop down and out of occasional drainage swales; there's too little rainfall here to bother building actual bridges. Mountains grow up on either side of me. Saguaro stand sentential to my progress. Not another vehicle, not another creature, not another soul.

The land lays strong and silent, though not in peace. We are turbulent people, riddled with power and yearning. Is there any way to satiate our unease?

One two three. Quick as an eye blink, out of the south, tractor-trailers whiz past me. "Save money. Live better." A six-stroke sunflower—or is it an asterisk—blooms on the side of each container full of stuff, likely manufactured in Mexico. The trucks shock me out of my reverie; they pull me forward in their wake.

We are a want society, and that's how we'll be tomorrow.
We live on instant gratification. We cater to that.
—Colleen Thompson, food vendor, Edinburg, OH

Spokane, WA—August 18, 2015, 11:00 a.m.

Five days into my journey, on the eve of my first direction change west, I stay with Jim Merkel and his family along the Maine coast. Jim wrote *Radical Simplicity*, a guide to creating a small footprint on our earth. In the decade since the author was a single man and bicycle advocate, Jim got married, had a son, travelled the country to find a community of choice, and settled in picturesque Belfast. He purchased 40 acres on the outskirts of town, built an energy-efficient house and greenhouse. Got a car and a boat. The Merkels lead an environmentally conscious life. They grow much of their own food; they heat their house with wood from their land. Their life is sustainable by some definitions, but it is hardly simple. Before I leave the following morning, Jim tours me around their spread. "I don't know where to put it all, and I wrote a book about it."

In my imaginings, my pilgrimage is a leisurely exploration of people and places. But the morning I turn west, my principle direction for the next 115 days, I realize the third key component to my survey course of America. Our country is not just about people and places. It's about stuff.

We have so much stuff. We buy so much stuff. And we throw so much stuff away. Our stuff is so important to us. Sometimes it's more important than other people. Sometimes it's more important than our selves.

Benton, Maine, has more square feet of self-storage than retail. People open the doors of their bulging garages on sunny Sunday afternoons and sell stuff to each other.

I pause on an overpass near Ligonier, Pennsylvania, to watch a freight train. Over a hundred cars of shiny black coal rumble beneath me. All across our nation I see long, full trains pulling raw materials, component parts, and finished products. We don't just like stuff. We like to move it.

Yard signs lead me to a Kiko's auction in Edinburg, Ohio. Pickup trucks line both sides of a residential street. Michelle sells tickets to guys who inspect and fondle another man's lifetime of accumulated tools. I hear the ghost sounds of a whirring lathe and grinding saw crafting hardwood coat racks and bookshelves. Where is the man whose hand guided these machines? Retired, for sure, maybe in a home, perhaps dead. Colleen sells cold pop and grilled sausages. She runs a tab for big-bellied men in camouflage caps, auction regulars in the hunt for a deal. A fast talker with a smooth stream of superlatives sells drills and presses to the highest bidder. This is not a distress sale; it's a nice home in a solid neighborhood. Colleen explains it is the first of three auctions at this property: tools today; home furnishings in two weeks; the house itself four weeks hence. Many people, especially downsizing retirees, sell everything by auction. It's easier to walk away from the accumulated memories than hand the stuff off piecemeal.

In St. Cloud, Minnesota, I chat with a construction crew installing a third set of railroad lines. Our rail system, battered ever since the Interstate Highway System made truck transport a breeze, is actually expanding.

In Ovando, Montana, the skies are sooty grey with smoke from raging forest fires. The National Fire Service has ordered evacuations, but many people refuse. Their homes and their stuff are their identity. They will survive, or perish, together.

The more a body living out of two panniers observes our affection, our obsession, with stuff, the more he wants to understand what he's missing. Every town I travel through, no matter how small, has a self-storage facility. Some are no more than a single metal structure surrounded by chain link. Others are elaborate campuses; castle fortress security towers overlooking menacing gates with a solid wall that encloses rows of garages chock full of possessions with separate pavilions for boats and RVs.

By the time I reach Spokane I itch to understand the phenomenon of locking our stuff away. I pedal over the rail yards and pass miles of light industry to Self-Storage of Spokane. I press the intercom button and announce my meek presence. Steel gates swing open to allow me entry with the quiet awe of approaching Oz. A treasure trove of wishes and dreams are sheltered behind these locked doors.

Running a self-storage facility, like most jobs, is more complicated than it first appears. Sharon Wiggins, manager, is well organized. There are leases and locks and limits to liability; a retail section that sells packing supplies; cameras and security codes and 24-hour access; liens for non-payment; and auctioning abandoned goods. Its no wonder reality TV thrives in this arena. Sharon has even categorized her four major client-types, each with their own particular bent on stuff.

First are people who need temporary storage between permanent residences. They rent a unit, fill it, and don't return until they empty it. They might rent for two to three months between houses, although that can stretch to years for servicemen and -women deployed overseas. These are Sharon's easiest renters: out of sight, out of mind.

Small business owners who run their companies out of a storage unit are quite the opposite. "We see them everyday, tradespeople and landscapers. They get their equipment in the morning and return it at night. Basing their business out of here is much cheaper than renting a storefront."

Other types of continuous renters, usually apartment dwellers, augment living space by stowing their seasonal belongings here. "We have the snow blower and skis in the summer, the lawnmower and canoe in the winter. It's cheaper to rent a unit than buy a house with a yard. It's a cost effective way to upsize."

The flip side is just as important. "Downsizing is a lot of our business. People going into nursing homes or assisted living rent large units. Parents have the satisfaction that their possessions are still intact while the children can delay having to decide what to do with them." Most of the time, heirs sell off the stuff after folks die. The children don't want the stuff, and nobody's feelings get hurt. Self-storage as mediator and grief counselor.

Sharon doesn't mention another type of renter I observe the morning I visit: a family of three, obviously homeless, with a modest stash in a small unit. Businesses aren't inclined to highlight their connection to the down-and-out.

Sharon helps me understand why these places thrive everywhere. As rental space goes, storage units are cheap. From the landlord's perspective, they're easy and profitable. No plumbing to break; no tenants to complain. Just stuff, sitting idle, generating income.

It's amazing what people have and what they move. Junk that means so much to them.
—Zander Chanin, paper artist, Eugene, OR

Carson City, NV—September 28, 2015, 11:00 a.m.

Flynn and Savannah Gabriel live a particular vision of tomorrow: a post-consumption world. Their modest ranch house a few blocks away from the Nevada State Capitol is easy to find: the driveway and yard is cluttered with stuff. At first glance, the place is chaos, but upon closer inspection their mini-fridges, bicycle wheels, and copper pipes are well ordered. Flynn explains, "Ninety percent of what we have, someone else was throwing away. Our neighbors don't complain because we keep things neat and give them anything they might like."

Flynn and Savannah are immersed in a world of stuff, though they don't purchase much, and never buy retail. Flynn, age 31, is a scrap man; Savannah works at a local thrift shop. They find what others discard, then fix it and resell it through eBay, Craigslist, or The Penny Hoarder on Facebook. During dinner the night I stay with them, the doorbell rings and Savannah collects $25 from the top bidder in an auction for a printer she's found and repaired.

Flynn's pickup and trailer are loaded with 88 microwaves he purchased for 3 cents a pound. Total cost: $68. I watch him dismantle one, strip resalable metal, and separate copper from aluminum from brass. He keeps the motors intact: resale value of 15 cents per pound. The carcasses will go to the landfill for a half-cent a pound. It takes Flynn 10 minutes to tear apart and separate each microwave's components, about 15 hours for the whole load. He'll gross about $300 for his effort, less than $10 an hour after you deduct his initial investment, the cost of transport, and time for resale.

But Flynn finds it interesting work he can do on his own time, and it doesn't require interacting with other people. As a man with Asperger's syndrome, Flynn's not keen on working with others.

At two in the morning Flynn slips in and out of the living room where I sleep. He rises early for his twice-weekly morning paper delivery route. He's also got a regular gig hauling trash for a few local motels. Erratic hours don't seem to bother the man.

He's back home in time for breakfast with Savannah and daughter Aria. We take group photos before Aria leaves for school, Savannah heads to the thrift store, and Flynn returns to his microwaves. "I've worked since the day I graduated high school. Of all the jobs I've had, I like scrapping best. I do what I want when I want."

I pedal away from the piles that litter this corner of Nevada's capital; eyesores that appear to be part of our unending accumulation of junk. But Flynn and Savannah don't add to the problem. In fact, in repurposing our discards, they're part of the solution.

I am interested in proving the hyper-loop concept: supplying things and transporting people via a magnetic vacuum tube.
It's very expensive to build but then very inexpensive to operate.
Objects will move up to 700 miles per hour. As long as it's straight, you can put it anywhere, in the ocean, in the sky.
A friend of Elon Musk is building one in Dubai. You can get anything built in Dubai.
—Joseph Gilbert, art history student, Gainesville, FL

Long Beach, CA—November 3, 2015, 10:00 a.m.

Flynn's piles of scrap are quaint in the face of the vast expanse of pavement, canals, and cranes that constitute the Port of Long Beach. What are 88 microwaves in the face of a single ship hauling 14,000 containers, each packed with thousands upon thousands of manufactured goods, from dental floss to tractors to microwaves? Every year, nearly a million containers arrive at this port in the futile attempt to satiate our American appetite for all things new.

Lee Peterson, Director of Communication for the Port of Long Beach, meets me at the administration building and tours me by car; Surly is not welcome along the docks. Container ships, the largest manmade objects on earth, exist for the sole purpose of shuttling stuff. Today's titan is the 14,000-container model; an 18,000-container behemoth is on its way. Each larger boat requires bigger docks, more sophisticated off-loading, and deeper ports. Long Beach, which superseded all East Coast ports when it adopted container shipping in the 1970s, is committed to expand however necessary to stay abreast of an economy and culture tied to moving stuff all the time. The port tripled its container volume in the 1990s, took a hit in the 2008 recession, but is back on track to offloading ever more goods. By 2030, the Port of Long Beach envisions doubling its capacity. As a good communications man and sensitive Californian, Lee emphasizes the port's net energy reduction despite this growth.

The success of the Long Beach port and its Los Angeles sister right next door, is all about optimizing the twin drivers of business: time and money.

There are only two ways to get from Shanghai to Los Angeles; 14 hours by plane or 14 days by boat. Since planes are prohibitively expensive for bulk transport, business reluctantly accepts the shipping time required to cross the Pacific. But the Port of Long Beach must beat the competition on our shores. Ships pass Seattle, Portland, and Oakland well before they get to LA/LB, but Long Beach's superior off-loading and truck/rail interface recoup that differential. Ships going through the Panama Canal to Miami, Savannah, or New York take more than a week longer to deliver goods to the East Coast. It's faster to offload in Long Beach and then railroad freight across the continent.

This is not a one-way route. We ship wood pulp to Japan, which they turn into paper and ship back to us. We ship computer chips to China and receive assembled electronic devices in return. We import more than we export, and, in general, the value of what we import exceeds the value of what we export. That's why it costs $1,200 to $1,600 to ship a container from China to Long Beach, but only $450 to send one in the other direction.

If we can get to the point that we stop trashing our planet, that could be a start.
—Robert Solos, sound engineer, Fort Worth, TX

Santa Ana, CA—November 5, 2015, 11:00 p.m.

Two days after I visit Lee at the Port of Long Beach I stay with Reza Barkholder, a man who deals in stuff at a mega-scale. Reza's a jocular guy with a Berkeley degree whose dream of becoming an attorney was deferred by life and children. Money needed to be made. More than 20 years ago he took a job managing trucks for a disposal company. California's integrated waste management plan, with a 50% recycling goal, put him in the right place at the right time. "I've tried to reinvent myself many times, but I've never been successful. I keep coming back to scrap."

Reza makes scrap more exciting than law. He whisks his truck along the Santa Ana Freeway on a crisp autumn night in a streaking blur of headlights. My stomach rises into my mouth; it's been months since I moved so fast in the dark. We park along a deserted stretch of industry and walk beneath a looming galvanized gate. Searchlights on stanchions make glistening piles of twisted metal shimmer as if they were jewels for giants. The jagged forms cut deep shadows. I step carefully in the lurking danger. It's not enough to keep my eyes set downward; the crane swinging wads of steel overhead demands attention as well.

Gnarled debris. This is what the greatest nation on earth sends its Communist cousins in exchange for all the finished products they deliver to us. Every morning six dump trucks leave Santa Ana, collect scrap from LA construction sites, and deposit it here. By mid-morning a crane operator begins sorting through the pickings. He clamps down on the debris, raises it in the sky and drops it into dumpster-size hoppers. A forklift driver fills hoppers and tosses their contents into the mouth of a shipping container. Then, a bobcat operator rams against the jumble to compress the metal shards into the 8-foot x 8-foot x 40-foot shell.

When Reza and I arrive at 10 p.m. a delivery truck drops off its final load, while the sorting crew is at max frenzy to fill containers. The crew will not stop until they've packed all the scrap delivered that day, well after midnight. Tomorrow morning, semis will haul the containers to the Port of Long Beach while Reza's six trucks return to the streets of Los Angeles to collect more scrap.

Reza's contract requires he deliver a minimum of 12 containers every day, filled as close to the 45,000-pound legal limit for transporting goods on US highways. Why? Most containers returning to China are empty. The ships need Reza's heavy scrap for ballast. What the Chinese do with it is anybody's guess.

Eugene, OR—September 12, 2015, 11:00 a.m.

The mammoth amount of stuff crisscrossing the globe that I witness in Long Beach and Santa Ana turns me numb. There's no feeling in so much hard metal. Our emotional connection to stuff, how it litters our psyche and contorts our behavior, emerges in the more intimate setting of weekend brunch.

Brail's is a Eugene, Oregon, institution. The place buzzes with college town cerebral chatter; a progressive vibe cossetted in coffee, hash and flannel. Saturday morning wait times are long, but the French toast is worth the queue. I am in deep conversation with Sherri McCutcheon, a robust woman with loose grey hair, and her slender, eloquent son Zander Chanin, well before the three of us squeeze into a cluttered table.

Zander graduated with a degree in architecture from the University of Oregon, though his terminology is foreign to a guy who earned the same degree 35 years earlier. Whereas I was infused with the notion of architecture as a conduit to a better world, Zander's perspective is ideologically neutral, even abstract. "Architecture is just one step of cycling materials from earth for our use. We borrow materials from the natural world. During the process of creating the built environment, materials are taken from their natural state, manipulated by man, and then they're returned to their natural state." Zander's detached assessment of human intervention seems benign, maybe pure, but it lacks passion. He has no urge to make a permanent mark, to build for eternity. In fact, Zander has little interest in making buildings at all. I appreciate that his analysis is a more sustainable perspective than, say, a zealous master builder, but I cannot reconcile his idea that we return materials to their natural state with the reality of litter and trash and landfills I see everywhere I go.

Zander spent a few months backpacking in Japan. "I felt completely liberated from stuff. I began to value things as potential art objects, particularly fragile things like paper." His experience in Japan informs his principle interest, creating art installations, often incorporating paper in large-scale, structural ways. Zander's day job is working for a moving company, an ironic counterpoint to his ambition to keep things light. Uncomfortable with the machinations and permanence of traditional architecture, he doesn't want to fabricate more stuff. Instead, he shuffles it around.

If Zander spends his time postulating about, and acting in opposition to, our material world, Sherri's relationship to stuff reveals the emotional power of physical objects.

Sherri moved to Eugene from Denver after she inherited her father's house. She planned to remain long enough to settle his estate. But she was uncomfortable living in and among her father's possessions. Her daily activities disrupted his presence. So, she rents a separate place and works two jobs to keep both houses afloat. Instead of turning her father's assets into her own nest egg, Sherri has become curator of a personal museum. She realizes, intellectually, it is not a viable long-term way to live. But she is unable to relinquish the stuff of memory.

"I need to sell my Dad's house, but I can't, yet. Every piece in it has to be touched, picked up, assessed. The candlestick is meaningless when you're not there. But when you're present with it, it's valuable."

Don't leave scoop in container

Monroe, MI—June 1, 2015, noon

You might think that a man living out of two saddlebags carries only essentials, but even I tote stuff whose sole function is to trigger memory.

People give me things all the time. Candy bars, cookies, and cold water are always welcome, fresh fruit is bulky, maps and brochures superfluous. In order to be polite, I accept whatever items I can fit, and usually give them away at my next stop. The fabulous ladies who organize the world's largest motorcycle rally in Sturgis, South Dakota, cram my panniers with T-shirts and caps. Fortunately, I stay with a household of teenagers in Rapid City who love all that stuff.

Still, some tokens become welcome parasites: the rub stone I keep in my shirt pocket, the suede lanyard from an Oneida Indian I wear around my neck, the lucky penny from a Steamboat, Colorado, rancher that lines my wallet. Six officers from the Racine Police Department give me a brocade emblem that I haul over 10,000 miles. The extra effort it takes me to power that patch through state after state is scant compared to the meaning it triggers of our generous conversation about community policing. While the media runs divisive poison about Black Lives Matter versus Blue Lives Matter, this memento reminds me: lives that matter cannot be an either/or proposition.

Many people ask me if I am riding to raise money. I am not. Actually, I loathe how our society has devolved into elaborate forms of begging to finance important needs like disease research and primary education. If I'm feeling cocky I tell folks, "I'm not raising money, I'm raising consciousness," but most of the time I am smart enough to curtail that smarmy attitude.

People also want to pay my way. Early on, I decline everyone's offer by explaining that I have enough money. But one noon, Martin Lujac, owner of Fino's Restaurant in Monroe, Michigan, joins me for lunch and shares his Iron Curtain immigrant tale. When he insists on comping my gyro and fries, I object. Until Martin thunders, "You're living the dream, man. You have to let others participate."

After that, I graciously accept free food and drink, though I never accept actual cash. For just as my relationship to stuff is different from people who are rooted, so is my relationship to money.

Money doesn't buy me anything I want. Actually, money obscures what I'm seeking. When I stay with an interesting host or lunch with a quirky local, we share stories; we build a relationship. But once I pull out my wallet, we spiral into mere transaction.

I have enough money to buy my own meals, repair my bike, or pay for a motel room. I don't seek something for nothing. But my richest days are the ones when I share nourishment with one fellow human, sleep on a scrap of carpet offered by another, and don't spend a cent.

What's memorable about Martin Lujac is not that he saved me $7 on lunch. It's his tale of escaping Yugoslavia in 1969. It's why he employs several of his eight children at Fino's ("It keeps them busy and let's me keep my eye on them."). It's the cross-country travel tips from a man who's motorcycled the same 48 states I'm crossing. It's his unbridled immigrant enthusiasm. "America, America, even now. Everyone wants to come here. That never changes." The man's attitudes and insights cannot be tallied on a meal tab.

When I was near Milwaukee I stayed with Shane and had a great conversation over delicious beers about how to live tomorrow, all thanks to the guest he had the previous night.
Today I made it to St. Cloud and saw a couple of business cards sitting on some gold-colored bananas asking the same question. So I wanted to let you know, from your perspective at least: I am tomorrow.
— Zachary Shiner, Dickinson, ND

Cashmere, WA—August 22, 2015, 11:00 a.m.

Though it's difficult for a guy on two wheels with two bags to reciprocate hospitality, I offer it whenever I can. Zachary Shiner's unique "I am tomorrow" response to my question shows up in my email queue in Fargo. I inquire about his route, and discover we're riding more or less parallel, one day apart, for the next week. Zachary catches up with me on a layover day in Dickinson where I "warmshower host" this former Chicago schoolteacher pedaling to his new job in Seattle: dinner at the local chicken joint and a solid night's sleep on a rollout at the Oasis Motel. Next morning, I head south toward Denver while Zachary keeps on west.

Weeks later, I arrive at Missoula, Montana, home of Adventure Cycling: aka bicycle touring Mecca. I meet a bunch of young guys, including Peter, a 19-year-old from New Jersey, who catches me the next day on highway 200 outside of Dixon. We chat and he pedals on. My warmshowers hosts that night warned they'd be driving up from Missoula and would pick me up along the way. Although I always prefer to cycle when weather and strength allow, if someone offering me dinner and a bed wants to pick me up, I'm not a prig about it. Near 5 p.m., a pickup passes me and rolls onto the shoulder just south of Plains. There's already one bike in the bed. Peter sits in the jump seat of the cab. "We thought he was you; stopped, and invited him along."

Next morning I leave after pancakes. Peter lingers behind. By midday the weather looks stormy, so I text him an offer to share my motel in Noxon if he doesn't want to camp. Noxon Motel has eight basic rooms, mostly for hunters. No restaurant for miles. I check into my room just as fat drops start to fall. There's a full storm raging by the time Peter shows up, wet and hungry. He has nothing but tortillas and peanut butter in his pack. I augment his

foodstuffs with PowerBars, trail mix, and crystalized ginger. Feast enough for two fellows thankful for the thin walls that separate us them from a driving rain.

Next morning is bright and sunny. I head toward Sandpoint, Idaho, where I'll bunk with some Mormons. Peter's on to Heron where a rancher he met day before invited him for lunch. Touring cyclists go where we're invited, where our quirks and our stories are appreciated.

I meander, according to my custom, across the gorgeous Idaho panhandle. I linger at Spokane's downtown falls, and detour to Grand Coulee Dam. I pedal through apple harvest in Brewster and along the spectacular Columbia River to Wenatchee. On a short day's jaunt to Leavenworth, I'm lured off Highway 2 by a pair of enticing diversions: factory tours and sweets. After a thorough tasting of the samples at Aplet's candy factory, I determine their harvest bars are the best energy snacks I've found. I buy a dozen. Handy, because as soon as I reconnect with Route 2, there's Peter and four other cyclists, some of whom I already know. I pass out the bars. We ride west together. Within a few miles they are far ahead; I can't keep up with young bucks one-third my age. But I'll likely see them again. It's late August. Cross-country summer cyclists from all over our land are converging on that urban cyclist's dream: Seattle.

You live in America. You sit on the sidewalk drinking beer.
You got to have a conspiracy theory.
—JJ, owner of San Rosendro Crossing, Marathon, TX

Bozeman, MT—August 8, 2015, 6:00 p.m.

Conspiracy theories are an eccentric yet persistent part of the American ethos. Obama is about to invade Texas; illegal immigrants are poisoning our food; the Chinese add arsenic to our water. I've never found satisfaction in extrapolating an evil into a universal threat, but if I ascribed to a conspiracy theory here's the one I'd choose: mighty forces conspire to keep us all in debt.

I sense a good story the moment a middle-aged man opens the townhouse door at a married students' housing complex at Montana State University. This is no 20-something guy juggling a wife, a baby, and a dissertation. Dr. Don Funke has leading man looks—Marcus Welby meets George Clooney—an attractive wife, Karen, and two college-age children. So why's he living in married students' housing? Because Karen's returned to school to pursue her master's degree, and it's a step up from the double-wide the family previously occupied.

When Don graduated from chiropractic school in upstate New York in the 1980s, he owed $88,000 in education debt. Through 15 years of practice, and a shift in medical reimbursements, that debt kept increasing. "We had $275,000 in debt and no way to ever get out from under it. I'm a good chiropractor, but not a good entrepreneur."

Funke family lore is they came west to start clean. "We arrived with no job, no house, nothing." Don never says the word "bankrupt." I read between the lines. Don gets a job, a trailer house, and more debt. Debt is the constant, chronic condition of the Funke family existence; an economic allergy that cannot be escaped or cured: only managed.

Don and his family are not poor in mind or spirit. They pursue their aspirations, even as they add to their debt. Karen's graduate study is education financing, the first major debt of many people's lives. "Everyone needs an education, but at what cost? Pell grants used to cover 75% of a college education. Now they cover 24%. People graduate with debt levels they can never repay. Or worse, they incur debt and never graduate."

Don and Karen see no end to the burden they bear, and will bestow upon the next generation. "We come from families that managed debt, used it to gain positions and security. But it's a different paradigm for our generation. The debt is eternal. And it's not going to change for our kids."

Son Walter minimizes his debt by living at home and attending a state school to study art, but like most college graduates, he will get a payment schedule with his diploma. Megan will spend junior year in France though it costs more than remaining at MSU. At some point, when debt becomes your permanent reality, you shrug the monthly statements and go on with life.

From one perspective, debt liberated Don and his family. It prompted them to pursue their dream of Bozeman, a place they love.

To be sure, there are many more tragic stories of debt in our nation than the Funke's: people who spiral into homelessness, disease, and destitution until eventually they drop out of the system and live beyond credit.

People like Flynn and Savannah Gabriel in Carson City, Nevada, who use their local pawn shop as a bank because they can't get conventional credit.

People like Kevin Cipolla in Crescent City, California, so disengaged from our financial system that he doesn't even own anything to pawn. Kevin's got a bike, a set of clothes, a thirst for beer, and an addiction to butts. If he can land a day job and get some cash, all good. If not, he gets by.

What makes the Funkes' story resonate is not that they wallow in the bottom of our economic barrel. It's how, despite their middle class aspirations, they teeter on the economic edge. Though their actions pretend away debt's grip, it infiltrates our conversation from so many angles, I suspect it's always on their mind.

Debt is pernicious. It makes us vulnerable. One random accident, one illness, one economic reversal could land Don's family in dire straights. Their story could so easily flip from a tale of striving to a debacle of defeat, extinguishing all illusion of middle class life.

And so the Funkes continue to borrow and toil, to rest uncomfortably in an economic limbo, fueling the fastest growing component of our economy—financial services—by paying more and more interest for goods and services already consumed. They occupy the conspiratorial sweet spot of perpetual debt: not so disenfranchised that we resort to revolution, just enough to keep our heads down and our interest payments flowing.

The future is going to be tiny houses.
We need to downsize.
We need less stuff.
    —Lisa Frame, dog owner, Houston, TX

Glendale, AZ—November 17, 2015, 8:00 p.m.

Our devotion to stuff and the shackles of debt intersect within that cherished American fiefdom: the single-family home.

Off the thoroughfare grid, the residential streets of Glendale follow gentle curves. Low-slung brick houses: two-car garages, four bedrooms, a scattering of baths, and the requisite Great Room, all capped by enormous roofs. I imagine a real estate agent describing a string of pearls laced over the desert. Phil Campbell's house is more like a noose.

Phil is single, a Southern transplant with an easy smile. He owns a spacious house with a fireplace, a well-appointed kitchen, and a beautifully landscaped yard. I ask Phil "How will we live tomorrow?" He laughs and says, "I want to have a good time." But the more we talk, the more his smile strains.

Phil is an HVAC mechanic; he loves working with his hands. Over 30 years, Phil has made a series of investments geared toward a secure retirement. This is the third home he's purchased, each larger than the last, "because owning a house is a good investment." He also purchased a local home air conditioning company. At age 60 Phil is working more than ever, though beyond flipping our burgers with point guard dexterity, he doesn't work with his hands anymore. He has a mortgage, rent on his shop, and payroll to meet. He took a few business calls during dinner, and when I went to bed, settled into a stack of paperwork.

Owning a home is a cornerstone of the American Dream. It roots us to our community; it provides financial security in retirement. But trading up—buying more than we need—distorts the dream. Real estate agents, banks, and retailers don't make much money off people who buy a modest home and stay put. They promote the idea that buying an ever larger home will result in ever-larger gains. More often it simply results in ever-larger debt. When we trade up instead of pay off, the cycle of consumption and debt grows bigger with every move. The investment logic—pay down a mortgage rather than pay rent—deteriorates with each "trade up." When we apply the costs that never get factored into real estate appreciation figures—furnishings, heating, cooling, and maintenance—the investment value of real estate actually shrinks.

Phil is fascinated by my trip; envious would not be too strong a word. He reminisces about a long-ago adventure. "I hiked the Shenandoah's, along the Appalachian Trail. When on tour, your life is simple. You get grounded to the earth. You get back here and the world is ugly."

There's something wrong in a society where a hard-working middle-aged man is so burdened by obligations that he pines for a single month in his past while so much of life renders a bitter taste.

Next morning, as I meander out of Glendale's curves, I murmur what passes for a prayer; that I caught Phil on a bad night; that he finds more enjoyment in his house and its comforts than I witnessed. He's bound to them for the long haul. Like so many who bought real estate in the early 2000s, Phil monitors his home's present value. Years after assuming the debt, his investment is still falling short.

73

Would Phil be content if he had stayed in his first home, paid it off, and kept fabricating ductwork rather than taking on obligations that, so far, have brought neither profit nor security? We can never know. Life is not a double-blind controlled experiment. We make a choice, it guides our path; we endure, or enjoy, the consequences.

What we do know is that our culture doesn't applaud modest ambition. Against the drumbeat of bigger, better, newer, mere content seems a feeble objective. We are conditioned to always want more.

It's not about money.
It's about the treasure of the experience along the way.
   —Tom Wann, cyclist, Cheyenne, WY

Norwalk, OH—May 30, 2015, 11:00 a.m.

I don't owe anyone a dime, yet I am deep in debt: the debt of gratitude to everyone I meet along my way.

Odd how the same four-letter word—debt—conjures such divergent meaning. Monetary debt divides the wealthy from the poor, the powerful from the beholden; it reinforces hierarchy and privilege. The debt of gratitude binds us through generosity and shared experience,

Ominous clouds shadow me along US 20 West out of Norwalk. Sunday morning traffic is light. The wind picks up. Rain splatters my parka. I could feel sorry for myself, a yellow smudge braced against grey gusts. Instead this weather emboldens me. I feel strong. I feel radical.

I think of the hundreds, thousands of cars that have already passed me on this journey. I'll never know which driver has observed my slow progress and thought "now there's a guy living his own set of rules." I am not supposed to know. Yet I am confident that it's happened, that I've changed someone's perspective.

I am a tiny testament to a different way of being.

The ancients worked with vibration, song, and dance to address any problem.
They worked with nature. We work against nature.
We have to find the vibration that allows us to work with nature.
We have to find the song.
　　　　—Bob Boyce, home-schooled energy guru, Rice, VA

Redig, SD—June 29, 2015, 10:00 a.m.

Now somewhere in the Black Mountain hills of Dakota ...

Bicycle touring, like most of life, is routine. The legs spin. The hands grip. The eyes keep watch on the shoulder, avoid big rocks and strips of metal, stay clear of the rumble strip. Ears stay alert to traffic, though mostly they're occupied with bird chatter and the wind's ceaseless sigh. The body is raised above the ground, but the skin's riddled with sensations from all that wind. The nose shifts into overdrive as well. Stiff breezes bombard with scents we never behold behind a windshield: fecund fields and damp forests. A guy on a bike inhales the stale dust of a strip mine, miles from view.

US 85 from Buffalo, South Dakota, to Spearfish, on a 95-degree glorious June day, is cycle touring heaven. Dazzling sun warms my forearms; a robust crosswind prickles the hair thereupon. Hardly a car. A dry, acrid smell rises out of the tawny plains. Spring fresh is already turning to brittle summer in this land of scant rainfall. The fertile farms of Ohio and Michigan are hundreds of miles behind me. The massive fires that will enflame such brittle grass are yet miles ahead.

Eighty-four miles equals eight hours in the saddle. The proprietress at the Tipperary Motel metes out the emptiness. "It's 20 miles to Redig; there's a convenience store there. Then 50 miles of nothing until Belle Fourche." The stretch to Spearfish is a coda.

The first 10 miles of every day are the hardest. It only takes a mile or two for my body to settle into cycling rhythm, but my mind protests. It demands that I check my odometer too often; it argues that my pace is too slow. Mental complaint is like pedaling into a headwind. Eventually, my body's discipline vanquishes my head's lazy yearnings. My brain concedes to another day of pavement. My psyche falls in sync with my legs. Everything spins in balance.

But what can my mind do for eight hours while my body burns forward-motion calories across a landscape that even local innkeepers describe as empty? It absorbs the sights, the sounds, the smells in ever-finer detail, until my senses fuse with the world around me.

Emptiness dissolves. It's opposite—subtlety—blossoms. Every blade of grass, every flickering insect comes to life. The world dances. My mind gets so crammed with minutiae it expands. It embraces everything around me. It bursts open and flows across the prairie. My head becomes empty. Then it fills with song.

Once a tune streams into my head, it swishes around there all day long. For reasons I cannot discern, the longer the ride, the more majestic the scenery, the sillier the lyric. Though I admit there's a certain logic to The Beatles' "Rocky Raccoon" hounding me across South Dakota.

I learn to accept whatever lodges in my head, whether it's Jackson Five purgatory (*A-B-C, easy as 1-2-3...*) or Leonard Cohen heaven (*Now I've heard there was a secret chord / That David played and it pleased the Lord...*). Whether I actually like a song is irrelevant. Once a tune aligns with Surly's sprocket, it plays in continuous rotation.

Thanks to Rocky and his catchy love for Lil, I come upon Redig before I even recognize my thirst: three-dozen abandoned vehicles; two mobile home shells; and a small building with the words "Cold Pop" painted on the side. I prop my bike beneath the letters and enter. No one responds to the tinkling of the door. I stand in the dust-laden remnants of a post office. A refrigerator commands the solitary center of the space. I open the fridge door to find bottled water, pop, and ice tea, cool and fresh. I gulp down a tea and leave a buck on the counter, along with a card bearing my question.

I pedal for 50 more miles; spinning, singing.

In the middle of the bleak nothing I stop. I stand astride Surly and scan the horizon. I absorb the silence. Beyond a distant butte I hear a chorus of cattle, their bellows like ancestral vibrations. The music of time and space.

D'da d'da d'da da da da
D'da d'da d'da da da da

That's how I spin my day.

We cannot know, and you can quote me on that.
—Bob, moving from CA to FL with an improvised trailer, Cameron, LA

Merced, CA—October 5, 2015, 7:00 p.m.

"Your question cannot be answered. It is mathematically impossible to analyze a system of which you are a part." Somesh Roy, a 34-year-old post-doc at UC Merced, Calcutta native, and excellent cook, takes an analytically tough stance on my query. "We think of ourselves as more important than other aspects of nature. We forget that we are part of the environmental system. We cannot manipulate the system from the inside. We should not think we can shape the future. We don't know what will be good in our future."

Even though I lack a PhD from Cornell, I know Somesh is right. Immigrants understand our country with greater clarity than those of us born here. People from abroad are both more critical and better humored about our habits. They are from outside the system.

For the first 50 years of my life I never considered how we live in this country. Then I went to Haiti and witnessed a different normal. Since then, I cannot stem the curious questions about the United States that rise in me like pimples on an adolescent chin.

Somesh studies soot, an unclean by-product of combustion. Over superb curry, I learn more than I ever cared about the stuff. Combustion takes place in a gas state; soot is solid. Some of it comes from the yellow part of an exposed flame; other soot is produced beyond our visual range. Although we have relied on combustion for hundreds of years, we don't know much about the soot it creates. "Combustion engines are everywhere and are not going away. A small improvement could have a large effect. Ideally, we would understand the physics of soot first and then apply it to combustion engines. But we can't wait. So there is a lot of research where we tinker with combustion engines, and from that, maybe, inform our understanding of the physics."

Somesh is comfortable inverting the scientific process. Ambiguity, so discomforting to citizens hell-bent on certainty, falls comfortably on this guy's shoulders. For a man steeped in flux, nothing is fixed.

Somesh's scientific bent flows into social and cultural realms. He likens our expanded social capability to "quantum engagement," in which two atoms have no direct attraction, yet an action on one instantly affects the other. "The industrial revolution freed up time for each individual. The struggle of daily life came under control and initiated a desire for more social interaction. Now, we are expanding those social connections to a virtual realm." It's a logical extrapolation, to a man savvy to the physics of probabilistic position, that our social networks should expand beyond personal interactions.

As a Hindi and a PhD, Somesh is both a man of science and of spirit. "No human can be 100% analytical, but I try to be. Coincidence is just coincidence. But we must accept that we cannot know everything about our world. Science is our religion. But there is always a higher power."

I bow to Somesh's mathematics: we cannot understand a system of which we are a part. Yet, as I pedal north and west on J7, through Winton and Cressey, past succulent gardens tended by Hmong grandmothers and miles of uniform tomatoes harvested by machine, I realize that I live as far outside our system as a man can while physically remaining within our borders. My actions, my aspirations, are at odds with the dominant culture.

I travel slow, untethered from money. I wield no power. I create nothing. I tell no one what to do. Quite the opposite. I spend my time asking—for shelter, for conversation, for ideas. This is my work. And like more and more people in the United States, it doesn't look anything like a traditional job.

Back in the 60s this question would have been presented by GE or Westinghouse.
—Bill Korn, state building inspector, Orcutt, CA

Watsonville, CA—October 21, 2015, 11:00 a.m.

Ten thousand years ago humans began farming; we remained in one place; our population soared; our dominion over other animals climbed. Three hundred years ago the industrial revolution mechanized work, created things we call jobs, and exalted the time clock. One hundred years ago our industrial capacity exceeded demand; world wars gobbled up goods until we created the consumer economy. Today, everything keeps humming as long as we buy stuff, but it takes fewer and fewer people to make more and more stuff.

In 1928, it took 100,000 men at the River Rouge plant in Dearborn, Michigan, to assemble Ford's Model A, the most popular automobile of the day. Today, a mere 1,000 workers make its equivalent, an F-150 pickup, one every 43 seconds.

A crew of four runs an Arkansas cotton plantation that supported 30 families two generations ago.

In Alabama, one man and a few hired hands raise six million pounds of Tyson chicken. We don't even have an historical precedent to compare to that level of efficiency.

Politicians clamor for more jobs, but we don't need people to make stuff anymore. Machines do it faster and better. The most fascinating thing about the F-150 plant is observing which tasks are allocated to people, and which by machines. Sealing the windshield, fixing the cab to the bed, mounting the engine block—the most precise tasks are fully automated. Humans snap in dashboards and interior ceiling panels. High touch is for accessories.

The chasm I observe between the machine and the human labor is most pronounced in corporate agriculture. Tomatoes, walnuts, and cotton are fully automated crops, never touched by human hands. But fingerprints are all over Washington apples; Hispanic men climb triangular ladders and fill giant bibs with those delicious red orbs.

Strawberry harvest near Watsonville, California, appears stuck in the Middle Ages. Buses line the edge of San Andreas Road; picnic tables and porta potties sit in their shade. Dozens of Mexicans, all ages and genders, stand small, right-angle bent at the waist, spread across the field. Their hands pluck berries from dawn to dusk, directly into the clear plastic Driscoll containers we find stacked in our supermarkets. A manager rolls a cart along the furrows, collects filled containers from the hunched figures, places them in corrugated flats, and distributes new plastic to be filled. The pickers never even raise their eyes.

All sorts of people fondle boutique food, a trendy yet growing alternative to corporate raised calories. College agronomists tinker with heirloom characteristics; permaculturists balance animal grazing and plant yield; WOOFER's dance euphoric over a pea shoot, encouraging it to sprout. But from Vermont to California and back through Florida, the only hands that I ever see touch industrial scale food are brown ones.

In general, tasks are automated based upon how repetitive they are, how much strength they require, and how much precision they demand. The Louisville Slugger bat we buy for our Little Leaguers is shaped on a hand lathe, but computers shape the custom bats the company fabricates to within 1/1000 of an inch of each Major League players' unique specifications.

Automating strength and dexterity means that, to date, robots eliminate traditional male jobs. But as automation runs deeper into our society, robots will be able to replace us all. Tomorrow, truck drivers, home health aides, and retail clerks will be automated. We will walk into the grocery store, put items in our cart, and be debited when we leave the store. Actually, Amazon already does that today. Tomorrow, a drone will deliver the whole shebang. And the day after tomorrow, the chip in our brain will anticipate a yen for sushi, transmit that desire to a mechanized chef that will create a fresh roll and deliver it in time for dinner.

What will we do when machines do everything for us? We will keep each other amused.

Consider the inverse correlation between need and compensation. We've always paid the people who address our most basic needs—food, clothing, shelter—the least. Yet we pay extraneous people—entertainers, athletes, hedge-fund managers—the most. Automation will gobble the bottom of the food chain until our economy won't even be measured by the stuff we make. Rather, it will be the experiences we create.

This is hard for the son of a blue-collar worker to swallow. But the most interesting dichotomy at the Louisville Slugger factory and museum is not which bats are made by hand and which by machine. It's observing how many, many more people work in the museum than in the factory. Humans give tours of machines that make bats.

We will live tomorrow as robots.
There's going to be a time when there's a robot that's smarter than us.
We'll live in fear of our place in the world.
　　—Karan Patal, construction management student, Tempe, AZ

Pittsburgh, PA—May 27, 2015, 6:00 p.m.

Simon Huntley grew up on a farm. He still works in farming, though he doesn't till the land. Simon's a computer guy with a specialty software business for small farmers and CSAs (community supported agriculture). His expertise provides his family with life's two greatest assets: money and time. A year ago, Simon and his wife Melanie purchased a 1950s-era contemporary home on a peak in Pittsburgh's desirable Squirrel Hill neighborhood. The view from their kitchen window of the sun setting over the skyline is striking. Melanie is a nurse practitioner, on extended leave to care for their two young boys. The afternoon I climb their steep hill, Simon has just returned from a weekday afternoon Pirate's game with their older son.

Simon's company has three employees; he works about 10 hours a week. A generation ago, Simon figures an operation like his would have up to a hundred employees, with ancillary departments for HR and PR. Today, "I have machines for all of that."

Simon views his good fortune from an historical perspective. "Look at the industrial revolution; 90% of the people lived on farms, now it's 3%. We are only in the middle of the computer revolution. The software revolution will continue for some time, and the robotics revolution is on the horizon. Within 10 years we will have autonomous truck driving: 6% of Americans have jobs related to truck driving. What will it mean when those jobs are gone? There will be disruption, but I don't believe in the idea that we will become a leisure economy. People will need jobs.

"My work in farming has reached a plateau. I have set up my business to pretty much run itself. So now I ask, 'What do I want to be involved in next?' I am interested in automation. Pittsburgh is a robotics center. Uber is here, developing autonomous cars. Autonomous cars will be good. We are just not that good at driving. What are there, 30,000 auto-related deaths per year? But automation will go so deep in our economy. It will have tremendous effects on our lives. Everyone will need an education to work. From an economic perspective, how are people going to live? Will we get a 'draw' just for being citizens that will allow us to live?"

Simon is not some tech billionaire making money for the thrill of adding zeros to his balance sheet or cashing in on some vanity app; he's a sharp guy with admirable ambition and family focus. He provides a useful service that benefits many, and he wants to further explore how technology can improve our lives. Yet even he is flummoxed by the contradiction of how a world run by technology interfaces with a society that defines us by work. He states that, "People will need jobs." But within moments he wonders, "Will we get a 'draw' just for being citizens?"

Many tech champions envision a world beyond work. The more challenging vision is articulating a society that not only eliminates unrewarding tasks, but also transcends work as our principle measure of economic and personal validation.

84

We don't have a connection to the stuff of our existence.
I live in a house and I know nothing about anyone who made it happen.
—Jesse Tillotson, Anadarko Energy employee, Uvalde, TX

Oakland, CA—October 14, 2015, 1:00 p.m.

A cyclist cannot simply stop by The Crucible for a quick visit. This mystical place of heat and muscle, the catalyst of the maker movement, is too large and too fascinating. The staff suck you into their enthusiasm, and before you know it you've whiled away an afternoon amidst glass furnaces, arc welders, molten iron, and drill presses; drenched in the intoxicating buzz of creativity.

The Crucible is a health club for minds and hands. The analogy is logistical: people purchase memberships to The Crucible, sign up for classes, and take turns using equipment in a giant open space. But it's also philosophical. Back when people performed manual labor, we didn't need to pump iron and pace treadmills to stay fit; physical activity was integrated into our daily tasks. Now we sit in front of screens all day and must purposefully exercise our bodies lest they atrophy. Similarly, back when we forged metal and blew glass and spun yarn, our hands shaped the components of daily life in a direct, often creative way. Today those same hands peck keyboards and rotate joysticks for our livelihood. Our effort is passive, our product abstract. We crave to create something tangible, something real, something that bears the imprint of our touch. At The Crucible, we keep our hands supple; we exercise our creativity.

Kier Lugo, general floor manager and glass-blowing studio head, tours me through The Crucible's 18 studios. Kier was a volunteer who became an intern, now on staff for 10 years; this place grabs hold and draws people in with magnetic force. Kier explains the rudiments of participation: safety sessions, equipment training, procuring and storing materials. When he opens the kiln door in the glass studio, 2,600-degree air blows me back to the Industrial Revolution: the magic of heat transforming silica into a transparent delicacy.

The connection between basic manufacturing and current technology is integral to The Crucible's lore. "We get tech people here. They get enthused by doing things with their hands, develop it into an avocation, then a career, and they bring their computer background with them. These techniques are not obsolete. They are actually more relevant than ever."

The Crucible's founder, Michael Sturtz, studied art, ceramics, and engineering at Alfred University, followed by graduate work at the Art Institute of Chicago. "I never found the teacher I wanted, so I decided to become that teacher." At age 26, this lover of fire got a $1,750 start-up grant to create a mixed-use workshop on a side street in Berkeley. Fifteen years later, The Crucible occupies a 50,000-square foot former factory within sight of West Oakland's BART station: the nation's largest non-profit educator of industrial arts.

A few years ago, Michael moved on from The Crucible and tried what he calls being, "California retired," but it didn't stick. Now he's applying his hands-on creed to the epicenter of San Francisco Bay academia as the executive director of the Stanford Creative Ignition Lab, a mash-up of high-tech and voc-tech, ivory tower and grease pit, digitally generated and hand crafted. Or, as Michael posits in collegiate-speak: "Our mission is the exploration of visual, experimental, and embodied thinking to influence the future around design and making."

By the time Kier tours me through glass polishing, TIG welding, MIG welding, neon, ceramics, leather, textiles, kinesthetic, stone carving, carpentry, and a made-from-scratch bike shop, I've lost track of where one industrial specialty begins and another ends. Which is the point. "We bring materials handling knowledge together rather than keeping each discipline separate." Collaboration among people and projects is fundamental to The Crucible ethos.

I've also lost track of time. More than four hours have ticked away and I'm supposed to be in Pleasant Valley for dinner, 28 miles away. I give over to the reality that sometimes, a bicycle is simply too slow to accommodate all the fun a day offers. I hike Surly on my shoulder, mount the BART station stairs, and join the ranks of commuters on their journey home.

As a species we're going to go away in evolutionary terms. I don't know what we'll become,
maybe a computer. It's okay, it's part of the evolutionary chain.
I like 2001, the three parts: the ape, the humans, and Hal starting to think for himself.
It is not an extraordinary extrapolation.
—Jason Malinowski, Restoration Hardware executive, Novato, CA

Susanville, CA—September 24, 2015, 6:00 p.m.

Simon Huntley flourishes in the tech economy. The Crucible thrives on providing techies tactile creativity. But our computer culture is not an equal-opportunity benefit. It provokes fear in huge swaths of our population; people who are poor or old, uneducated or simply timid. They may not know how to use a computer, but they're keenly aware of their deficit. The world is moving, fast, in a direction opposite from where they stand.

This is another form of division, another bifurcation among us. Beyond the haves versus the have-nots of money, property, education, status, and looks, people who have technology—access and capability—possess an inside track to success that people without technology cannot attain. Tech deprived people often feign happiness that they are unhinged from the burdens of constant communication and distraction. They proclaim technology as a sour grape largely because they lack the opportunity to savor its sweetness.

That's a fine perspective for Eris, clerk at the Susanville Motel, who checks me in by hand and says, "I don't use the computer. I just sit and watch the clouds." After all, Eris is 90 years old. Unfortunately, a 20-year-old who exercises that same luxury will lag her entire life.

Rockdale, TX—February 11, 2016, 4:00 p.m.

There is, however, a small group of folks I meet who occupy the far edge of the work/technology continuum: People who have access and technological capacity but aren't driven by it. People who understand how our economic system operates, but choose to exist outside of it. People motivated by non-economic incentives.

Some folks I meet who make life decisions according to economic advantage are happy. Not all of them, not even most of them. But everyone I meet who pursues her passion, whether it's a geographic ideal, a lifestyle choice, an artistic burn, or an idiosyncratic yearning, is happy. Every single one. People whose dreams dictate their actions, and let the economic chips fall as they may, manage to get by, and do it with satisfaction. Whether they are courageous or foolish is not for me to say, though I am impressed by their spirit.

Victoria Everett makes more bold personal choices than anyone I meet across our broad continent. Unlike youths, who champion a personal passion before they assume responsibility for others, or older folks like me, who spread their wings after conventional family and careers, Victoria is in the thick of life, with a teenage daughter and an infant. Those responsibilities did not stop her from leaving everything behind to strike out on a new path.

Ten years ago Victoria was a 34-year-old Idaho native and mother of three middle school children. She weighed 250 pounds. "I could barely get out of bed. Doctors just gave me more pills. I prayed to the universe and it gave me a message. I woke up one night during an infomercial for a food book. I bought it. That's where I was."

Within a year Victoria lost 120 pounds. She parented her three children to independence. "Everything I had was in Boise; my cleaning business and my family. But I was done with winter. It didn't bother me when I was fat, but it did when I was thin. I decided to move south. Two years ago, I picked Austin. But when I got there I couldn't afford it, so I moved to Rockdale. I love it here."

Victoria arrived in Texas pregnant and jobless. She put her life in the hands of the universe, and the universe provided well. Within a few months she found community and sustenance. "Seven people participated in the birth of my daughter. After she was born, I was very weak. A man from France I had met stayed with us for two months while I recuperated."

Today, Victoria is a micro-entrepreneur with a baby in tow. "The 9-to-5 thing is not working for people. I follow my heart. I live my passions. I am going to trust that I will have everything I need. I am going to live my life in love and compassion, which is so much easier when you are happy." She works in a greenhouse where she recently earned a partner share. She is also a housekeeping companion for an elderly man. She rents out her spare room through Airbnb (or shares it for free to itinerant cyclists like me). She is a fruitarian who grows produce in her backyard. She makes kale chips to sell at the local farmers market. She is a devotee of the inspirational speaker and author Esther Hicks. "All you need to do is manifest money and money is there. I do what I like, I grow plants and I care for my baby. I am confident that money will come. I follow my heart and the doors open. I'm leading a life without resistance.

"All beliefs are true to the believer. We can change our beliefs and have new truths, but some truths are fixed. The laws of nature are infallible and cannot be changed. I don't worry about Monsanto or Dow because they're going against Mother Nature. That's why Monsanto can't win."

Libertarian radicalism is where we need to go. We need to rethink the basic concepts of our society: private property, money, debt. We need a change in scale. We need to get more local. Do we need government? It was invented to protect those who have.
Only if we question everything can we get to the basics. It's okay to be Utopian.
You have to be Utopian to think real change is possible. Everything else is just fiddling around the edges.

–Alex, Auburn Rural Studio, Newbern, AL

Pines, IN—June 6, 2015, 2:00 p.m.

Weekends are different from workdays, even to a guy on a bike. Saturday, the world is a happier place.

Everything about my spin from Stephenville, Michigan, to Gary, Indiana, is perfect; 61 miles of easy terrain on a sunny, 70-degree day along the shore of Lake Michigan. I stop to inspect sand castles along the beach and taste local honey at a crafts fair. I veer off Red Arrow Highway to pedal Lakeshore Drive through Grand Beach, Michiana, and Long Beach. Brilliant blue stripes of water pop into view between tight-packed houses claiming their slice of shore. Weekend warriors stoking lightweight frames overtake me. They spin alongside for a mile or two. We chat until their thighs clamor for a harder workout, then they speed ahead. I am in no rush. The day is so perfect I repeat an entire hour. Welcome to Central Time.

Zach Nelson stands on a raised platform framed by the gaudy items of quick sale—a rack of candy bars, a canister of Slim Jims, bags of Funyuns, and Lottery tickets overhead. He's a burly, bearded guy who attacks my question as savagely as I devour half a dozen Little Debbie donuts.

"How will we live tomorrow? Without a monetary system. When we get rid of the Fractional Reserve we can move forward to equality. Until then, every man will just chase money and we will all suffer. There are only three countries in the world—China, Iraq, and one other—that don't use the monetary system masterminded by the Rothschilds. There's more debt in this world than money. Debt is created out of nothing. But more people have gotten on their knees to it than to any Messiah."

After Zach lambasts every Rothschild and all messiahs, he cracks a self-satisfied smile. "I bet you never thought you'd get so much from a convenience store clerk."

Actually, waitresses, farm workers, and maids often provide more thought-provoking responses to my question than academics and entrepreneurs. The conclusions they reach, however, tempered by direct experience rather than observational distance, are more hard-nosed than their intellectual counterparts. A libertarian peddling smokes and ice cream on a hot summer afternoon places change in so many palms, flesh becomes unseemly.

I relish guys like Zach, who tap the radical potential of my question. People who parrot platitudes of harmony lull me complacent, while folks who proclaim the end of private property or the inevitability of one-world government or a return to hunter-gatherer mode jolt me to attention. Responses that subvert the existing order provide the most satisfying fodder to my pedaling.

Ideas, grand as the swaling Indiana dunes, emphatic as my freewheeling legs, spin through my head. The sky is clear but my mind brims with the big concepts—and big dichotomies—that underpin our social order: the rifts between man and nature, the battles between man and man.

We live in a time when capitalism has emerged as the dominant economic system. We proclaim the virtue of private property because it motivates economic growth. Yet unfettered possession accelerates inequality.

We sing patriotic anthems to discrete nation-states and highlight the differences between democracy, communism, socialism, and dictators. Yet global economic interdependence supersedes political differences.

We romanticize our ancestor's ecological balance. Yet we shudder at the cataclysmic disaster required to retrieve that equilibrium; to decimate our numbers 10 times over, to reduce our population from billions to mere millions.

Rapid City, SD—July 1, 2015, 8:00 p.m.

Except for a single black afternoon when thunderstorms slant water so hard and fast it careens off the tarmac, not a drop of rain falls on my path in all of June. Every day is hot and sunny. Humans celebrate a glorious day, we exalt in a sunny week, but a full month of sun after sun after sun with no moisture in sight casts a shadow. Everywhere I go, people's parched lips fret about the weather.

Climate change is the most persistent theme people discuss when I ask, "How will we live tomorrow?" Concerned citizens wring their hands over human intervention in global processes; deniers protest too hard that nothing is happening. The synopsis of all these opinions is simple:

Is our natural environment changing? *Yes.*

Are humans responsible? *Mostly.*

Can we do anything about it? *Probably.*

Will we do anything about it? *Probably not.*

Although I strive to accept all responses equally, I chuckle when a well-intentioned soul says, "I worry about our planet." Our planet is not endangered. Humans are. The earth has withstood fire and ice and dinosaurs. It will keep spinning regardless of how we deface it.

The science of climate change is solid, but in a sound-bite world, its easy for fear drummers to cast doubt about shifts expressed as probabilities that spread over years. They coopt meaningful discussion by tangling the debate at its root, insisting that climate change doesn't even exist.

Consideration of our environment falls into two major camps: technologists and balance-seekers. The technologists advocate more technology: desalinate water; sequester carbon; tap the sun and the wind; frack the rocks; conquer hydrogen. The more gargantuan the challenge, the more the technologists salivate. Seed clouds. Cover glaciers with reflective coating. Colonize other planets. If they pause to catch their breath, they acknowledge that every technological fix creates unforeseen problems. But new dilemmas are simply opportunities for new solutions in a drawn-out chess game between Mother Nature and human ingenuity. Technologists relish the challenge.

The balance-seekers strive for equilibrium between man and nature. They can identify environmental devastation and rattle off alarming statistics with moral certainty. Problem is, they're Luddites, pining for a past that was never as sanguine as they imagine, offering solutions antithetical to our economic growth machine.

Then there are the arguments that fall more than two deviations beyond the norm: revelationists pray for the Second Coming; science fictionists believe evolution is accelerating so fast that we will physically change to adapt to our changing earth. The more elaborate the description of a steady-state habitat, the more it piques my funny bone, considering that we've done almost nothing to cool our overheating planet.

93

Everyone proclaims he is sustainable, because we all tailor the definition to our own behavior. Rapid City architect Fred Thurston explains, "I use a wood stove. It is more work than turning on the furnace. I want to show people that I care about our present and our future." Fred is a conscientious guy, more environmentally aware than most Americans to be sure. He lives in a passive solar house with low-flow toilets; he drives a Prius. He points out these admirable features, and then describes the energy improvements he'll make at the new house he and wife plan to build, 10 miles farther out of town. I listen with the true interest of a fellow architect: we live to build. Yet I know, objectively, that Fred will consume more energy, and add more carbon dioxide to the atmosphere, by building his new home and driving his Prius farther to reach it, than he will burn if he just stays put. In the face of grand plans, conservation is simply no fun.

Many people tell me I am sustainable, riding my bike, living small. But they're wrong. On any given motel overnight I generate a wastebasket full of trash: a plastic container from dinner; cardboard cereal box from breakfast; discarded brochures; a spent tube of sunscreen. Nobody is sustainable in the United States, not even a guy on a bike. Except maybe the Amish.

How will our marginally democratic government and skewed capitalism address our environmental crisis? They won't. Our checks and balances, vested interests, loopholes, and safety nets, for all their shortcomings, have enabled the highest standard of living for the greatest number of people ever to inhabit the earth. But the incremental nature of democracy is lousy in the face of any disaster that isn't timed to the quarterly business cycle. So far, environmental damage has just been too darn slow for it to

register economically. And by the time that change is rapid, it will be too late.

Responses to climate change require radical "convenience store clerk" philosophies. If we truly want harmony with nature, we have to return to being hunter-gatherers. If we want to address environmental hazards that defy national borders, we have to embrace more shared governance. If we want a product's sticker price to reflect its true cost through its lifecycle, we will have to redefine cost and value. If we want to balance human appetite with our planet's bounty, we need to invent a new economy, one whose cornerstone is parity rather than growth.

None of that is going to happen—tomorrow.

As I pedal west I notice the price of gas goes lower and lower. I make a game of checking it every few days. Although the price bumps up on the West Coast (at 44.5 cents per gallon, Washington has the second-highest state gas tax in our nation) and then drops fast when I enter Arizona (gas tax of only 19 cents a gallon), the more I pedal, the cheaper gas becomes. It bottoms out in New Braunfels, Texas, where I can fill up my tank for $1.359 per gallon. If only I had one.

As long as we live in a society that celebrates economic incentives, and as long as gas is so cheap, we won't change our fossil fuel habit. We won't stop pillaging our environment until we make it more profitable to keep the environment clean: another thing that's not going to happen—tomorrow.

I've lived here my whole live and never seen North Dakota like this. Things that would never have been proposed 10 years ago—creative ideas—are being discussed and embraced. The upside of the boom is visible everywhere. The downside is, are we caring for the land the way we need to for the next generation? It's the question we all ask. But the freight train is out of control, so we just hang on.

—Beth Campbell, Heritage Center of North Dakota, Bismarck, ND

Richardson, ND—June 25, 2015, 4:00 p.m.

My blue ribbon route through North Dakota climbs north and then west across US Highway 2. I want to visit Williston, epicenter of the state's oil and gas boom. But I heed warnings delivered in Fargo: cyclists should stay south of that narrow road overrun with truck convoys servicing fracking operations. Instead, I buck the headwinds on ND 200 through Glenfield, Goodrich, and McClusky; shrinking farm towns insignificant against the immense Plains. I dip down to Bismarck, a charming place with a quirky Deco state capitol, eat the only bad meal of my journey in a German restaurant in Mandan, and persevere 40 miles of I-94 shoulder; the longest Interstate stretch of my trip. Riding the Interstate is not unsafe: it's just unpleasant. The wide shoulders and rumble strip keep vehicles at bay, but trucks roaring past at 80 miles per hour pull a bicycle into their wake, especially the triple trailers allowed in North Dakota.

In 2015 North Dakota is the second-highest energy producing state in our nation, surpassed only by Texas. Production has tripled within five years. A state with less than a million people sucks a million barrels of crude from beneath its grassy surface every day. Oil is the new caffeine, and this place buzzes with energy. People worry about the havoc they're wreaking upon the land; the fracture of their community. Crime is up; inflation is rampant. A four-room house in Mandan, circa 1950, is listed for $425,000, 10 times more than a comparable home in Iowa. But such worries can't dampen the giddiness of so much oil, so much money. Folks' biggest fear is not the impact of the boom, but rather how long will it last. The number of new wells is decreasing; the price of gas is falling. Fracking is expensive extraction that depends on premium prices. That house in Mandan may be pricey, but a year ago it wouldn't have even needed a "For Sale" sign: it would have been

95

sold, cash, to the highest bidder, in a single day. I ride a boom that is already past peak.

Black clouds threaten as I exit I-94 in Richardson. I come upon a new, upscale grocery with prepared foods and free Wi-Fi, a kind of rural Whole Foods without the aura of virtue. The $7.49 special is two fried chicken breasts, mashed potatoes with gravy, fried rice, and a whole-wheat roll. I ask the food lady if she has any vegetables. She can't be bothered. "There are vegetables in the fried rice." I count three peas and two diced carrots. No matter. Ingesting three mounds of starch is a small price to pay for a solid roof. Rain lands hard and fierce.

I have a reservation at the Oasis Motel in Dickinson, 24 miles west. The skies clear above me, though menacing clouds loiter on the horizon. It's already after five but so far north, in late June, I still have hours of daylight. I strike out on 36th Street SW (an east-west road 36 miles off the state's centerline, in the southwest quadrant according to North Dakota's statewide numbering system). No one else travels this strip of pavement within parallel earshot of I-94. The tiny town of Taylor could be a movie set for a TV Western. The prairie bucks into gentle swales. More black clouds gather on my left, and my right. They fill my peripheral vision. They pinch closer and closer to the road. They reach overhead like giant tentacles; they touch; they merge their dark energy. Straight before me is a void, a tunnel of pure light. The sun shines, blinding, brilliant, through a tiny aperture of calm surrounded by turmoil. I pass through the vortex, delivered safe to the Oasis.

Look at NPR. They have a sponsor that says, "Natural gas; think about it."
I don't want to think about it. I don't want to consider the pros and cons of fracking.
I want to acknowledge that every time we extract a resource that is forever gone, we are not sustainable.
   —Jim Merkel, author of Radical Simplicity, Belfast, ME

Dickinson, ND—June 26, 2015, 2:00 p.m.

I am enthralled with fracking. It's so elegant. Take a nine-inch diameter pipe and drive it two miles into the ground, then bend it 90 degrees and run it two more miles horizontally. Like pushing a silk thread through a watermelon.

Whiting Oil and Gas occupies a broad metal building tight against an expanse of parking; steel and blacktop sizzling in the High Plains sun. It's cool inside, airy and spacious. A receptionist guides me left, then right, then left again to corridor's end. Blaine Hoffman sits in his gigantic office, behind a plane of well-organized mahogany, in front of a shelf-wall of photos, statuettes, and plaques commending 39 successful years in the business. Blaine explains fracking to me with a teacher's patience and a believer's zeal. The man, North Dakota born and raised, lives on 40 acres northeast of town. Apparently I passed his place in the eye of yesterday's storm. Blaine will retire soon—his collection of accolades will undoubtedly increase—but not until he rides out the current boom. "This is he hardest work, and most fun, of my prospecting life."

Blaine begins with a geology lesson. The Bakken Formation sits beneath northwest North Dakota, eastern Montana, and southern Saskatchewan. It contains over 3.5 billion barrels of oil. "The Bakken is a tight rock formation with horizontal fractures. The oil-rich zone is between 6 and 70 feet thick. We use MWD (measurement while drilling) directional tools to drill straight down to that zone and then horizontally to tap into the transcendental fractures. Longitudinal drilling is easier, but vertical production in a place like the Bakken would yield very little. The Middle Bakken is the target zone. We pump a mix of water and sand, six pounds of sand per gallon, into the well at 8,000 psi pressure.

That deep in the ground, the hydrostatic pressure of the slurry is 14,000 psi or more. The water/sand mix infiltrates the fractures and releases the trapped oil."

Then, like all good teachers, Blaine reiterates at a deeper level. "We start with 9-5/8-inch surface casing that we drill about 2,500 feet deep, to get below any potable water. We fill that casing with cement to eliminate any leaks. We run an 8-5/8-inch bit filled with oil-based mud to keep the hole stable to a depth of 10,000 feet." Blaine tosses out these two dimensions in a single breath, but my engineering mind calculates that a 9-inch bore over 10,000 feet is a slenderness ratio of 14,000:1.

Unfazed by my astonishment, Blaine continues. "We cement that hole in a 7-inch casing, and then drill a 6-inch horizontal bit with a 4-1/2-inch liner up to 20,000 feet, nearly four miles. We insert a series of P-valves along the length of the horizontal bit." After the well is drilled, fracking begins from the end. Open the last P-valve, pump in the water/sand slurry, and open fractures. Stop the slurry flow and allow the released oil to flow up the well. Pull back to the next valve. Repeat.

I know little about geology or resource extraction. However, after a career in healthcare design, the medical analogy is clear. We are performing an endoscopy on mother earth.

According to Blaine, fracking is benign. I ask why people are so worried about it. "When this started in Pennsylvania, there were no rules in place to protect groundwater. They didn't always cement the surface and intermediate casings. Now, 99.7% of states have some rules. North Dakota leads in writing many of these

rules." Blaine stresses safety and precision over groundwater contamination or residual earthquake activity. He makes the case that fracking satisfies our energy appetite. It's also his livelihood.

Since I'm interested in tomorrow, I ask Blaine how fracking technology will change. Like so many, he references the past before projecting forward. "Fracking is an evolving process. We used to incorporate sliding screens along the horizontal casings." My medical analogy would call them stents. "But P-valves and plugs proved more accurate. The next thing is secondary recovery. When we run parallel well bores we can get maybe 25% of what's there. Parallel wells run between 300 feet and 700 feet apart, sometimes at different elevations to access different oil strata. But at some point they reach diminishing returns. We are always looking for ways to capture more oil."

I walk out of Blaine's cool office and retrace the labyrinth past reception. Outside, the building's metal exterior is hot to the touch. Heat vapors rise off the pavement. The wind blows steady from the south. In that instant, I realize our folly.

There is so much energy in this world. It radiates from the sun. It blows our hair. And thanks to eons of compression, we've got combustible stuff right beneath our feet. Invisible power on demand seems so much neater than towering windmills and solar arrays that deliver haphazard bursts of energy. We've created an economic engine for extraction, one that produces big, corporate profits. We don't monetize something as diffuse, as decentralized, and as democratic as wind and sun nearly so well.

Burning oil in 2015 poses pesky problems that John D. Rockefeller and Henry Ford never reckoned: the CO2 exhaust that's cooking our planet. Fracking creates induced pressures that could lead to additional havoc, just as wastewater disposal wells have jostled Oklahoma into our nation's most active seismic region, in quantity if not in Richter value.

To a man with a hammer, everything looks like a nail. When we ask a company called Whiting Oil and Gas to provide us with energy, they don't look up at the sun. They drill into the earth. That's what they know how to do, and we shouldn't find fault with them just because they keep finding better and better ways to do it.

The oil and gas industry has enabled industrialized society to flourish. But now that we know the downside of burning all that carbon, we have to slow it down, even bring it to a halt. Exxon Mobil is not going away anytime soon. Maybe it doesn't need to go away. We just need to move it in new directions. Get its head out of the ground and into the sun.

We have to design a future that will serve us all.
If we use our imagination we can create a world
that works for everybody.
We can't just do what we've been doing.
　　　—Tim Holmes, artist, Helena, MT

Tempe, AZ—January 13, 2016, 1:00 p.m.

Nothing is more enjoyable than sitting in the sun at an outdoor café on a balmy January afternoon shooting the breeze with a bunch of futurists. I could earn a degree from the School for the Future of Innovation in Society at Arizona State University, an institution that is rethinking higher education by expanding online course offerings, emphasizing cross-disciplinary study, and focusing on the future. How cool is that?

There's both irony and logic in studying the future in metro Phoenix, often cited as the least sustainable place for humans on earth. Dave Guston, the dean of SFIS says, "The Salt River Valley has supported human life for over 2,000 years. Now 4.5 million people live here. It is unsustainable by many measures, but here we are. We create more externalities than other places: it takes a lot of energy to get our water; we use a lot of fossil fuels. We have long-term water/energy nexus issues. How sustainable we are depends on where you draw the boundaries of the sustainability circle. Yet in some ways living in a place that is considered unsustainable sharpens our focus. If we can articulate a realistic vision for inhabiting Phoenix, it bodes well for humans most anywhere."

In addition to the School for the Future of Innovation in Society, ASU also supports the Center for Science and the Imagination. CSI staff produces a journal, *Future Tense*; teaches classes like "The History of the Future"; and pursues research funded by ASU, NSF, NASA, and The World Bank. Four members of CSI—not the Tempe version of the popular TV crime show—treat me to lunch at House of Tricks on a day so perfect even an enlightened future cannot eclipse our present.

Ed Flynn, CSI's founding director explains, "The point of CSI is to create agency—to give people choice and responsibility. We are lazy in our storytelling. It's either post-nuclear apocalypse or some other Michael Bay movie. The dystopian scenarios are rote. They replace agency with disillusionment. The best stories are the ones we inhabit.

"Breaking out of the present allows us to create new perspectives. A drone delivering stuff in one hour is a great thing. But where does it lead? What is the logical conclusion of it? Faster? More? Sustainability is a good narrative frame for discussing the future. But it's only one way to look at the world we live in."

Ruth Wylie ties CSI's work to my own. "Our focus is creating a shared vision of the future. The future is not waiting to be unveiled. That's why your question is so valuable. It's accessible: a simple question to ask that is difficult to answer. I believe that you don't ask a question unless you think there is an answer that you can enact."

Between nibbles of fish taco and lemon water—I kicked my diet coke addiction back in Nebraska—I savor the warmth of being surrounded by like-minded souls. Folks at ASU and I seek the same thing: getting a fix on tomorrow. There is, however, one really important difference between us. They get paid and I don't. In our capitalist world, money is influence. When people get paid for contemplating the future, we stake a claim in their effort. When more people get paychecks in the solar and wind industries than in coal, oil, and gas, that's when our energy priorities will change. That's when Big Sun and Big Wind will have the lobby power to move Big Oil.

This is Texas. I am a Democrat with a gun.
—Susan Negly, Jungian psychologist, San Antonio, TX

Altoona, PA—May 25, 2015, 2:00 p.m.

Sometimes, a question catches you so off guard your initial response is absurd. An elderly woman at a McDonald's in this aging railroad town is the first person to ask if I'm carrying a gun. My mind flashes to logistics. Where would I put a gun? In my bike-shirt pocket? Do I tell a mugger, "Hold on while I dismount and pull a pistol out of my bag?"

I'm from Massachusetts, a state among the lowest in gun ownership and gun-related deaths. Guns in New England are historic artifacts, muskets that guys in tri-corner hats tote around Lexington Green on Patriot's Day. I don't know a single soul who owns a gun, let alone carries one, let alone carries one on a bicycle.

But on Memorial Day in Pennsylvania—34th among states in rate of gun ownership and in the middle of the pack for rate of gun deaths—guns are in the present. Silhouettes of a contemporary soldier on bended knee before a cross grace every VFW Hall. Photos of local men, died in recent wars, hang from every downtown lamppost. Sweet old ladies fret over unarmed cyclists.

The farther west I go, the more guns I see. I arrive in Texas the week the state's open carry law takes effect. Adam Turcotte of Ranger Firearms in San Antonio explains the rules surrounding gun sales, why he considers registration futile and waiting periods unnecessary because gun shops effectively block sales to agitated people. "The State of Texas allows us to delay or deny selling a gun to anyone. If someone comes in agitated, I can tell him that his background check has been delayed." Why am I uncomfortable placing the decision of whether a person is too agitated to purchase a gun with a guy whose livelihood is to sell guns? My mind wanders to hen houses and roosters.

I meet a group of Austin liberals who bemoan the NRA's power. "We can't have a discussion about guns; we can't even research the problem. The NRA will not allow it; no politician will fund it."

The first guy I see with a pistol strapped to his jeans strides up to the fountain machine at McDonald's in Egypt, Texas. I figure if some guy's going to carry a gun 'round a bunch of young kids and soda pop, we're all better off seeing it.

Wyoming has the highest rate of gun ownership in the country and the sixth highest rate of gun deaths, in case the correlation between those two statistics is still elusive. My host in Cheyenne is Tom Wann, veteran Master Sergeant in the Special Forces. He advocates allowing qualified gun owners to carry arms anywhere. "If psychotics know that trained, armed people are everywhere, they will stop killing." Tom is a thoughtful, reasoned man. But I don't believe that fear of being shot will stop mass-murderers, so many of whom turn their guns on themselves.

Of all the issues I confront along my journey across these United States, none is more contagious, or divisive, than guns. The facts are clear; the more people have guns, the more people die from guns. No matter. More than 400 years after the delusional Don Quixote exclaimed that, "Facts are the enemy of truth," we each define our own truth according to a concoction of personal beliefs, myths, and hunches. Then we select "facts" to support our truth.

There is no objective discussion about guns in this country. Guns are a religion in a culture where faith trumps fact. If a gun makes you feel safe, you want one.

When I am gardening I am hurting no one.
I am on my knees, in a position to meditate.
It makes me a better man. Be humble. Be small. Live simply.
    —Larry Walters, motel clerk and gardener, Rochester, MN

w

Medicine Bow National Forest, WY—July 8, 2015, 10:00 a.m.

The quickest route out of Cheyenne on a bicycle is through Francis E. Warren Air Force Base. I queue up in the line of cars being waved through the gate on a weekday morning. But I get turned back. Apparently, an unarmed cyclist in bright yellow is a threat to national security. As a result, I'm forced to ride Interstate 25, which doesn't feel safe at all, until I reach the exit for Happy Jack Road. A stretch of blacktop just as pleasant as it sounds.

I climb a plateau, long and steady. The cloudy morning turns somber grey. I enter Medicine Bow National Forest. The atmosphere turns to mist. Distant trees grow faint, sparkly. Visibility shrinks to 50 yards, maybe less. I tune my ears for traffic but no one drives this road anymore; I-80 parallels just a few miles to the south. It's not raining, yet I'm moist. The altitude is high but the air is dense. I traverse a mystical threshold to an enchanted, inviting, frightening land.

I reach Sherman Summit. A small city nests in the valley below. I cannot see it through the haze, yet it beckons me to descend. Happy Jack Road terminates into I-80: my second foray on our nation's vaunted highway system in one day. The eight-mile descent takes a mere 15 minutes, knuckle-braked the entire time, body braced against the cross draft of unclutched semis whooshing past. I coast off the Grand Avenue exit, jittery and trembling. It takes a few moments for the tension in each limb, each rib, each vertebra to dissipate. By the time my body is relaxed enough to fathom where I am, I have already arrived.

Back in March, one of the very first pushpins I stick in my route map is Laramie, Wyoming. I have business here with a dead person.

MATTHEW WAYNE SHEPARD
DECEMBER 1, 1976 - OCTOBER 12, 1998
BELOVED SON, BROTHER, AND FRIEND
HE CONTINUES TO MAKE A DIFFERENCE
PEACE BE WITH HIM AND ALL WHO SIT HERE

We are going to download our consciousness and live forever.
　　—Bryon Gibson, video gamer, Slingerlands, NY

Laramie, WY—July 9, 2015, 3:00 p.m.

Matthew Shepard would be 38 years old now. He could marry the person of his choice, even in Wyoming. He never got that chance. When Aaron McKinney and Russell Henderson murdered Matthew in 1998, I had been an out gay man for five years. Coming out in Cambridge was easy. No prejudice at work, no rejection at my children's school, no personal violence. The true discomfort lay beneath my own skin. I shattered the straight man I'd contrived, but the gay guy who replaced him was no more convincing. I'm a father, an architect, a writer, a cyclist, a yogi, and a curious wanderer who just happens to be gay; an analytical thinker who's never been able to figure out how that puzzling piece fits.

I feel certain Matthew has something worthwhile to tell me.

Laramie keeps Matthew Shepard under wraps. He doesn't exist beyond a commemorative bench on University of Wyoming campus. The bar where he met his murderers has a new face and a new name. The streets where he was strung up have been renamed as well. But I am not the first pilgrim to seek the site of his carnage. When the "No Trespassing" signs grow menacing, I know I've found the place.

What's unsettling is how public it is. Matthew Shepard's killers did not remove him to some remote, misty scene, easy enough to come by in these parts. Matthew was tied and tortured in a residential development, the kind of 2- to 5-acre plots where people pretend they're on a ranch even though they can clearly see their neighbors. Matthew was beaten close to several houses. Did no one hear his cries? Eighteen hours passed before he was found, a full turn of daylight. Did no one see his body?

It's an uncomfortable place, where Matthew Shepard was murdered: scrawny plants; gravel; a few utility stumps. The place doesn't lend itself to reverie, or lingering. I contemplate the underbelly of human behavior this soil has witnessed. I try to conjure meaning. Which means, of course, that no meaning appears.

A deer walks over the rise between two houses, crosses the road and stops to graze. A second one joins. Less than a hundred feet separate us. The second deer picks up her head and looks straight at me. I wait for her to reveal something profound. The only truth she betrays is that Laramie deer are very accustomed to people.

The graceful does turn and leave, and so do I. A quarter mile down the gravel road, Leonard Cohen springs into my head: "Bird on a Wire." A song I've known for years. Yet in this moment it acquires completely new meaning.

I always identified with the man in the song, the beggar on his crutch who warns against asking for so much. Asking little protects us from hurt, it sidesteps disappointment. But Matthew Shepard's spirit compels me to heed the woman in the song, the woman in the door, who taunts, Why not ask for more? On my gravelly retreat, I understand the woman's virtue. We have to go out and demand what we want. We may not get it, we may come up short, but we must try.

What did Matthew Shepard ask for the night he died? More than was allowed in his place and time. Asking for more got Matthew killed. Yet, his savage death forced us all to acknowledge a right from a wrong. Matthew Shepard's death made it forever unacceptable to beat up on faggots.

Since Matthew Shepard died, the rest of us have received more. Not more than we deserve, just more than we had. No one could predict, in 1998, how fully gay people live today. I don't have to be a man hobbled by a crutch, content with what I'm given. I'm free to ask for more.

Everything is going to go faster and faster. Distances will matter less.
I see things getting more fragmented and bureaucratic.
Different forms and players will each have their own systems.
—Sophie Feldstein, high school senior, San Francisco, CA

Langtry, TX—January 31, 2016, 1:00 p.m.

Personal bests are eternal in the record book of our minds. Six months ago my balance, and nerves, hit a downhill maximum at 27 or 28 miles per hour. Once I hit that speed, fear stepped in and forced me upright in the saddle. It commanded that I brace against the wind and pump my brakes to slow my descent. Fear is a stern master; I accepted its limit without complaint. But no matter how much we do something, the more we do it, the better we get at it; even something simple as riding a bike.

Today, 11,170 miles into my journey, with perfect conditions and not a lick of traffic, I sail down West Texas slopes on US 90, cruising smooth at 30 miles per hour, sometimes more. I crouch low on the straight stretch leading to the Pecos River and let gravity accelerate me beyond experience. My odometer tops out at a resounding 39 miles per hour. In the world of bicycle racing, that's not a speed of any consequence. Yet I am proud of my personal best; confident it will stand for some time.

I was a chubby kid. Uncoordinated. It took me almost a year to learn how to ride a bike. I couldn't control my shifting weight. I nearly wore out the training wheels bouncing right, left, right, off the pavement. Finally, my father took them off. "You've had them long enough, short one. Time to ride or crash." I crashed. But I mounted the curb, threw my leg over the bar and tried again. And again. Something in me knew to keep at it. With balance comes freedom.

There was a hill at the end of our street, which led to an even steeper one that bottomed out in a gulley. I kept my circles small so as not to get drawn into that gravity. Until one day, miracle of miracles, I spun six, maybe eight, pedal strokes in a row. Giddy to be upright, my wheels rolled to the slope before I could turn round. I stopped pedaling. Momentum gathered. I backpedaled to brake, unsteady against the rim. I came to the turn: nothing to do but lower my shoulders and lean to the right. Just before my wheels flew out from under me, I pumped my fat left thigh. My body rose. My bike stayed firm beneath me. My heart raced, faster than my wheels. I wheezed through the gulley and up the other side.

The rising slope slowed me down. I nearly toppled to a stop. But my legs kicked in and pedaled, hard, to keep moving. By the time I reached level ground, I was three blocks from home, beyond anywhere I'd ever been on my own. I wondered if maybe I needed to turn back. But my mother wouldn't notice me gone until dinner. My brothers and sister weren't about to get all whoopee because I biked the hill; they'd been doing it for years. I basked in my private glory, and pedaled on.

Ever since that afternoon, I am never so free as I am on a bicycle.

107

Our ancestors came here on foot. They experienced nature's subtle changes.
When they arrived they had the feel of the land. You must get that on your bike.
In our cars, whoosh, we zoom right by everything.
  —Kathy, Utah Visitor's Center, Jensen, UT

Tioga Pass, CA—September 30, 2015, 3:00 p.m.

I know how to drive a car. It's a useful skill. But I experience no thrill seat-belted behind a windshield. Freedom is the wind in my face, a leisurely pace, and time enough for a detour along the way. Why is my slower mode so much more enjoyable? The answer is higher mathematics.

Consider a tourist in an automobile, traveling from New York to Yosemite National Park, a four-day drive from a man-made wonder to a natural one. At 70 miles per hour, the space between these two attractions is a blur of highway interchanges, roadside meals, and beige motel rooms. What sticks in our mind are sheer walls created by man, and sheer walls created by nature. It's an integer experience: New York + 3,000 miles = Yosemite.

The same journey on a bicycle reveals the beauty of calculus. The earth's contours, the birdsong, the scent of fresh hay, the factory fumes, the gravel shoulder; they form a continuous flow of imprinted memory. I appreciate New York's glitz and Yosemite's majesty, but they're not isolated places. They are the apex and saddle point of an immense continuum. The guy on the bike absorbs it all. Sometimes, the connective tissue clings to memory even more vividly than the destination.

Fairhope, AL—February 29, 2016, 5:00 p.m.

Mobile, Alabama, is a tough city for cyclists. Cars bear down on me along Dauphin Street. I am not allowed in the river tunnel. The eight-mile detour up and over the bridge leaves me pedaling the causeway across Mobile Bay in the first pulse of afternoon rush. The road is a mere six inches above the water. The I-10 fly-over rises up like a serpent. The wind is so loud it merges with engine roars; the sea scent so strong it fuses with exhaust. I spin taut between forces of nature and forces of man.

On the east side of the bay, I climb stately cliffs and turn south on US 98 to Fairhope, a town recommended for its architectural beauty and genteel charm. My host is the friend of a friend of a friend, a woman who produces local music concerts.

The breeze through the pines is a heady fusion of pitch and salt. Traffic is noteworthy, but I'm in sync with its pulse. I am in tune with my surroundings, yet I am not a specific point in time. I am the continuity of man and nature and pedal and wheel. I peel onto Scenic 98, deep forest shade, cadenced by a parade of American flags. I mount a shallow rise; I roll into a gentle hollow. I flow.

A Porsche turns left, sharp across my path. Surly hits his side door. I fly through the air; my bike ricochets behind. I hit the pavement. Calculus cut short.

I am one discrete pile of pain.

PART TWO
RELATIONSHIPS

The strong who survive will do so
by the strength of their relationships.
Genghis Khan conquered the world by
gathering the world in,
not by shutting it out.
Our connections are our strongest asset.

Krys Holmes, Myrna Loy Center, Helena, MT

We are the agents of evolution.
If I say, "I love you" to everyone I meet for 24 hours, that creates an evolutionary energy.
If I sit home by myself for that time, that creates a different type of evolution.
　　—Andrew Wood, Buddhist, Cambridge, MA

Mansfield, CT—July 12, 2016, 8:00 p.m.

Sixty-three uphill miles. Finally, I'm back in the swing of things.

Willimantic is a classic New England mill town with a proud history and tenuous present. Massive, granite structures rise straight out of the river, sturdy still, more than a century beyond their original purpose. Hundreds of identical windows punctuate the walls. The architecture of our frenetic age, all idiosyncratic bumps and obtuse variety, will never unspool a plane of such noble proportion. Downtown facades harken the city's prosperous past. Rows of modest worker howusing are covered in vinyl, as are the mansions commanding the surrounding hills, gerrymandered into apartments for immigrants no longer offered the opportunity to stand for hours before a loom in search of the American dream.

American Thread relocated manufacturing from Willimantic to North Carolina in 1985, later to Mexico. The city slid into a rut. By the early 2000s, the city's renown had flipped from manufacturing might to heroin haven. But things are looking up. Structures have been stabilized and renovated. The mansions may by wrapped in vinyl and cut up into apartments, but at least they're occupied. The Frog Bridge is charming. Like me, Willimantic is trying to climb out of a bad place and figure out where it's headed tomorrow.

I meet Alice Rubin, manager of Connecticut's oldest food co-op. I appreciate how they've repurposed an old A&P, even turned the front parking lot into a garden. What I love most about Alice, about Willimantic in total, is that no one here knows about that Porsche back in Alabama. Today is the first day I am not required to relive my altercation. It's a great relief.

There are two things that people love, particularly affluent people of a certain age without a lot of real problems on our hands. They love to trade stories about their health: aches and pains and chronic conditions; and they love to give advice. Even when it's not requested. Especially when it's not requested. I find "organ recitals" of personal health indiscreet and tedious, and I strive to only give advice when asked. But for the past four months I've endured hefty doses of both medical curiosity and unsolicited advice.

On the afternoon of February 29, I lie face down, sprawled across an intersection in Fairhope, Alabama. Traffic stops in all directions. An off-duty EMS crouches beside me and coaxes me to remain still. A bystander calls 911. The driver of the car that hit me mills about my peripheral vision. Broken bike, cracked windshield, police cars, ambulance, blood on the pavement: the usual gore that slows people to a gawk.

I spend five hours in the emergency room at Thomas Hospital. I tolerate all tests and refuse all pain meds. Hardly wince when Big Nurse yanks chunks of bituminous from my left arm. As shock dissipates, new regions of pain pulse. Question of the day: "Can you move your toes?" To everyone's paralytic relief, I can. When my handsome doctor greets me, his chiseled face and warm hands make other stuff twitch. That's when I know I'll be all right.

I am transferred to Sacred Heart Hospital in Pensacola, Florida: the ICU for neurological observation, then step down, finally, to a basic inpatient room. Maladies are confirmed and catalogued. Popped the AC joint in my left shoulder, nothing to do about that beyond accepting a Frankenstein silhouette for the rest of

my days. Broke the fifth metacarpal in my left hand, which the orthopedist sets, finds unsatisfactory, re-breaks, and surgically re-pairs. Fractured my L2 vertebrae, which triggers debate between surgical fusion and rehabilitation. The neurosurgeon decides an operation is "indicated but not required" since I am in such good health. I concur, get a nifty custom brace and start walking every-where the nurses allow. I pace the hospital courtyard for hours in Florida's March balm.

Eight days later, Jet Blue flies me home with kid gloves, and the real work begins. Fixing the body. I turn my den into a home gym with pulleys and straps and putty. Manipulating three body parts, 30 minutes each, four times a day equals six hours of rehab, plus five miles of walking. Fixing the mind. I recoil against every car horn; flinch at accidents on TV; fear that every cyclist banking the curve outside my window is spinning toward disaster.

Time passes; spring warms. Fear turns to longing. Those same cy-clists appear lyrical.

Three months after Fairhope my spine is stable, but I'm dizzy. Who knew reawakening muscles discombobulate your head? I keep walking. I lose my hand cast. I lose my sling. I start swim-ming. I take my brace off at home. I climb stairs without it. I ven-ture out of doors without my hard shell, fragile as a chrysalis. What's impossible one week proves merely difficult the next. The difficult becomes commonplace. Equilibrium returns. I remount my bike. Not Surly, god rest her soul. My around-town bike is a friendly Giant.

Leaning forward creates an odd angle for my back; there's strain on my broken hand; my shoulder aches. I acknowledge these frailties but embrace the breeze. I marvel that my legs still spin.

Every day, everywhere I go, everyone demands the tale of the Porsche and me. After 12,000 miles of cycling, I have so many stories of benevolence and humor, of strength and wisdom to share, but people only want to hear about the accident. Then, after they've listened as long as they care to, they tell me what I ought to do. "You've travelled far enough, you don't need to ride anymore." "Take at least a year off." "Don't get on that bike until you have full medical clearance." "You are working too hard, let your body rest."

The consensus in favor of leisure and delay is overwhelming, which only proves my hunch that advice reflects the attitude of the giver more than the condition of the recipient. I am allergic to leisure and delay. Comfort teaches us nothing; extended comfort turns us numb. One by one my doctors and therapists sign off on my abilities, astounded how quickly I've recovered. My neurolo-gist asks me to touch my toes; I put five fingers on the floor. He gasps, "I can't even do that." But I recall yoga days when my entire palm met the mat, and I yearn for that flexibility.

In a culture that champions getting by with the least required, cli-nicians are unaccustomed to patients who perform every exercise they prescribe. Yet that's exactly how I get better. I'm fortunate to have the luxury of time; not everyone can spend six hours a day fiddling his body. But motivation and discipline are deep bless-ings, and I itch to get back on my bike. During all those hours of putty massage, lateral pulls, and back twists, I hatch a plan.

My original blue ribbon stretched in a continuous furl around our nation's perimeter: cross the north in the summer of 2015; descend west that fall; Gulf Coast through the winter, all the way down to Miami. Then stream north along the Atlantic, backtrack the "inner loop" across the Deep South, return to Colorado for another round of Courage Classic, meander east along the Ohio River Valley and finally return to New England in the autumn of 2016. Despite repeated advice to hold off a year and then pick up where my route was interrupted, I decide to navigate the last third of my journey in reverse: leave Cambridge in July and head south to the Carolinas, turn west through Atlanta and Birmingham, north to Louisville, across to Saint Louis and Denver, then back through New Mexico and the Ozarks. I can end in Florida before Christmas. I shave two months by eliminating the Florida peninsula and skirting Appalachia, but I can still sleep at least one night in each of the 48 contiguous states.

By June I ride the Minuteman Trial near my home for 10 miles, then 20, then 40. I ease into Phase Two on July 9, with short cycling days on flat terrain: Onset and Berkley, Massachusetts; Kingston, Rhode Island. I stay with friends, each of whom demands the story of my accident. Only when I arrive in Connecticut, beyond the sphere family and friends, am I finally liberated from that obligation.

Tony, my Mansfield host, is a vegan body builder. He invites a group of friends, mostly fellow librarians from University of Connecticut, to share dinner and discuss tomorrow. Tony's a great cook and Vitamix master. The gazpacho is spicy, the lentil/walnut tacos delicious, the Modelo icy cold. I take only a sip of Plum Palinka, Rumanian liquor so strong the vapors knock me back. I'm feeling no pain. Not because I drink too much: just because I don't have to talk about it.

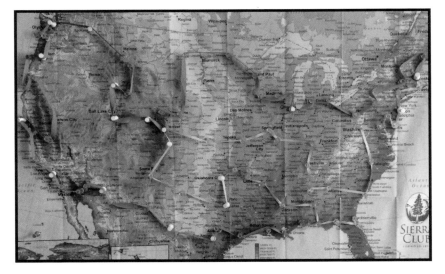

In Utopia, everyone is valued.
　　—Teresa Winslow, DuPont Learning Center, DuPont, WA

New Harmony, IN—September 6, 2016, 6:00 p.m.

Utopia! Sir Thomas More invents a perfect, imaginary place and coins a new word based on the Greek root for "nowhere."

Utopia! In 1600, 10 million people are spread across North America in communal tribes that revere the spiritual power of nature.

Utopia! The English create a colony in Jamestown to extract the resources of this faraway place.

Utopia! Pilgrims voyage to Massachusetts Bay in search of a religious sanctuary.

Utopia! It's a fiction, an illusion. But there's this New World beyond the horizon where wealth, salvation, and nature coalesce in perfect unity. It's difficult to attain, but heaven on earth is worth the effort.

The United States is both geography and idea, a country based on an enlightened view of man rather than fixed boundaries. We are exceptional. We determine our destiny. We do not consider these to be opinions. We consider them fact.

The rugged individual is the central figure of American mythology. The nuclear family is his backbone. It's an appealing myth to recruit immigrants to our shores, to lure Easterners out West. But multiply this autonomy 300 million times and we end up at miles upon miles of single-family houses with three cars in the drive: quarter-acre fiefdoms of independence, affluence, and moral virtue. Nature's bounty bent to man, ad infinitum.

The United States has always been large enough to harbor competing visions of what our heaven on earth might be: collective experiments in chasing perfection. Utopian fever reached its zenith in the 19th century when economic prosperity and religious zealotry peaked in the Shaker's frenzied dance, the Oneida community's group marriage, Adventist's fiery tongues, and New Harmony's focus on discipline, shared work, and education.

Where are the descendants of these utopian communities today?

There are new, secular, variants. Chrysalis Cooperative in Boulder, Colorado, thrives on the idea that collective living is both economically and socially preferable. Cohousing is scattered among our left-leaning cities, but it's mostly upper middle class people who can afford common space in addition to private dwellings. Buskers Bunkhouse in New Orleans is an anarchist alternative to private property; the proprietress, Ms. Pearl, bucks the establishment, however defined. A gated community in Scottsdale is a sort of Utopia, walled-in to keep the haves from the have-nots, to separate the blessed from the damned.

The great 19th-century experiments have become museums, artifacts in a world that moves with accelerating speed away from collective experience. Seventh-day Adventist Village in Battle Creek, Michigan, is a mecca for devotees of Ellen White's prophecies. The Oneida Community Mansion House in upstate New York is an odd mix of restoration and residential rentals, stripped of its collective consciousness and scandalous sexual attitudes.

New Harmony has a museum quality as well. It's a bit too neat to be a real place. Yet it's more extensive than one large building or an historic recreation. Joseph Rapp, the Robert Moses of Utopias, founded New Harmony in Indiana after creating and abandoning Harmony, Pennsylvania. Ten years later he essentially sold New Harmony to Robert Owen and led his Rappist flock back to Pennsylvania to found Economy. Owen, a social theorist, championed collective effort and enlightened education in his bucolic town on the Wabash. Although New Harmony never grew large (apparently, Owen was a lousy farmer), or spread its ideas wide, the town remains a pristine enclave of 750 deep thinkers set apart from the fertile farms that surround it.

Owen Lewis, Robert Owen's great-great-great grandson, and his mother, Docey, welcome me to New Harmony like the long-lost Utopian seeker I am. Robert's first comment to me establishes the analytical, cerebral tone of the town. "Your succinct question lays upon my mind. We are compelled to live here where we, in a microcosm, explore how we can live, and extrapolate that to the larger world."

Docey and Robert put me up in Poet's Cottage, a 19-century worker dwelling turned retreat refuge. They host a salon in their own home, where more than a dozen strivers share food, drink and ideals through the night.

New Harmony is a lovely place. Unfortunately, it's too ideologically removed from the rest of our country to impact how we will live tomorrow; and in the last decade, the town's philosophical dissonance with the rest of our nation has become a physical reality. The State of Indiana closed the deteriorating bridge over the Wabash. Indiana highway 80 terminates at Richard Meier's stunning metal and glass Athenaeum, poised like a steamboat along the riverbanks. New Harmony has literally become a dead end.

The closest I come to a contemporary utopia is a single-story swath of Arizona desert built by a private developer to turn a buck. When Del Webb sold an experience rather than a product, he not only changed the way we think about growing old, he created a hive of leisurely perfection.

I could retire now but I don't know what I'd do. I don't have any hobbies.
—Alan Stuckey, grandfather, Waubeka, WI

Sun City, AZ—November 15, 2015, 3:00 p.m.

I arrive in Sun City in the rain. A downpour. My hosts, Trudy Bryson and Larry Vroom, have just returned from an afternoon concert. I clean up, dry off, and join them in the great room overlooking the backyard pool and golf course. Trudy explains, "In the 1960s I came home from college to Northbrook, Illinois, and my parents had moved here."

Trudy and her two sisters started coming to Sun City for holidays and vacations. The spanking new Arizona town became the center of their family life. In time, each daughter retired here. "I have such faith in this community. It will last through my lifetime, my children's lifetime, and my grandkid's lifetime." Trudy bought the house across the street from her folks. After they died, she and Larry expanded the 1,000-square-foot house her parents had bought for $10,000 into a spacious, though not lavish, place to live. Sun City is not showy.

Del Webb hated straight lines. He graded the desert into concentric circles lined with pastel houses, sprinkled eight recreation centers and seven golf courses at the interstices of his arcs, and excluded anyone under the age of 18. He reimagined retirement as a new beginning and thousands upon thousands of people from all over the country affirmed his vision. They collected gold watches, left snow and children behind, and flocked to the desert sun. After all, who reinvents themselves better than Americans?

To be sure, Sun City is a skewed Utopia; a social security–based economy with age discrimination and lively people with time on their hands. But don't sell the place short. The golf carts that tote people within the village are energy efficient. Security's a snap where everyone knows her neighbors. The vibe is middle class white, but there's little economic stratification. People in Sun City move; they live longer, healthier lives.

Trudy is the president of Ukeladies, an 80-member ukulele band. The morning I leave, she's excited about taking her very first voice lesson, to bolster her sing-along abilities. Anyplace where a 69-year-old woman embarks on new pursuits must be doing something right.

We took a year to ride around the country on a tandem bicycle, and it changed us.
Small is beautiful, old is beautiful, slow is beautiful, safe is beautiful.
Just because we can do more things than ever before doesn't mean we should.
— Claire Rogers, 44,000-mile tandem cyclist on six continents, Tucson, AZ

Cape May, NJ—July 23, 2016, 8:00 a.m.

Bicycles are like dogs; they reflect their owners. Tom, my new bike, earned his name because his maroon frame is the exact color of my high school mascot, old Indian Tom. Not very PC, but back in the day, no one quibbled about Indians and Chiefs and Warriors. Tom is functional rather than flashy. He's got a hefty steel frame for stability and a low gear ratio that makes climbing easy. He grips the road tight and can handle a patch of gravel if necessary, though he'd rather not. Like me, he prefers pavement.

Tom is the same make and model as his cousin Surly, yet he's a completely different bike. Kind of top heavy: as if having a boy's name shrank his hips and bulked his shoulders. When I prop him against a fence he topples. It takes me a thousand miles, and several falls, to lean his wheels wide. Tom's got swagger.

Other cyclists pass us by. Guys on mountain bikes stand in their pedals and pivot their handlebars side-to-side, antsy for dirt. Weekend racers flatten their backs parallel to the road and pump carbon fiber frames too fast to even greet me. Which is fine. Just thinking about leaning that far forward hurts my back.

I'm partial to cyclists who simply meander. The slower you go, the quirkier you are.

Obese trike guys need the stability of three wheels. Recumbent riders lay low and let their flags fly high. Tandems are magic. The person in front steers more than she powers, the person behind powers more than he steers. Each couple I meet discovers their unique optimization, in sync with one another as they journey the world.

On an early Saturday morning, before the lifeguards shoo bicycles off the boardwalk, I *dit-dunk, dit-dunk, dit-dunk* along Cape May's cedar slats; blazing sand and listless waves to my right, Victorian gingerbread to my left. Tom and I roll in rhythm, content with one another. A tandem approaches: a patrician thin woman in a pink shell with a wisp of gray hair wrung loose from her bun pedals in front of a knob-kneed gent with a Yankee hat covering his close-shorn head. We nod in passing. A tincture of Chanel Number 5 and indeterminate after-shave waft beneath the shore breeze for just the briefest moment. Strong sea air balloons my nostrils with salt before the comingled fragrance fully registers. I may be missing something.

124

I was homeless for six years. Now I stay in a trailer on a piece of land after my boyfriend got out of prison. We don't have electricity or running water, but we have each other. We're not strung out on drugs anymore. We're doing better.
— Mindy Malloy, walking with a broken bicycle and a purse inscribed "Peace and Love," Long Beach, WA

Lawrence, KS—September 18, 2016, 7:00 p.m.

"We got engaged last year. We even set a date, September 12, though we haven't done anything else to plan it."

"Char's been engaged three times."

"Yes, but each time something wasn't right. Within a month of meeting David, I knew this was the man I wanted to marry. He rubs my arthritic hip."

"And she rubs my arthritic hands."

Middle-aged Charlene Toncrey and David Klippell of Naperville, Illinois, strike a chord in me. Not because their devotion is unique, though the arthritic angle's a fresh twist. Rather they illustrate the many, many loving interactions I witness among couples I meet: uncharted depth for a man with no personal reference for such affection. Though I have never felt it in my fingers or in my toes, love is all around me, and it tickles with delightful exhilaration.

Immediately upon arriving at a host's house I can tell whether a couple is happy. Discord weighs heavy in the air; contentment is light and fresh. This sweet scent of joy is new to a boy who grew up between menacing walls. My parents' ill-matched temperaments transformed an aching love into malignant torture; we ricocheted off our split-level's acute angles like pinballs in a maze of rejection. As an adult, I loved my wife best I could, I still do. But the conscious maneuvers required to deny our fundamental dissonance forbade the instinctive abandon, the trust, true intimacy requires. We cannot miss what we have never known. So for 60 years I function pretty well, ignorant of what I lack: until this adventure reveals the wonder of couples who feed each other strength instead of heartburn, whose commitment is so strong and deep, its binding force gladdens even a clueless stranger.

"Danny, are you going to be warm enough?" Patrice Parsons, who goes by Pete, asks her high school sweetheart as he prepares for bed. He replies in a deep voice, "As long as you're next to me, baby doll, I'll be warm and fine." Pete and Danny were high school sweethearts in Victoria, Texas. They broke up, as young lovers often do, and then searched hard to find true soul mates, as lost lovers often do. Danny was married and divorced three times; ditto times five for Pete, until they found each other again. Pete and Danny are in their 60s now. Excited as young lovers, mellow as aged whiskey.

I've known Kay and Kenyon Morgan for 35 years. Kenyon and I launched our architecture careers together. Kay, his vivacious wife, kept two sapling architects from taking themselves too seriously. Before I arrive in Oklahoma City, Kenyon emails that since our last visit, everything's changed. Kay slipped on ice, which triggered early dementia. I can't envision what a disease I ascribe to the next generation will look like in someone my age, someone who made me laugh so hard. I pedal to their home in apprehension and absorb a new reality. Kay is like a firefly on a moist June night. We are eager, joyful, when her welcome light flashes, and chastened when, just as mysteriously, it extinguishes. She loses track of our conversation and withdraws behind a quizzical stare; aware that something's missing, unable to pinpoint what it is. Frustration is Kay's biggest foe. Fortunately, the couple's difficult present is bolstered by many years of shared joy. "I am her security." Kenyon tells me. "She always wants to be with me. But I tell her I need her, too. And it's true."

125

I witness a long litany of love's power. Seven job relocations in nine years toss Vicky and Phil Weinheimer into so many strange places, among so many new people, they lean into each other as one inseparable whole. When John Cawley's wife of 46 years dies a lingering, painful death, he buys a Miata, tours the West, exorcizes the demons of loss, returns to Cazenovia, New York, seeks a new love, and at age 70, he finds a keeper. Kim and Eddie Feeley, a young Seattle couple, are locked tight beyond their years; their affection seeps into shared gestures, joint sentences, and complementary sympathies.

The almost mystical devotion I find within Flynn and Savannah Gabriel's hand-me-down Carson City home reminds me of *The Enchanted Cottage*, where love conquers obstacles the outside world condemns. Flynn reports that when the family obtained health insurance through the Affordable Care Act, "Savannah went to her first appointment. The doctor just wrote 'obese' on her form without even talking to Savannah about it. Look at her, she's a big girl but she's active, she moves all the time." Our society has little patience for Asperger syndrome men who speak with Flynn's clipped abruptness, or praise for women of Savannah's proportions. Yet, within their haven of second-hand stuff, Savannah and Flynn create a sanctuary of mutual admiration and affirmation.

Not all nurturing couples face uphill battles against our cruel world. But they all navigate conflicts, concede preferences, and make sacrifices: the dance of give and take. The key to the inspirational couples I meet is, no matter how they tally the score, each always feels he's come out ahead.

Margaret and Ashton Lambdie are an opposites-attract couple. Ashton's a gregarious bike-repair junkie whose watermelon thighs pump out records in long-distance dirt-bike racing: the first man to complete Kansas' infamous Dirty Kanza in under seven hours. Margaret is a soft-spoken, composed woman pursuing a PhD in flute. Ever optimistic, Ashton finds advantage in their differences. "We'll go wherever Margaret can play; there are bike shops everywhere."

The couple's worldview is similarly bifurcated. For Ashton, "I love it when shit hits the proverbial fan. Global warming, overpopulation, our political situation—it's all fascinating to me." Margaret recoils at the idea. "I hate it when everything breaks. Everything that's good strengthens me. System failure bothers me extraordinarily."

Margaret and Ashton are a "traditional" couple, American Baptists who bake their own bread, yet they embrace very different intellectual spheres. Though not yet 30, they consider what's lost in our cultural freedoms greater than what's gained. "50, no 70, years ago, you went to church because it's what you 'did.' It was your social life. It represented the need to belong. That's not important anymore. Nobody wants to commit to anything anymore." Margaret and Ashton make commitments, to each other, their church, and their community. Being married is important. "We know so many people who have taken every step—dated a long time, live together, even buy a house together, but they don't get married." It evolves from 'what are you waiting for' to 'what are you afraid of.'"

We sit in their tiny, grad student–size living room, between bikes stacked in one corner and bulk grain tucked in the other. We nosh on protein infused cookies that Margaret bakes for Ashton's races. He washes them down with maple syrup. Given that energy, and those quads, it's easy to see how Ashton leaves spandex dudes sucking down packaged gel in the dust. As we talk, Margaret knits a sweater. Ashton holds his hands out and skeins her wool. The yarn binds their mutual appreciation, their concurrences, as well as their differences.

Plan for tomorrow, but enjoy today. Too many people bellyache about today and worry about tomorrow but they miss what's happening now.
I remember when my boys were little.
Where did that time go? That's what I want back.
—Merrill McGee, HVAC contractor, Poland, OH

Corydon, IN—September 4, 2016, 6:00 p.m.

The extension of the happy couple is, of course, the happy family.

When I accept a host's invitation for the night, I typically offer, "I'll arrive around six o'clock unless another time is more convenient for you." Sometimes a host has a long workday and suggests a later hour. Only once do I hear, "Oh, I was hoping you could come earlier." Ever obliging, I climb the front porch steps of the aging row house in Altoona, Pennsylvania, in mid-afternoon and knock on Deb Greene's door.

"My cyclist is here!" A tiny creature with huge red hair runs at me with her arms high. She leads me through a kitchen where every surface is covered with food and drink, to a deck that fills half the back yard. At least 20 people give me a quick once-over. Deb's mom, sister, in-laws, nieces; I can't keep track who's who and what they do, but it doesn't matter.

Altoona is long past prime, a dying railroad town wallowing at the base of its famous horseshoe curve. Anyone with gumption leaves. Deb's family stays. They work hard: at Target, at the gas station, as home health aides. They have jobs rather than careers. They avoid the itch to move up and out. This is where they are from; this is where they will stay, together. Defined not by what they do or what they have. They have each other.

Janice Feldstein, of Scottsdale, Arizona, tells me straight out, "Family is the most important thing." Yet, her two children live on opposite coasts, her five grandchildren are scattered; attorneys, doctors, people of asset and influence. For Janice the primacy of family is not measured by proximity; it's optimizing each individual's opportunity. Janice's attitude is more prevalent in a nation that prizes independence, especially among the educated and affluent who step up and out to ever loftier ladders. But facilitating your grandchildren's self-actualization is a more abstract satisfaction than showing off your cycling guest to the whole clan at an afternoon barbeque.

Katie and Nathan Bloom bring a focus on family full circle. The pair moved to Oregon, as did Katie's sister Mims and her husband Dan. After starting families, both couples returned to southern Indiana to raise their children near their mother, their siblings, and their children's cousins. Indiana's lower cost of living sweetened the pull. Katie and Nathan bought a house and live comfortably on her nursing salary; Nathan stays home with the children.

The evening I arrive, the two couples, plus mom and some old friends, gather for chili and beer. An assortment of children, aged three to eight, present an impromptu musical on piano, harmonica, and accordion for dessert. Corydon, Indiana, may not be a hip as Portland, but it offers more of everything the Bloom's desire.

It used to be you would look out for your own, your tribe. Now, that's not enough.
We have to pay attention to people beyond the mountain, beyond the ocean.
We are all connected.
—Tom, Marine veteran, San Diego, CA

Athens, GA—August 18, 2016, 8:00 p.m.

Beyond the tight circles of partner and family, the ripple effect of our connections runs into 21st-century turbulence. Humans are tribal creatures. We trust those within our tribe. We take their words as truth, their actions as beneficial. We doubt, even fear, those beyond.

For generations, our expanding circle of trust, our tribe, aligned with geography. The closer we resided to others, the better we knew them; the more we trusted them. That correlation is history. Blame the Industrial Revolution, blame immigration, blame public education, blame the World Wars, blame the Interstate highway system, blame racial integration, blame television, blame Levittown, blame rock'n'roll, blame corporate agriculture, blame the "Me" generation, blame Walmart, blame the internet, blame Fox News, blame MSNBC, blame Twitter. Blame whatever shadows of change provoke your personal angina. The ideal community we pine for is a fantasy rooted in romanticism over any reality, present or past. Today, our lives, our community, our sense of who we are and where we belong are unhinged from geography. City dwellers, numb to crushing density, may not even know their next-door neighbor; while communities defined by work, ideology, or social media bind people across the globe.

Wherever I travel, social media is alternately pillared for destroying community, or championed for creating it. Detractors are often those who flourish in a face-to-face social system—the homecoming queen who married a local insurance agent—or people who lack computer access or skills. Advocates of internet communities are computer savvy, or, more important, people whose physical communities lack support: Muslims in Douglas, Arizona; homosexual teens in Scottsbluff, Nebraska; and single Jewish farmers in Walterboro, South Carolina, reach beyond their physical bounds of community to find their tribe.

As a slow moving wanderer, I appreciate, and access, virtual communities along my path. For warmshowers' hosts, the bond of cycle touring eclipses conventional prohibitions: they open their door to a stranger just because he's on a bicycle. But after months of trading bike tales, I realize the limitations of a community disproportionately affluent and white. If my objective is to mingle with the broadest possible range of Americans, I must dive into a deeper pool. So I start couchsurfing.

Couchsurfing is a concept: people let others crash on their sofas. It's also a website, couchsurfing.org. While warmshowers has over 80,000 members, couchsurfing boasts more than 12 million "friends you haven't met yet." This leap in scale ensures that couchsurfing is more plentiful and more diverse. It's also beset with more pitfalls. Couchsurfing.com is littered with deadwood, people who signed up and never host or even reply. My hit rate on warmshowers is one in three; on couchsurfing it's one in five, maybe more. The bigger the city, the more inquiries I need to make in order to land a place. Yet I avoid over-requesting. It's unseemly to seek hospitality and then, once invited, turn it down because something else comes along. Even online communities deserve a modicum of etiquette.

Despite the extra effort, I begin to prioritize couchsurfing hosts because they offer such a wide range. I stay with the son of illegal immigrants in Fresno; an African American in Harlem; a working cowboy in Portal, Arizona; an Indian IT guru in Dallas; and the sole Turkmen at the University of Missouri. Welcoming folks with fascinating perspectives on tomorrow that lay outside the cycling community.

Couchsurfing also promotes socializing among members within a local community. When Jon Pierson invites me to stay with him within a week of his moving to Athens, Georgia, he capitalizes on my visit by setting up a local couchsurfing event. Six "friends we haven't met yet" show up at the HiLo Lounge in Normaltown to meet the bicycle junkie. We share beers and bites and stories of surfing.

Jon's backstory is a telling example of how the nature of our relationships has changed. Jon and a former girlfriend had a child together. "I never felt a lifelong commitment to her. I feel that for our son. I am the child of divorced parents. When I get married I want to be married for the relationship, not the child." Since the couple was never married, they never got divorced; there is no formal child support. Jon gives Ben's mother regular payments, and after she moved to Athens, he relocated to be close to his son. A generation ago this arrangement would have been peculiar, two generations ago it would have been scandalous. Today, it is just one of the myriad ways individuals, couples, and families navigate life's terrain.

Jon is "social glue," an easy-going extrovert who values connections. Within days of arriving in Athens he's organizing meet-ups and building a new life. Social media facilitates his transition to a new place where the only person Jon knows is one very special five-year-old.

What brings out the best aspects of our military are our shared hardships. How do we manufacture that in civilian life?
In Ranger School, the challenges were great in difficult conditions.
I am a good soldier, but in Ranger School I was so exhausted I would have cut corners if I could.
But I couldn't. My community wouldn't let me. We need more of that in politics and in life.

—Anonymous, US Army captain, Joint Base Lewis-McChord, WA

Santa Fe, NM—October 7, 2016, 8:00 p.m.

How do we define community stripped of geographical underpinning?

The desk clerk at the Oasis Motel is a life long North Dakotan. She's also chatty. Ann tells warm stories of growing up in Dickinson, of family in Bismarck. I ask, "Is the entire state of North Dakota your community?" She hesitates; then laughs. "Except for parts of Fargo." Like all jokes, her response revels the underbelly of truth; a wistful phrase tinged with dissonance and loss.

Ethel MacDonald, a septuagenarian from Missoula, Montana, talks tomorrow well past midnight. She throws her arms wide and proclaims, "The community I am concerned about is the whole world."

Francie Marks is a mother with four children who raises chickens and vegetables in Sandpoint, Idaho, to be "more self-sufficient." Like thousands of other preppers, Francie considers survival an individual endeavor; her tribe is very small, her suspicions of outsiders fierce.

These three women represent different ways of drawing the boundary between who's in our tribe and who's outside of it. It's a boundary every one of us creates because humans simply cannot encounter every being with a blank slate. Unfortunately, evolutionary trust and social cooperation move at an anthropological crawl compared to the speed at which contemporary life changes.

Where are the boundaries of my tribe? A new question haunts my travel, for within it lays our propensity to cooperate and the extents of our fear. In keeping with our bipolar nature, we em-phasize the extremes. Ethel MacDonald may claim kinship with all, and Francie Marks may aim laser focus on nuclear family, but I'm pretty sure that Ethel interacts with her Missoula neighbors differently than from Asian villagers, and that Francie is involved with groups and causes beyond her immediate family.

What about Ann back at the Oasis Motel? She faces a conundrum. Fargo is the fastest growing city in North Dakota, while rural areas are losing population. As more and more Dakotans move to Fargo and become city folk, does Ann's community grow to include them, or does it shrink to embrace only those who remain behind?

So often I hear people's yearning for constancy in our land: a wish that things will slow down, be stable. Stasis is an illusion. Ann cannot preserve a steady-state community. Either she expands her tribe through affinity or geography, or it will shrink.

My worry for Ann, for all of us, when change turns from excitement to anxiety, is heartfelt. But it does not linger. The great salve of the bicycle traveler is that deep concerns evaporate under my light load. Legs spin; endorphins expand, I can't stay bummed for long.

CB and his comrades, Randy and Barb, roam our nation in RVs. They call themselves a band, "a group of people that is small enough not to have a leader," and I'm delighted to join them for a night in their community shaped by movement.

On September 9, 2009, CB drove away from his suburban Atlanta home towing an Airstream trailer. Though the guy's a great talker, he shares nothing of his life before that date; I don't even know what CB stands for. The man focuses on the present and future, not the past. What I do know is that for the past seven years CB has lived in his trailer, usually near Randy and Barb. The trio crisscrosses the United States like tokens on a giant board game, seeking bonus points for warm climate, good scenery, solar power, and internet access. They make music together. Sometimes their roving village expands, especially in winter when so many kindred spirits are drawn to Arizona. Sometimes it's just the three of them, which is how I find them encamped along the road to Albuquerque. CB and friends live light upon the land; less than one kilowatt-hour of electricity per day. They are well versed in the laws and strategies of inhabiting National Parks and Forests and are careful not to flaunt rules or violate 14-day camping limits.

They are an intentional community, a physical community, released from the constrictions of geography.

Tomorrow is where most of us live.
We also live in yesterday.
Very few live today.
— Mike Sliwa, Progressive Radio Network host of Nature Bats Last, Gila, NM

Murfreesboro, TN—August 29, 2016, 10:00 a.m.

My phone rings along the bike path that follows the West Fork Stones River in Murfreesboro. It's a convenient place to stop. Susan Ruth introduces herself, explains how she learned about my trip, and asks whether I would like to participate in her podcast series, *Hey Human*. My media outreach is even goosier than my route. If someone asks me to do a podcast, newspaper interview, or TV spot, I do. But I don't seek them out.

I'll be in Nashville a few days, but it's difficult for Susan and I to find a compatible time to meet. "How about tonight?" She asks.

"Fine with me, but I try not to travel at night. Would you mind if I crash at your place? I have a sleeping bag."

"That works."

Susan Ruth and I share five degrees of separation. A friend of mine in Boston connected me with Pete Parsons in Texas. Pete's husband Danny told a songwriter in Nashville about my trip, who thought Susan might be interested. Yet within minutes we go from complete strangers to overnight host and guest.

The more I travel, the bolder I become in finding shelter. Only once do I initiate a cold request for floor space, from an IT guy I meet at the community table at Figueroa Mountain Brewery in Santa Barbara when the hour is too late to pedal around for a motel room and authorities are cracking down on beach sleepers. It takes Kerry a few moments to absorb my bald request. Nevertheless he agrees, we trade stories well into the night, and he sends me off with a hot breakfast.

When I am more cautious, and more sober, I know how to nudge the envelope of a connection toward an invitation to someone's home. After all, the best conversation happens around the kitchen table.

The hierarchy of where I like to stay becomes clear. First preference is family: four brothers and sisters; a dozen grown-up nieces and nephews—the only people I bunk with for more than a single night. Next comes 60 years of accumulated friends. Third preference is friends of friends: people like Susan separated by two, three, even five degrees. Referrals beget referrals; the longer my trip unwinds, the more friends of friends I meet. When I have no personal connections to a place, I default to couchsurfing or warmshowers. If no social media host accepts, I stay in a motel. Last resort: sleep outdoors.

I spend exactly four nights outside, all early on. One each in Yellowstone and Yosemite, where accommodations require years-ahead booking but the National Park Service ensures a campsite to anyone who hikes or bikes into the parks. One night each in Livingston, Montana, and in Helena, after I miscommunicate with crusty hosts whose hospitality extends only to the back door. No problem that I travel without a tent; those two August nights are warm and star-filled. By the time I reach Nashville, a year later, I'm so smooth in seeking accommodations that I never again get stuck sleeping outdoors.

Staying with family and friends is great fun; we rekindle memories. And I appreciate every website host, even though their open generosity skews my survey of a nation steeped in privacy and laced with suspicion. But I develop a special affinity for "friends of

friends," fresh encounters that represent the widest cross-section of all my hosts. "Friends of friends" come from every quadrant of the political spectrum: addicts and amputees, corporate farmers and urban gardeners, academics and amusement park operators. These folks don't open their doors to strangers on a regular basis; I'm welcome because someone in their tribe vouched for me. They're the closest I get to the heartbeat of America.

I bring dinner to share with Susan. She tapes me for an interview of *Hey Human*. I listen to Susan's song that Reba McIntyre covered on a recent album. A generation ago, that level of fame that might have prompted a songwriter to quit her day job, but those days are gone. There is little money in Susan's songwriting, or the cartoons she draws, or her podcasts. She has no illusion that art will earn her a living. She creates to express herself, to be fully alive. We celebrate our Monday evening; two people doing what we love. I ask Susan, "How will we live tomorrow?"

"We will likely hold our breath for a while. We are trying not to drown. We will likely venture off this rock and find another rock. If we can understand each other—understanding and compassion are the keys—we will find a way to continue.

"I am an alien, not in the science fiction way, but in the sense of being 'other'. I'm part of something bigger than me, than my community, than this earth."

Susan gives me a copy of her CD, *All I Ever Wanted Was Everything*. I have no way to play it on my bike, but I tote it 5,000 miles and listen to it when I get home. Worth every extra ounce of transport: it's that good.

Tomorrow is Aggieland Saturday. My day is mandated.
    —Cadet Faukhaber, Texas A&M Corps of Cadets, College Station, TX

Fort Worth, TX—October 22, 2016, 11:00 p.m.

We can pursue empathy by walking in another man's shoes, but it's more exhilarating to step into his banana suit.

Steve Culver tosses our bikes in the back of his pickup. We drive out to Azle for a barbeque with his friend Ryan: three racks of ribs, cheese biscuits, and local brew. A bowl of salad gets passed around for show, the vermouth of our carnivore martini. Ryan and his wife live in a nice three-bedroom ranch, the kind of house you can pick up in Texas for $150K or so; it would go for half a million or more on either coast. They don't have kids; two giant dogs own one spare bedroom, the other's furnished with a pair of beer fridges. A large framed photo of the happy couple on their wedding day hangs over the mantle, standing proud in tuxedo and long dress, smiling at each other, rifles propped on their hips.

"Are you Steve's dad?" Ryan kids. For the rest of the night, everyone calls me "dad." After we're ribbed-out and tap more beer, Ryan dumps a huge box of costumes and accessories on the living room floor. Banana suits of all sizes. Everyone scavenges for something fancy. We stack a bunch of bikes in three pickups and drive back into town: three former marines, two active-duty jarheads, a pair of girlfriends, all pushing 30; and me, twice their age and half their muscle.

We park near the Convention Center. Assemble our bikes and adjust our suits. Ryan straps a boom box to the back of his bike. He leads us to the Winter Garden, where we practice riding in rotation, carving loops that echo our loud music. Folks gawk our way. Some applaud.

Once our formation is tight, we pedal out along Fort Worth's sidewalks on a clear and animated Saturday night. The office towers are outlined in colored lights; pedestrians high-five us along the way. We stream up Commerce and down Main, bobbing onto cross streets in no particular order. The police are surprisingly kind; our leader Ryan is a sweet-talker. Even in a banana suit he looks like the handsome Marine he is. Officials won't let us invade Sundance Square, but otherwise we get free reign. Grumpy folks might call us sidewalk terrorists, but everyone's in a merry mood. Passersby are just happy enough and just drunk enough to encourage our antics.

We pedal to the Tarrant County College campus, a paradise of hard, sloped surfaces. We spin up the ramps of the Sundance Garage. From the top, the obscenely large angel trumpet reliefs on the Bass Performance Hall float above bacchanal revelry below. We share tricks with a group of skateboarders and race them down seven stories of spiral ramps, back to the street.

Ryan's soused. He crosses the street to a couple of men holding hands and gives them a bear hug, praising their love. I cringe. I imagine that, among the hundreds of couples holding hands on this lovely night, gay couples want to fit in, not be singled out. But Ryan sees himself as generous and noble, as befits the top dog of our dominant culture. He can dress up, hug guys, make a racket, and disturb the peace: everybody still loves him. And he knows it. I marvel at his confidence, I wonder what it must feel like.

Sometime after midnight we breeze by a middle-aged couple. They ask if I'm the chaperone. I laugh at the joke, but its underlying truth bursts my energy. In a moment, nothing's funny.

Ryan's boom box falls off his bike. A speaker pops out. The silence is like the giant sucking of a shop vac inhaling our good spirits. He tries to repair the damage, but it's after 1:00 a.m. Our buzz evaporates. The banana boys and girls are ready to head home.

I thank the group for letting me join the fun. No one gives me a hug; that would be awkward. I'm a one-off tagalong, a quirky visitor, not a member of the tribe. On the drive home Steve turns philosophical.

"We used to run patrols with rifles in Iraq. Now we ride around downtown in banana suits." I'll take that as progress.

Pueblo, CO—September 18, 2016, 7:00 p.m.

Just as I navigate the internet to find hosts in new cities so too I search the web for interesting people to profile. A few days before I arrive in Akron I cruise TripAdvisor to discover what's unique about Ohio's fifth-largest city. Turns out that Dr. Bob, the co-founder of Alcoholics Anonymous, is from Akron; his house is open to public. I know many men and women who credit AA for turning around their lives; I decide to visit.

Back in the 1980s I attended Al-Anon, AA's associate arm for people touched by alcoholism. My father was a deep alcoholic. Anger, temper, rage, contrition, requite; we never knew what emotional roulette he'd spin as the bourbon streamed through his arteries, only that its effect would be fierce, unassuaged by kindness or reason. Al-Anon helped me understand how my father's unpredictable behavior contributes to my own shunted emotions. Not as an excuse to justify isolation so much as motivation to transcend it.

Dr. Bob's Home is a Mission-style bungalow circa 1915, built when the Rubber Capital of the World was rolling into its heyday. It's a modest place, serene and well tended. Volunteers do everything. My guide, Wayne, weaves the history of the house, the program, and his personal story. "Looking back, I knew who I was when I was 16. A friend of mine and I wore long coats with interior pockets, into a local store. He took a Playboy, I took a bottle of cheap booze."

Every room of Dr. Bob's Home is anointed with compassion and dignity; every person there manifests content. The humble security derived from the fortitude to confront our demon and tread a disciplined path against it.

"One day at a time" is the most frequent response I receive to my question. It's also a cornerstone slogan of AA's 12-step program. Not everyone who tells me "Tomorrow we will live one day at a time" is in AA; but everyone in AA delivers that response.

Isley Worthy stands beside me on the promontory above Spokane's spectacular rapids. He delivers a puzzling response to my question. "Tomorrow will be different from today." Many people predict that tomorrow will be just like today; even more describe change, good and ill, that evolves from our present actions. Isley is the first person to proclaim sharp change without suggesting a route to get us there.

Isley talks staccato, his eyes dart, he's riddled with nervous energy. He's the first obvious drug addict I meet. I encounter others like him: in downtown Portland, along Waterbury Connecticut's Main Street. They all proffer disjointed responses. I realize that addicts' reality is skewed, they lack the continuity of time. Past, present, future are unrelated incidents. The fundamental pretense of my question—that tomorrow flows from today—doesn't apply. Addicts are passive bystanders of experience shaped by external substances. Chaotic highs and lows obliterate cause and effect. They are not agents; they do not influence their circumstances.

Colorado, the first state to legalize recreational marijuana, offers a glimpse into a world that tolerates, if not embraces, altered substances and addiction. On my first pass through Denver, I visit Medicine Man dispensary. Elan Nelson tours me through an efficient, vertically integrated marijuana growth and sales facility. I come away impressed by how carefully lawmakers structured production and sales. I'm flabbergasted at the money involved.

Medicine Man's profits, and the state's share, are stupendous. An ancillary take away is that I stink of pot and must shower before I can meet anyone else. The media carries a few naysaying stories of Colorado's experiment, but most people seem happy with the rollout. It's hard to argue with coffers full of cash.

More than a year passes before my second visit to the Centennial State. The buzz has shifted. The economy is booming, thanks in part to legal marijuana, but many companies who require drug tests cannot fill open positions. Since marijuana lingers in our bloodstream up to 30 days, fewer and fewer Coloradans can pass drug tests.

In Pueblo I stay with Allen Ungerer, more than 10 years my junior. Three years ago Allen quit an insurance business in Delaware, left his wife, flipped an annuity into a monthly payment, and struck out West. He lived among homeless in Ventura, California, and then settled in Pueblo, enticed by legal cannabis. Allen suffered *necrotizing facilitis* at age 12; one of his shins is a twig. He also survived a wicked motorcycle accident in college. The man is in constant pain; marijuana offers his best relief. "I used to take six prescriptions. Now, I manage my pain through various mixes I grind myself."

Allen lives in a squat stucco house in a low-rent district near the Fountain Branch of the Arkansas River, proximate to floods, within earshot of constant sirens. A pair of upholstered chairs dominates his living room, flanking a TV table littered with jars of ground leaves, papers, and clips. During our 14 hours together, Allen sits in his chair and chain-smokes joints; often lighting the next joint off the ember of the last. Allen sold his car. Everything

he needs is within four blocks of his Pueblo home, including his dispensary, though I gather he goes days without leaving home at all. Allen has created a haven from a life of unsatisfying work, a nagging wife, and constant pain. "I want to be untraceable, untrackable. When I get self-sufficient I will be able to disappear."

I'm an advocate for legalized marijuana. Alcohol does just as much damage, maybe more, to super users and their families. That booze is legal and marijuana is not reflects cultural bias rather than any objective measure of harm. Regulating victimless activities, and collecting tax revenue from them, gives us more control over the product and distribution. It's a safer system. Allen Ungerer smoking himself into hazy oblivion is no worse than an alcoholic passing out drunk. Which is not to say that's its good, for Allen, or for our society.

The tragedy of Allen Ungerer, of Isley Worthy, and of my own father, isn't the legality of the substance they choose. It's that our world is such a cold and scary place that so many of us turn away from fellow humans and seek refuge in chemical escape.

There will be a lot more people.
We have to learn to accommodate them.
And dogs.
With more people, there will be more dogs.
> —Tymer, dog owner, Seattle, WA

Locust Fork, AL—August 26, 2016, 2:00 p.m.

Chased by dogs
Pithy slogans on church signs
Rebel flags on trailer houses that never move
Propane farms
Chased by dogs
Get the US out of the UN
Jaxson Smokehouse smackin' hot bar-be-cue
Fresh rain rising off blacktop steams the sweat right up my neck
Making good time
'Cause I'm chased by dogs

This is where states rights were born.
We want decisions to be made at the most local level possible.
—Kelly, fair-skinned smoker, Florence, SC

Rixeyville, VA—August 3, 2016, 2:00 p.m.

Ever since that early morning I wake up in a yurt in Maine, I'm struck by how the past colors our prospects for tomorrow. Today, past, present, and future coalesce into a single current.

I hale from a region rich in history. In daily life I stroll by Old South Church where the Adams boys, Sam and John, roused the rabble. I cross the intersection where the Boston Massacre occurred. I pedal past the Lexington Green and Concord footbridge: "The shot heard round the world" echoes still. Washington's Brattle Street Headquarters during the siege of Boston is a few blocks from my house. These places rest easy in my mind, unambiguously positive landmarks commemorating our nation's independence from England. The Revolutionary War is settled history: the pomp and celebration belongs to us, the victors.

As I pedal over Chester Gap from Front Royal to Flint Hill and along Ben Venue Road, I am touched by an altogether different weight of history. Here in Virginia, the Civil War is ever present, though its message is murky still. Huge clouds, occasional sprinkles, and intermittent sun create thermal updrafts and cool undercurrents. The earth itself sighs under the ambivalent burden of a glorious land tainted by ignoble defeat.

The Confederate Army marched from Culpepper to Gettysburg along the route I traverse—twice. First they headed north: 60,000 confident, strong men; four abreast and three miles long, trailed by artillery and support in a bold move to take an offensive stance against the North. A far smaller number returned along the same route, in the direction I spin, in defeat.

One local tells me, "After Gettysburg, everything fell apart. The rest of the war was defense and retreat. If we could have just stopped then, perhaps the destruction would not have been so great. But fighting continued and we were humbled."

One hundred and fifty years later, the land is lush, bountiful. The stately plantation houses (refurbished), and extant slave quarters (whitewashed), offer fresh-painted accents to the verdant scene. There is no evidence of pillage, no clue that hardly a tree stood in all of Culpepper County. But the natives remember. "There was a dance of etiquette between the races. A desire for order that is gone." Kathy Ellis is the fifth-generation Crisler to live at Clifton Farm. She is a conscientious steward who has not only restored the property but also reached out to others, former slaves, who lived there. I doubt they long for that lost order in quite the same way.

Time romanticizes a way of life out of step with the march of equality and justice. A century and a half after Appomattox the gentry remain baffled why the remedy came so hard. They relive the Civil War, yesterday, today, and tomorrow, in a ceaseless struggle to fathom, to reframe, what transpired in a way that can reflect their honor.

142

We, society, must pull together with empathy
and compassion for all,
or we will crumble from greed and ignorance.
—Brad Simkins, father and online college student, Madera, CA

Levelland, TX—October 15, 2016, 11:00 a.m.

The morning haze leaches into my room, burnt orange, thanks to the scrim of dirt on the Budget Inn windows. No friends; no couchsurfing hosts. I don't have a thread of connection in this out-of-the-way town where I used to know so many people. Once upon a time, I lived here.

In the 1970s, I spent a year as a VISTA volunteer in Levelland, Texas, providing housing and energy conservation assistance to the poor and elderly of the South Plains. The work required a disparate set of skills: absorbing arcane government eligibility regulations; palling around with cowboy-booted USDA agents; learning Spanish; designing solar hot water heaters; driving 2,000 miles a month along lonely two-lane highways; praising jalapeno cornbread and Jell-O salads at covered dish luncheons; getting stoned; shooting a gun for the first time; and shooting tequila for the first time (though not at the same time, thank goodness). I dispensed hundreds of thousands of dollars in energy and housing assistance funds to a smattering of whites, blacks, and Latinos, early settlers and their direct descendants.

For four days I don't cross a river, or even a wash. This high, dry land, *Llano Estacado*, thwarted settlement until the late 19th century. Real development occurred only within the last hundred years, after we tapped the Ogallala Aquifer and irrigation turned flat brown grass into commodity crops. When I first arrived, the towns were ugly, squat, and dusty; the people friendly and accommodating; the land a vast canvas of speckled white cotton and brilliant yellow sunflowers undulating across an immense prairie sea.

For the past week I've tried to find some of those good folks on Facebook or Google with no luck. So I strike out in no particular direction, determined to see how reality squares with memory.

Downtown looks the same, though with more empty storefronts. The courthouse square, with library anchoring the southwest corner, looks unchanged. Ditto the community college. Highway 385 has more fast food. Ace Hardware distributes free coffee. The small metal shed of a church I attended sports a brick front. The migrant worker housing court where I lived has been razed; funny how the step-down shower that drained directly outside has become a fond memory. The 7-11 around the corner is now a Mexican grocery with excellent pastries. I stop at Tienda's for a burrito, because I'm nostalgic rather than hungry.

In the 55 years before I arrived, Levelland's population grew from zero to 13,000 people. 38 years later, it's virtually the same. A place that grew from nothing now claws for stasis. Other towns in the South Plains are already shrinking, as is the Ogallala that gives this region life. The measure of human habitation on this arid plain may prove short, but Levelland will linger. It is the county seat; it has a McDonalds and a Walmart. Bungalows near downtown don't look like they've been painted since I left, but a subdivision of million-dollar houses has sprouted east of town. Levelland has become a refuge for wealthy folks escaping that den of urban vice next county over: Lubbock.

By noon, I exhaust my recollected haunts, save one. I pedal north of town to seek out any vestige of Emmer Lee Whitfield, my life's most unexpected mentor.

On a chilly November day in 1977, I canvassed the black neighborhood, across the tracks, in the shadow and stench of the soybean processing plant, to solicit applicants for an energy improvement / heating bill assistance program. I climbed the steps of a wide house with a long porch. A black woman opened the door, medium height, medium weight, medium expression; a few curler papers stuck to the ends of her damp hair.

Emmer Lee Whitfield leaned against the doorframe. She listened, nodded, and then spoke. "I could use that. This here house is so drafty and my bills is so high." I wrote down pertinent information. It took a long time. Emmer Lee reported that she was disabled; had two high school aged children; received food stamps, AFDC, SSI, and Medicaid; her son was enrolled in a job training program; her daughter in an education program. Emmer Lee displayed a discomforting knowledge of assistance. She knew income limits, eligibility requirements, funding cycles. I took an immediate distrust of her. She didn't look disabled; her house was more upright than others on the unpaved street; she was clearly smart enough to work. I completed her application and left, resolved to find some way to disqualify her from receiving yet another government program.

Back in the office, I asked about Emmer Lee Whitfield. Everyone smiled knowingly. A professional poor person, a welfare queen, she received virtually every form of assistance our Community Action Agency offered. And though it galled me, she qualified for energy conservation assistance.

The spring funding cycle arrived with more complicated requirements, including local citizen committees charged with evaluating applications and disbursing funds. Committees had to include members from the community at large, utility companies, and the "target population," a bureaucratic euphemism for poor people that would never fly in today's politically correct times. Top of my list to represent Levelland's target: Emmer Lee Whitfield.

I facilitated Community Energy Conservation Group meetings in seven counties; the process was predictable. I arrived early to organize the room: six folding tables set in a square with a dozen chairs set around the perimeter. No implied hierarchy. The utility executive arrived in a suit; as did whatever local businessman I cajoled to represent the community at large. They sat next to each other and created the de facto front of the room. I sat to one side with my stack of applications; target community representatives sat, in work clothes, in the opposite corner. There was tacit understanding that, as committee members, their personal applications would be approved. The process began. I selected an application, described the applicant, and passed the paperwork to the executives, who scanned and commented. The target representatives nodded agreement. Whoever the suits recommended got the money. Actually, they didn't get the money. The utility company got all the money. The poor people received a credit on their gas bill. We don't like to give real money to poor people in this country. We don't trust them.

The first meeting in Levelland was different. The vice president of the utility company set himself down. Emmer Lee Whitfield walked in and placed her purse right next to him. She wore a shirtwaist dress of satin sheen, small pumps, and a single set of pearls. Her hair softly curled. With the established power order disrupted, everyone else sat wherever. I started through the applications. Emmer Lee reviewed them first. She checked the name and provided an opinion. "Bertha Mae really needs this because her husband is laid up. … Wanda's boyfriend is working nights on a rig down in Denver City, they are doing fine. … Millie doesn't need the cash so much, but she could use some repairs that she can't manage now that her son has left home." Emmer Lee commented on every black applicant and a good number of the whites and Latinos as well. Emboldened, other target representatives spoke

up. The meeting took much longer than usual, but when we were done we had actually allocated the money according to a deeper understanding of need than application forms could describe.

I walked home near midnight, past the quiet courthouse square and the bank sign flashing time and temperature. The Texas sky never exhibited more stars. Within two months I'd leave Levelland, to return to Cambridge, to graduate school, to what everyone called "real life." Had my tenure here touched anyone? I had been touched, that night; my perspective forever changed by a woman of extraordinary ability at the top of her game.

Emmer Lee Whitfield was the most accomplished welfare recipient I ever met. That's not a skill we condone, yet I must applaud her ability. Perhaps in 2016 a well-dressed articulate black woman can sit beside an executive and be accepted as an important member of the proceedings. But in 1978, in Levelland, Texas, a poor black woman with scant education and few prospects commanding the attention of white men who dole out money was brazenly out of place.

Emmer Lee Whitfield understood her options with a clarity few of us can claim; she knew what the world offered, and reasoned her best opportunity lay in extracting the most from the welfare system. Without welfare, Emmer Lee would have survived; perhaps she would have even exceeded the constraints a welfare life imposed. But her decision to be a welfare queen was a rational one. Each of us, every day, absorbs our reality, assesses our strengths, our pitfalls, and determines our best move. The systems our society has established, whether Wall Street or welfare, influence how we act.

I joined VISTA to nourish some vague altruistic ideal. What I learned was the exact opposite. We all act in our self-interest. In fact, self-interest is always the best possible motive for action. The key is, how do we define our self-interest?

We live in a culture that defines it as maximizing profits measured in quarterly return. This propels many of us to personal prosperity, but also produces the ancillary effects of income disparity and social isolation. It shortchanges the long-term. It creates a world where a poor black woman's best opportunity is not work, but welfare. Emmer Lee Whitfield acted in her best interest, very astutely, as a welfare queen. If we don't like that, the fault is not in her, it's in the system.

The internet informed me that Emmer Lee Whitfield died in an automobile accident in 1996, the same year Bill Clinton killed "welfare as we know it." Still, I ride down her street, reminiscing. The street is paved now. Emmer Lee's house is gone. No sign of her children. The black neighborhood's a remnant of what it was; all the tarpaper shacks are gone. I take that as progress.

I pedal out of Levelland under a noon high sun, hollow with a hunger Tienda's cannot satisfy. A long time has passed since I was a blip in this place; whatever connections I had are long gone. I'm queasy about elevating Emmer Lee Whitfield to hero status. Being the town's best welfare queen is not on the same as being the best surgeon, or even the best quarterback. I just wish we'd offered a woman with so much spunk something better to perfect. I feel certain Emmer Lee would have extended her self-interest to a higher reach, if only the world allowed.

We are uniquely positioned to set an example of what progress and change can be.
We are viewed as a place of police brutality but we can transcend that.
Ferguson can offer a path out that others can emulate.
　　　—Wesley Bell, city councilor, Ferguson, MO

The lessons of the past have to be respected to give hope to our future.
Take what we learn, acknowledge the anger, leave it behind.
Keep what each of us has to contribute to the solution.
　　　—Linda Lipka, city councilor, Ferguson, MO

Ferguson, MO—September 10, 2016, 10:00 a.m.

Sixteen thousand miles after I first leave Cambridge I arrive at one of the very first push pins I place on my map: Ferguson, Missouri. What I encounter here is worth all the effort.

Ferguson looks nothing like the violent images etched into our televisions two summers ago when Michael Brown, an unarmed black teen, was shot by Officer Darren Wilson and left on the pavement for hours. It looks nothing like a place where riots erupted, nothing like a city bristling with police brutality or African American overreaction, depending on your niche along our political spectrum.

Ferguson looks like the quiet middle class community it is: modest houses with trim lawns, solid businesses, no-nonsense public buildings, and shady trees. I visit the Ferguson Farmer's Market, the public library, City Hall, and West Florissant Ave, where the worst of the rioting and looting occurred. Two Ferguson City Council representatives, Linda Lipka and Wesley Bell, talk with me about their work and respond to my question; the first elected officials who participate in my project. Everywhere I go in Ferguson, people release the exhaustive sigh of anger spent. In violence and turmoil's wake, I find transparency, tolerance, and respect.

Corliss and Carl Thorn, my Ferguson hosts, have lived on the same street of small ranch houses for 26 years. It's always been an integrated neighborhood, though over time that's tilted from majority white to majority black. Like everyone I meet in Ferguson, the couple believe the attention their city received after Michael Brown's shooting and Officer Darren Wilson's exoneration is unbalanced, yet they embrace the tragedy as a call to improve. Corliss offers her perspective. "Michael Brown was not about race. It was about respect. Michael Brown disrespected the police officer responding to a 911 call; the officer disrespected Michael Brown. A series of poor decisions on the part of the police made everything worse. Al Sharpton and the media turned it into race. Then we had riots and looting. I came home at night and heard the marches and the teargas alarms. It was scary."

Corliss and Carl treat me to dinner at Marley's Bar & Grill, where it's difficult to refute Corliss's assessment. Marley's is one of the most integrated places I've been; black and white staff, black and white customers. People greet each other without tension. Everyone humors a local drunk who wanders onto the deck begging cigarettes.

Toward the bottom of my locally brewed Ferguson Pale Ale, I realize that what transpired in Ferguson could not have happened just anywhere. It couldn't happen in a lily-white community, a pitch-black community, or a gated community. It could only happen in a community that was already on the road to integration, a community where whites and blacks rubbed shoulders on a regular basis. When a string of disrespect and bad decisions sparked that rubbing into friction and violence, a young black man died and a white officer was exonerated. We practice no equality of respect in this country.

The world reprimands Ferguson. But when do we reprimand the places that keep blacks out through wealth and privilege? Places so guarded, so fearful, so segregated, that racial discourse doesn't even occur?

Ferguson represents opposing truths of our polarized politics: that police unfairly target and abuse black men; that the black community will remain disenfranchised until it becomes more integrated in mainstream society.

Ferguson also represents the limits of my favorite pronoun. Because when it comes to race in America, there is no single "we." Skin color divides "us" and "them."

I can say that we, the white folks, have to stop passing draconian laws, enforcing them racially, and tossing so many black men in prison; that we have to stop shooting them and being afraid of them just because they're black. As a white person, I am allowed to weigh in on our groups' action.

But I cannot say that African Americans need to follow the course set by every other immigrant community: to join the dominant culture and bend that culture to what they best offer. I'm not allowed to say that because I cannot pretend to know what it's like to be black in America. I'm not allowed to say that because it doesn't matter if I acknowledge, or even apologize, for my ancestors bringing blacks to this country as slaves. I'm not allowed to say that because how many times before have white men said that, and reneged on the promise of equality. I am not allowed to say that because the burden of violence and distrust, of lies and torture and deceit, seems too great to overcome.

I cannot tell anyone what to do and what not to do; I certainly cannot tell the black community. I can only strive to make the possibilities available to my fellow black citizens as broad and deep as my own, and to respect that their actions reflect their own best interests. Neither more nor less than I learned from my savvy mentor, Emmer Lee Whitfield, nearly 40 years ago.

I ask Wesley Bell whether Michael Brown had to die in order to create the respect and tolerance I witness in Ferguson. The councilor struggles; he wants to say no, yet he cannot deny it. It takes tragedy to trigger change. But not all tragedy does. That's why I commend the citizens of this unassuming city. Under a microscope, they confronted death and its aftermath as a call to come together. Ferguson is far from perfect, but it appears to be further along the path of respecting all our citizens than most places I visit.

More freedom, less government.
> —John Baer, farmer's market shopper, Ferguson, MO

Limon, CO—September 25, 2016, 8:00 p.m.

Has there ever, in the history of civilization, been a citizenry with so much voice in their government, who disdain their government so much?

I lean into that question all the way across Missouri and Kansas like a bracing crosswind. Everyone I meet on my third foray across the Plains hates the government so much. Yet isn't it our government? What's the source of this gulf between the people and its representatives? Between the citizens of our states and the elites cocooned inside the Beltway? Has the government failed us in some tangible way? And if so, are we to blame? After all, we elect them. Or are we simply self-loathing masochists who like to complain?

Serendipity prevails. On my final evening of gentle uphill pedaling before confronting the mighty Rockies, I meet the perfect host to explore this conundrum. Ellie Bontrager and her husband Warren live in a pleasant home in this small farming and ranch community that has mutated into a major motel, gas, and restaurant intersection where Interstate 70 slashes across US 287. Warren's in Denver the night I visit; we don't get to meet. He recently started a new job as a bus driver for RTD, Denver's transit system, and bunks in the Mile High City most nights. His first career spanned 20-plus years with the Colorado prison system; first as a security guard, then maintenance supervisor, and finally as the woodshop instructor. When the woodshop program was defunded, Warren retired, with pension. After raising six children, Ellie took a half-time job as a postmistress in Agate. "There are 40 mailboxes. I work noon to four six days a week. Everything is manual; there are no computers. I like getting to know the locals. Some days I am busy. Some days I have no customers at all."

When I ask, "How will we live tomorrow?" Ellie responds, "There is too much government. The government was created to protect our borders. Now it is in every part of our lives." As a scribe rather than investigative journalist, I usually accept people's response to my question at face value, but I am intrigued by Ellie's inherent conflict. How can someone whose entire family works in the public sector harbor such a dark view of our government? I explore this dissonance. "I can't explain it; 35% of Americans work for the government, including me and my husband. It's too much; the government's reach is too deep. But we don't know how to pull it back."

I appreciate that Ellie acknowledges the conflict. A bit of fact checking reveals that about one-sixth, not one-third, of Americans work in the government sector. Still, it is a large proportion, and their toil extends well beyond protecting our borders.

The next morning I detour through Agate on my way to Denver. It's a dwindling town whose only remaining services are a school with about 25 students and Ellie's tiny post office. The private sector—that commercial world that deals with profit and loss and flexible response to market forces—has completely abandoned this faded place. There's no money to be made here, no reason for this town to exist anymore. But government lingers, beyond any reason save tradition and politics. It provides sweet Ellie a job that ought to be obsolete, though her appreciation for it is, at best, peculiar.

Levelland, TX—October 15, 2016, 11:00 a.m.

The dying town of Agate is but one example of government lingering beyond usefulness except to a small group of (probably vocal) folks. In Levelland, the apt-named Texas town where I served my year as a VISTA volunteer, I observe a different form of government creep.

The reason I first came to Levelland, nearly 40 years ago, was to initiate services for the elderly. One or two people had died in their homes and weren't found for days, so we started phone trees. Some were not getting proper nourishment, so we started meals on wheels. We offered rides to doctor appointments, insulated drafty houses, and opened senior centers to promote socialization. We used federal block grant money, though the scope of our work was local. The services weren't complex; extended family, neighbors, churches, or civic groups could have provided them. But they didn't. So our government stepped in.

The progression goes something like this. Some people don't have family or neighbors to care for them. We create programs to address the gap. The programs become the norm. Families and neighbors feel less responsible. More people use the services. Programs get larger, institutionalized. They develop bureaucracies, advocates, agendas; they take on lives of their own. As the programs grow, our sense of community shrinks.

Levelland's population hasn't increased since I lived here. If anything, the town is more affluent. But South Pains Community Action, the agency I worked for, now spreads over several buildings near downtown. One bears a sign: Senior Companion Program. An entire building to run a visitation program.

There's nothing wrong, in theory, with government-supported care. Except the American duality of individualism and compassion renders us uncomfortable with centralized social services. We think people should be independent, and when they can't be, we want them to be cared for locally. But families, neighbors, and churches don't have to serve everyone—only our government has that mandate.

It's a long stretch from a federal government formed to provide for the common defense to one that provides senior companions. We have three choices: step up in our communities and care for everyone locally; let our government provide services, and likely get bigger in the process; or retreat to a time when elders die unaccounted for in their homes. I hope we are humane enough to avoid the third option. We could get comfortable with government-supported social services. Or we could shrink our government by tending to our communities ourselves. Unfortunately, I witness far more talk about government bloat than individual action in my travels, so I suppose we will just keep complaining.

151

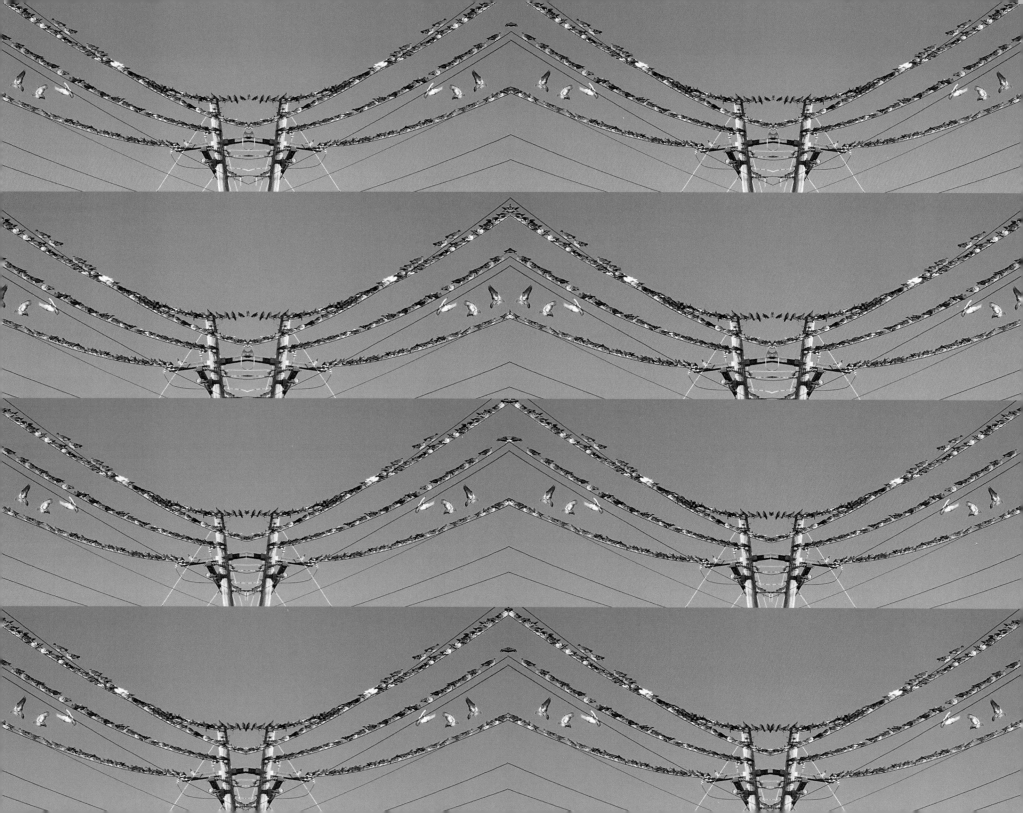

I think we're going to have to work together.
It's all about balance.
We need industry, that's not going to go away,
but we need the birds too.
—Jeff Henderson, bird watcher, Hayward, CA

Moriarty, NM—October 10, 2016, 6:00 p.m.

The view from my rear window at the Motel 6 in Moriarty, New Mexico, is a photorealistic painting of erratic light highlighting, and obscuring, discordant objects. In the foreground, just beyond my sill, yards upon yards of moldy carpet lie in loopy folds; the place must have gotten an upgrade and they skimped on hiring a dumpster. Rutted earth stretches several hundred feet toward the highway, punctuated by flat brown weeds and prairie dog mounds. Who owns these leftover acres wedged between commerce and movement? A tenuous fence marks the right-of-way to Interstate 40. The blacktop is no more than a flat charcoal line, my eye dead level with the road. Trucks stream along the taut line. The setting sun sparks the leading edge of gleaming silver trailers, so concentrated it should combust. This line of brilliant light and speed is the painterly focus. Above spreads a giant matte plane of cerulean sky. Five pencil-thin lines, telephone wires, stretch across the saturated, surreal color, spanning from pole to pole; measure marks of a musical score. The wires are thick with black birds, thousands of them, more grace notes than even Mozart would dare. They cluster on their perches. A swift wind agitates them to swoop up, twittering silhouettes against the syrupy blue. A flutter of frenzy, then they settle into a new formation. Do truck drafts displace these birds, or forces of nature? From within my room, I cannot tell. The wind possesses no visual component. I can only observe its effect.

Ever since Matthew Shepard channeled Leonard Cohen's "Bird on a Wire" back in Laramie, I am enthralled by these suspended creatures. I see them everywhere. Occasionally a bird perches alone; sometimes I observe a pair. More often they cluster in groups. Wire birds are social creatures. Often I can discern the logic of their perch, near a silo or a landfill or a nourishing cattle

yard. Other times, I have no clue why they gather in a particular place. They tend to congregate in morning and evening, when the light shows them to best advantage. I think they're vain.

I exit my motel room and tromp out across the desolate strip of land lost between the highway to the north and the usual franchises to the south. Human activity abounds within a hundred yards of me in every direction, yet I am quite alone. That discarded carpet might endure years of rats and rain before another person comes near it. I stride across the pocked plain, step over prairie dog holes, move toward the birds. I greet them; photograph them. I add their formation to the hundreds of other photos I've already taken of birds on wires.

153

People often turn the tables and ask me, "How will we live tomorrow?" I duck the question. I don't want to influence their response, or make them think I favor any particular slant. Collecting ideas on tomorrow doesn't give me an inside track on the matter.

Nonetheless, I promise to respond when my journey ends. Then I toss out a crumb of context. I explain the notion that spurred my odyssey; that the characteristics that have served our nation so well for the past 200-plus years—our land, our resources, our industry, our individualism—will prove less valuable moving forward. The frontier is gone, extraction has a price, other countries nurture busier bees, and collaboration is the key to globalization. I'm interested in how we navigate these changes.

As I watch these birds come together and soar apart, mesmerized by the collective choreography of their individual movement, I realize that my response to my own question has to derive from my experience of the road. And nothing has captivated, time and again, more than birds on wires. I have a mere 3,000 more miles to observe them and witness what they suggest.

I will have to accomplish something.
I have to accomplish something every day or I don't feel good.
  —Larry LaPadue, Miller Beach Arts District, Gary, IN

Baltimore, MD—July 26, 2016, 3:00 p.m.

Baltimore is a hard-edged town. I ride through block after block of flat-front houses where weary black bodies melt into sizzling shallow stoops. I have no business here, yet I travel unscathed. I nod and smile at the few eyes that lift my way, but poor people trying in vain to catch a breeze are unconcerned about the silly old man on his bike.

I could not do this trip if I were not a middle-aged white man. I'll never know which specific individuals would avoid my question or withhold an invitation to their home if I were bearded or ratty or black or brown; I simply know that people don't recoil from a guy who looks like me.

I wish it weren't so. I wish everyone enjoyed my access and my freedoms. But the world is not fair. I could pretend my privilege away: a common liberal trick. Instead I acknowledge it. It's an opportunity, a challenge, to show the same respect to everyone I meet, that the world gives me by default.

I feel a kinship with these folks on their stoops—neither of us doing much of anything this society values—though the eyes of the world see us differently. I've had my career; done my part: riding my bicycle is eccentric, maybe admirable. When you look like me, anything's legitimate, even opting out of the system. Not so for these quiet souls evading the sun.

We are a nation premised on doing, on making, on growing. "Expand or die" is corporate America's corollary to Darwin's theory. We are never allowed to simply be. Yet everyone competing to make his or her mark is rendering our earth uninhabitable. We have to start doing less. Not to get more. To find balance.

People can polish each other.
— Randy, founder of "Quest for Community," Santa Fe, NM

Abilene, TX—October 19, 2016, 4:00 p.m.

Intuition and trust are not zero-sum traits; they are expanding blossoms. The more we exercise them, the deeper they root in our psyches, the greater they flower in our countenance. As positive experiences multiply, they swell my trust in others. Perhaps I've enlarged their trust in return. I am not naive or reckless, though in Abilene I push my own comfort envelope.

As I turn onto Woodridge Drive, with its gentle curve, sumptuous trees, and expansive houses, it strikes me as one of the most attractive residential streets in America. In the next moment I catch my breath. Wait a second. I don't even know my host's name for this evening. I find the house number, prop Tom against the garage, and knock on the front door. A blonde woman opens it. "Are you Cara's mom?" How ridiculous. A question for a middle-school kid, come to play video games with his social studies partner. But "Cara's mom" is all I know, so what else I can say?

Officially, my host is Cara Hines, an artist from Anson, 24 miles north. But Cara suggested I come to Abilene, where she works at the Center for Contemporary Art. My visit coincides with the "downtownABI" design charrette, which Cara invites me to join. "Go by my mom's house. You can shower there and she'll bring you to the event. We'll figure out where you'll sleep later."

The blonde woman welcomes me. She laughs that I don't even know her name. Cara's mom, aka Laura Lee, takes in whomever her daughter sends her way in this former railroad town recreating itself as a center for art and culture. Laura Lee escorts me to an elegant guest suite in the far corner of the sprawling ranch.

I clean up. Feel pampered. Dress up in my single pair of long pants and sole collared shirt. Laura Lee pulls her 1966 pink Mustang out of the garage. Unrolls the convertible top. She tours me through Abilene: the National Center for Children's Illustrated Literature; the Grace Museum; the restored train station turned Visitors Bureau, the Dr. Seuss sculptures in Everman Park.

I finally meet Cara at the Convention Center. We join over a hundred others at "downtownABI." I watch and listen to this community engagement event, similar to ones I facilitated during my architectural career. When we come to the inevitable small-group discussion, I blow my cover. Depending on your perspective, I am either a ringer, since I've done dozens of similar exercises; or an interloper, since I'd been in Abilene all of three hours. Either way, the downtown restaurateur, the healthcare IT guru, and the Chamber of Commerce associate at our table don't seem to mind me being here.

Afterward Cara, Laura Lee, and I dine at Vagabond's, an urban eatery. Like most small cities, downtown Abilene's distant past was lively; it's recent past deadly. The pendulum is swinging back up. A handful of beautifully restored buildings, the linear park along the railroad, the focus on art; all contribute to increased life. A decade ago nothing was open past five o'clock. Now there are a handful of cool bars and restaurants. Non-franchise destinations. A new hotel is planned next to the Convention Center. The city is climbing up from its nadir. Abilene may be half the size of nearby Lubbock, but it's got twice the downtown.

We mustang home. Cara's late-working husband, Ernie, a detective as hard chiseled as that profession implies, joins us for a nightcap. We talk well past midnight. In a journey where the people I meet delineate memory, Abilene etches a generous niche in my mind.

Next morning, the winds bear down from the east. The plains give over to hills and grueling headwinds. I divert my mind from the discouraging task of pedaling hard for little gain by contemplating the difference between Abilene's past, when a handful of white men in 1880 determined the location of a railroad stop and shaped a town out of nothing, and Abilene's present, when hundreds of diverse stakeholders want a voice in how the place moves forward. Abilene is not the blank slate it once was. It possesses history, infrastructure, character; aspects that are both help and hindrance. Deciding what the city can be is a messy process, because of what's already here, because of who's already here; because revitalize and restore is more difficult than spanking new.

Abilene is a microcosm of our country as a whole. The task of making stuff and moving it no longer provides adequate economic or personal satisfaction. Abilene is climbing Maslow's hierarchy of needs, moving beyond physiological requirements and personal safety. Tapping the arts to propel us toward self-actualization.

*My plan is to tell our story, through arts, storytelling, meetings.
I want to explain why we are here. We want to share our culture and our food.
We aren't going anywhere anytime soon. We want to be friendly.*
　　—Muhidin Libah, Somali Bantu Community Association of Maine, Lewiston, ME

Santa Fe, NM—October 8, 2016, 1:00 p.m.

Strolling through an outdoor art exhibit in Santa Fe on a grey and chilly day, a mature woman in sculpted jeans and a glass jewel belt, exquisite grey hair tucked beneath a wide-brimmed hat, and too many turquoise adornments, stands in front of predictably bright, abstract landscapes. "Are you an artist?" She calls out, apropos of nothing. A flash of anger surges through me. I figure she's mocking my grizzled stubble and garish spandex. Just because she's broad brushed a few canvases, assembled a costume, and adopted an attitude of superior sensibility doesn't mean I owe her homage. "We're all artists." I reply without breaking stride.

I don't really believe we're all artists, for then the term becomes meaningless. I do believe all humans are creative; we can all depict our experience insightfully. But an artist is more than that. An artist devotes time and energy to studying, interpreting, reinterpreting, and presenting our world from her fresh perspective. Being an artist is not a job or a career, it's a calling, a vocation that may or may not yield economic benefit. Artists transcend commerce. They produce meaning.

Our educational system is a Prussian model.
Adhere them to the State and they will fight for the State.
—Stephanie Harren, home-school advocate, Port Arthur, TX

New York, NY—July 18, 2016, 10:00 p.m.

In a parallel vein, we are all educators, charged with instructing our children and sharing the particular skills we've polished in a specialized world. Yet for some, imparting knowledge is not an adjunct activity; it's the primary focus. These people are teachers, and they are under siege.

The purest reflection of a society's values is what it teaches its offspring.

Formal education in the United States—public, private, and religious—flourished in local communities even before the Revolutionary War. The General Court of Massachusetts Bay Colony mandated villages provide schools as early as 1647. Massachusetts continued to lead public education, creating the first public high school (1820) and free schools for all grades (1827).

By the second half of the 19th century, free, compulsory public education became the norm in this country. Education was hyper-local, often carved into neighborhoods more fine grained than city limits, until municipalities created Boards of Education that wrestled control from districts or wards to thwart the influence of immigrant groups. The classroom was the medium of assimilation; citywide curricula established a consistent set of cultural norms to the burgeoning throngs of newcomers and city dwellers.

After World War II, the United States was the most powerful nation on the planet and our schools the envy of the world. No other country enjoyed such universally high achievement— achievement we extended, if not equally, to college, thanks to the GI Bill. The mid-20th century marked the apex of monolithic American culture, and that culture dominated our schools. I learned how to read via Dick and Jane, who looked just like me.

But America circa 1955 did not embrace everyone. In the 1960s, our culture began to expand, or fray, depending on whether you consider diversity and multiculturalism an asset or a threat. As the voice of our nation evolved from a sage white man to a cacophony of accents and experiences, our schools struggled to identify which cultural norms to transmit. They have been struggling, and failing, ever since.

Every major conflict in our nation suffers its educational parallel: local versus federal control, minimum standards, unions, parental control, funding, religious influence, racial balance. And when children receive cultural lessons at odds with their parents' beliefs, families—especially affluent and religious families—seek other options.

American public education is no longer the envy of the world. Though the majority of children still attend traditional public schools, the proportion of families pursuing alternative models is expanding fast (private school, 10%; public charters, 5%; home school, 3%; sanctioned online programs, 0.5%). If you have a libertarian streak, this is all to the good. If you believe that universal public education made our nation great, you fear these alternatives cherry pick the best students and spiral already weak public schools into a secondary or tertiary abyss.

During my journey, I stay with, or profile, over 50 teachers, the largest group representing any one profession. Aside from a pair of lovely ladies in Laramie, Wyoming, and Conway, Arkansas (who are still enchanted by the energy and curiosity of the very young) and the hyper-energetic folks cheerleading BASIS Charter School in Goodyear, Arizona, to success, teachers are a disgruntled lot. Whether they teach in public schools, charter schools, religious schools, technical schools, or college, their complaints about standards and tests, paper work and bureaucracy, ill prepared students and intrusive parents, are as consistent as they are alarming.

In a bifurcated, argumentative society where opinion masquerades as fact, our education "system," if that word even applies, is devolving into a disjointed array of options. None of them offer the cultural cohesion that's been the hallmark, the reason, for public education over the past 300 years.

As a guy vested in tomorrow, I strive to highlight people who represent the vanguard of an idea, but I find few fresh ideas among the teachers I meet. Energetic ones push their pet perspective, be it technology or the Bible, Western Civilization or the Montessori method. Since the broad view is so bleak, they stuff their respective backpacks with narrow solutions. Burned out ones are simply, well, burned out. No one suggests how we can shape an educational system that conveys meaning and binds trust in a nation of expanding diversity and constant change. How can they, when our larger society has no idea what that looks like either?

Instead, I highlight Patrick Walsh because, despite his many complaints, his passion still rings true. Patrick is Irish Catholic, in temperament as well as genealogy, the literary sibling among a grand lineage of firefighters and police officers. The man's deep sensibilities absorb life's marvelous futility.

Patrick knocked around for several years after high school, studied literature at Rutgers, spent four years in Barcelona, and then returned to teach at his former high school on Staten Island. He was drinking, a lot. Ten Guinness's a day, until he renounced his barstool perspective. Patrick returned to Spain, walked the 500-mile Camino de Santiago, cleared his head, and returned home,

resolved to teach for good. He's a far-left liberal who lives in a fifth-floor tenement in the Lower East Side. The apartment has no proper bathroom; there's a solitary commode in a tiny closet and a bathtub that doubles as the kitchen sink. He's a night owl who strolls me through his neighborhood past midnight, when the immigrant ghosts of this working-class ghetto cast their shadows over the shiny condominiums that this friend of the workingman disdains by day. Patrick is a dynamo. Anger is his energy.

"Teaching in the past 10 years has become so difficult. Obama's 'Race to the Top' wants the best teacher in every classroom. It's like Bush saying he wants to bring democracy to the Middle East. Who can argue with that? But that's not what's going on. We're so burdened with student tests and teacher evaluations. The single person who most influences my job these days is Bill Gates. Who appointed him to dictate how we educate? It's his money."

Patrick teaches English as a Second Language in Harlem. Almost all of his students are black: African Americans and East African immigrants. "The two groups are so different. The Muslim children are true believers, very devout. The African American kids have no direction. I don't blame them. They were raised by corporate America. They're not interested in guiding people toward purpose or contentment; they just want to sell things. The Muslim kids' lives have form.

"Obama is a Manchurian candidate, symbolically important but not real change. Bush traumatized this country with his wars and his lies. Then Obama brings on Larry Summers and introduces 'Race to the Top.' I felt betrayed. It was the same stuff, repackaged."

The purest reflection of a society's values is what it teaches its offspring. Our once vaunted public educational system is crippled because our society does not know what we are about; we don't know what values we want to transmit. Teachers cannot help but fail as long as we expect them to transmit cohesive values that do not exist.

Our libraries are the most important institution we have; more important than the church.
—Chris Dykes, reference librarian, Hulbert, OK

Clovis, NM—October 13, 2016, 3:00 p.m.

The great thing about our bifurcated nation is that every thorny problem has its upbeat counterbalance. Our public schools may be failing, but our public libraries thrive.

I visit over a hundred public libraries along my journey, from the adorable cottage in Valentine, Texas (population 217 and fading) to the majestic reading room of the New York Public Library (population 8.4 million and rising). I stand in line with dozens of homeless men waiting to enter the bulky Fresno Public Library when it opens on a crisp morning, and I'm the last person to leave the upholstered chairs and upscale cafe nested within the library of Poland, Ohio. Although a library's quiet hush is less conducive to discussing my question than a boisterous McDonald's, I prefer to take my afternoon break in these secular sanctuaries whose noble intent inspires everyone who enters. Libraries are our highest and best examples of democratic ideals: information for all, for free. Libraries boost my spirit. They demand respect, and everyone who uses them rises to that call. I witness exemplary behavior in every library I visit.

Libraries in the United States are so well used. In town and after town I have to thread through the stacks just to find a seat. It takes me 20 minutes to find an available workspace at the Seattle Public Library; 10 stories tall with thousands of cubicles, all occupied by people chasing their silent pursuits. Fortunately, I have my own laptop; people who don't have a computer often wait an hour or more to get 30-minute access to a public one. Even in our most egalitarian forum, life is easier for the haves than the have-nots.

I am impressed, again and again, by our investment in libraries. The Coeur d'Alene Public Library in Idaho is reminiscent of a ski lodge on the edge of a lake. The failed shopping mall turned library in Nashville is spacious and bright. Even the concrete urban fortress surrounded by an iron fence in Lawrence, Massachusetts, braced against a deteriorating neighborhood, proves welcoming within. Libraries exude confidence, a civic pride missing from many contemporary public edifices. The Pelahatchie, Mississippi, library isn't much larger than a house: 2,000 square feet at most. Yet its prominent entrance, columns and symmetrical roof convey public presence.

More important than the structures, of course, are the people. Librarians may be trained in cataloging and reference, but they are our new social workers, our new guidance counselors, our new teachers. Every one of them treats me, and everyone else, with patience and respect.

San Francisco is awash with street people, often unwelcome. Police harass longhaired loiterers along Van Ness Avenue. But in the last hour before closing time at the Park Branch of the San Francisco Public Library, a stately building of yesteryear in which a single-occupant men's room is squeezed right off the reading room, a librarian taps on the door every few moments to encourage the fellow changing his clothes and scrubbing his body to finish up, so everyone who wants to wash up before nightfall has a chance. She is clear and firm, though never rude. Her tone is practiced; she does this every day.

Lissa, the reference librarian in Clovis, New Mexico, rises from her desk when she realizes a mother/daughter duo are having a difficult time during their 30 allotted minutes on the computer. The pair is Asian, perhaps Vietnamese. Lissa shows them how to log on, asks about their search, and discovers they need to set up an appointment with Social Security. She navigates them through a dot-gov maze. She explains what the local Social Security office can offer, and what complications will require a trip to Lubbock. She balances between giving these immigrants with limited English the information they need and letting them find it themselves. Together, they obtain answers before 30 minutes are up. Someone else is waiting for that terminal.

Libraries are not schools: they are elective rather than mandatory-use facilities. Yet I can't help but wonder if the attributes that make libraries so effective—that they serve across generations, that they invite independent inquiry, that they are staffed by people who support the scholar's interests rather than deliver prescribed content—suggest pathways to revitalize public education.

Having empathy is a difficult thing in an industrialized society.
We are passive and disconnected from each other.
 —Carlos Melendez, vegan cook, San Marcos, TX

Decatur, GA—August 19, 2016, 8:00 p.m.

"The Civil War was the first time the 1% coerced the 99% into doing something stupid, based on the fear that they would be worse off if things changed. At least the 99% of poor whites were above the slaves." One could argue with Mike Sheehan's timeframe: coerced slaves built the Egyptian pyramids and serfs built Europe's cathedrals. Still, he's got the right idea.

But isn't slavery is over; aren't we past all that? Hardly. The powers have just become more sophisticated in the way we pit the lower rung of society against the lowest.

As manufacturing jobs in the United States slip from 19 million to 12 million over 40 years, what's become of the men of modest education who traditionally work those jobs? They suffer to be sure, but many find positions in three growth areas: prison guards, Border Patrol agents, and more recently, TSA screeners.

It's better to patrol the border than try and cross it, better to guard a prisoner than to be one. We no longer need these workers to make things; so we hire them to make fear. When we spend eight hours searching out the bad man everywhere we look, that distrust follows us home. Our attitudes harden. We become nothing more than the bully in service to The Man.

Cartwright, OK—October 27, 2016, 3:00 p.m.

The "Native America" sign welcoming me to Oklahoma on Highway 91 just north of Lake Texoma is a joy to behold. It signifies success in traversing Texas on my bike—twice. Texas is a challenge for cyclists. The open highways are terrific, solid pavement and wide shoulders. But navigating the cities and towns is terrible. Everywhere, city streets are cast concrete with integral curbs. Without so much as one extra inch on the right, there's no place for me to be. I must occupy the right lane. Texas drivers, with gas pedal feet heavy as their F-350s, have no patience for that. And, being Texans, they broadcast their disdain. There are places with worse roads (the Carolinas) and places with worse drivers (Massachusetts) but the combination of tight space, aggressive behavior, and verbal abuse makes cycling across Texas look best in the rear view mirror.

To celebrate my escape from the Lone Star State, I spend a few hours contemplating the fine art of bicycle heckling. After almost a year on the shoulder I am an experienced, if inscrutable, victim of motorists' desire to intimidate me off the road. Since the road to Durant is uneventful, this proves an entertaining way to pass the time.

I catalogue seven different forms of heckling I've endured.

1. My least favorite, by far, is the ash flick. When the person in the passenger seat of an elevated pickup hangs their cigarette hand out the window and thumbs ashes on me, it stings.

2. Even unhealthier is the exhaust cloud. A truck—always a truck, usually a pickup, driven by a man, a young white man—passes me, shifts into the shoulder, and slows down. Just before I reach the vehicle, he guns the engine, rocketing a plume of smoke in my face.

3. Female drivers are less keen to prove dominance, more interested in shaping behavior. They like to scold. They slow down their mini-vans and yell, "Get on the sidewalk." An Hispanic woman in Houston tries to scold me to the sidewalk, even when there isn't one. She doesn't actually care if I am on the sidewalk; she just wants me gone from the road. Legally, of course, bicycles are supposed to be on the road, subject to the same rights and responsibilities as any other vehicle. A point I don't argue with angry drivers in larger, faster vehicles.

4. The car horn is the most common heckle, two beeps or one long honk. Truth is, some drivers may toot as a sign of solidarity or encouragement, but it is always annoying and never appreciated. A car horn signifies danger. If I am doing something wrong, use the horn as warning. If I am riding lawfully, please just pass me quietly as you would any other vehicle.

5. Showing off muscle does not require tossing a punch. Some guys slide past me, glide into the shoulder, and then peel away in a surge of benign testosterone. No exhaust plume, no danger. I laugh them off.

6. I get spritzed with a water pistol along Guadalupe Street in Austin: the perfect heckle in this self-consciously liberal town. Which is not to say that I like it. I carry my own water bottle if I want to cool off, thank you very much.

7. I receive one heckle I actually enjoy, though far from Texas. Two guys in a battered sedan come upon me in Grant's Pass, Oregon, and shout "nice ass" as they drive by. Unfortunately for them, the light at the next intersection turns red, so I catch up. "Glad you like my butt." I grin at their odd taste in men. The skinny guys, maybe in their 20s, maybe stoned, reply, "We like to shout to cyclists but always say something nice." Telling a 60-year-old man he's got a nice ass is beyond nice.

By the time I enter Oklahoma, my 46th state, I've travelled over 18,000 miles. More than a million vehicles have sped by me. The overwhelming majority treats me well; they give me space, they pass me quietly. The tiny few who spew anger and fear toward me are easy to recall. But I prefer to dwell on all the good drivers who treat me right.

What I hope for is the American dream—the human dream—food, clothing, shelter.
I live the status quo but I am so aware of people who do not have this.
—Cindy Reyes, Clinton Presidential Library, Little Rock, AR

Dallas, TX—October 24, 2016, 1:00 p.m.

Angelika Christenson, my host in Thousand Oaks, California, suggests that the Ronald Reagan Presidential Library is worth a visit. I love libraries and have time on my hands, so I pedal up the hill to the great communicator's lofty perch. Angelika's right. The place is fascinating. The exhibits spin a golden hue over the 1980s. Reagan's Air Force One commands its own giant hanger. My heart is warmed to learn that Ronnie always kept a chocolate cake on board in case anyone traveling with his entourage had a birthday. Reagan's fan base has expanded in the past 30 years: as many blacks and Hispanics visit the library as bouffant blondes. Beyond the objects and the stories and the audience, Reagan's library triggers memories of my own life during his presidency, that featureless period when I trailed my wife wherever her medical career led.

A week later, in Yorba Linda, I visit Nixon's library. The Rodney Dangerfield of presidents gets no respect. Nixon's aging helicopter cannot compete with Reagan's plane. Everything about the place is humble; any crowds long gone. I rather like his boyhood home; a 1912 kit house with original furnishings that Nixon's astute brothers preserved; they knew Dick would go far. Unfortunately, Dick went too far, though the library is light on Watergate and the first man compelled to resign our nation's highest office. Still, as with Reagan, Nixon's library offers a parallel set of memory triggers: my high school years. I stand before the exhibit of Nixon's 55 Time Magazine covers—the most of one person ever—and recall how often that pointed chin thrust itself at me from the end table of my youth.

After two presidential libraries, I'm hooked. I jigger my route to visit more: 11 of the 13 "official" libraries. I don't backtrack to Grand Rapids, rationalizing that Gerald Ford was never actually elected; and I forgo West Branch, Iowa, where Hoover's library was created well after the fact. I visit all the rest.

Before Franklin Delano Roosevelt created the first official presidential library and donated his papers to the United States, a president's records were his private property. Since then, every scrap of paper, every email, every 18-minute gap, is public information. Every president's legacy now includes a hybrid creature: a non-profit museum built with private funds attached to repositories operated by the National Archives. Every presidential candidate fantasizes how his library (never hers, so far) will polish his legacy, even before his first primary win.

I click off presidents like I click off states. I'm amazed how accurately each library reflects the man it celebrates, both consciously and unconsciously. LBJ's displays the most humor, FDR's the most inspiration, JFK's the most sophistication. Jimmy Carter's is humble to a fault; the low-slung building is literally in a ravine. Eisenhower's is mostly about World War II, which he clearly preferred to executive rounds of golf. George Bush's is as vanilla as his presidency: the man had little connection to Texas A&M, so what is his library even doing there? Clinton's is a sleek piece of architecture, the most like an actual library, until so many Little Rock locals compare its shiny proportions to a trailer that the "white trash" analogy lodges in my head. I hear that the George W. Bush Library at SMU is the grandest of all. I am prepared for awe. Only after I arrive do I recall that "W" coupled awe with shock.

"Are you delivering pizzas?" A broad shouldered gentleman with numerous pins on his blazer, former military to be sure, approaches me as I enter the library courtyard in my yellow cycling shirt, toting my yellow panniers.

"No," I reply.

"Then what are you here for?" His look is grave suspicion. He shifts position to stand between the door and me.

"I am here to visit the museum."

"I thought you were delivering pizzas."

My good cheer snaps. "That is presumptuous and rude." I regret my words as soon as they fly. Not because they're unwarranted: Mr. Medal Lapel is a pompous jerk. Rather I regret defaming pizza delivery guys who do honest work.

The plainclothesman steps aside, though its clear he'd rather not.

I proceed inside. The level of security at each presidential library directly correlates to the level of fear each president stirred during his tenure. The Jimmy Carter Library has none; I am deep into the place before I can find a spot to stow my bags. At FDR, JFK, Truman, and Eisenhower, an elderly ticket taker offers to keep an eye on my stuff. LBJ, Nixon, Reagan, Bush Senior, and Clinton have standard-issue detectors, tucked out of sight between the lobby and the exhibits. The first things a visitor to fortress "W" encounters are three guards and a detector.

"What are you delivering?" The first words out of the guard's mouth, a tight-haired, buxom woman.

"I'm not delivering anything." My tone is not pretty.

"So what's in your bags?"

"What's with you people?" I really lose it. Any sentence tainted by "you people" is doomed. "Have you never seen a bicyclist? You have a bike rack in front. Am I the first person to ever use it?"

The woman is taken aback, unaware that the courtyard guard already primed my sensitivity. "I hope you know you'll have to check them."

"Of course I want to check them. Why would I want to carry them through the museum?"

By this time every word uttered on both sides seethes in distrust. Several other blazer men scurry to put my bags in a remote closet, as if they would contaminate the regular coat-check. I spend 20, 30 minutes tops touring the place. It's hard to feel benevolent about "No Child Left Behind" in halls so unkind, so ungentle. I feel watched from every angle. Because I am.

I ride away, happy to part company with the George W. Bush Presidential Library. I send a letter to their website's comment link, explain that I've bicycled over 18,000 miles across 45 states and profiled over 400 individuals and organizations about our future. I point out that executives farmers, police officers, and homeless individuals have all greeted me with curiosity and good cheer.

"In my cycling clothes I look no more like a delivery person than you do in your office attire. However, I do look very different from people wearing street clothes. The message that your staff conveys loud and clear is, 'If you look different you will be treated with suspicion rather than respect.'"

Two days later I get a call from a staffer, who tells me straight out it's her first week on the job. Poor woman, saddled with the grunt work of calling irate visitors. "I watched the security video of the officer in the courtyard. He should not have asked you about delivery twice." I laugh, past anger about an incident 80 miles old. "You don't get it. When a person starts from a position of 'are you a delivery boy?' they assume privilege. The first question your staff should ask any person entering your museum is, 'May I help you?' Anything else is judgment."

During his tenure, "W" ratcheted up the politics of fear; it is fitting his legacy is shrouded in suspicion. This is the sole instance of prejudice I experience through my entire journey. Being unique for me only sharpens my sorrow that for others, disdain and derision are not isolated occurrences; they are the norm. Bullies in blazers treat blacks and browns and illegals and elderly and women and sissies and trannies and immigrant pizza delivery guys like that every day. They must get so worn down, they stop lashing out; they acquiesce rather than write letters of complaint. I can't pretend to know how people who are routinely belittled feel, based on one silly incident. The fact that I am incensed when mistreated, that I am emboldened to point out the prejudice, however ineffectively, is just another manifestation of my own privilege.

Just as I will not to let a handful of hecklers destroy the goodwill I feel toward the million motorists who pass me in peace, I don't let the humorless suits at the George W. Bush Library detract from the hundreds of people who receive me with open interest. I shake the dust of Dallas from my sneakers and I pedal on.

172

Ghost Ranch, NM—October 7, 2016, 7:00 a.m.

The longer this adventure continues, the more people ask, "What's your favorite place?" For months I reply, "North Dakota." I cite the state's stark beauty, challenging winds, and fine people. Actually, I also like the shock value—nobody expects North Dakota to be a favorite.

Truth is, my favorite place is always the next one. I wake up each day excited as a schoolboy on the first day of summer. I don't know whom I'll meet and what I'll see, but everything that lies before me is delight. I live in joy and satisfaction. When the unknown is so inviting, it's impossible for any actual place to claim preference. Until the morning I awake in Ghost Ranch.

During my travels, many people praise the allure of northern New Mexico. No magic clicks during my first few days; Taos is too self-consciously cool. But my heart warms as I head west, through the stark morning shadows of Rio Grande Gorge and Rinconda's fanciful Museum of Gas. I split off the highway along Rio Arriba County Road 40; tight-walled farms and brilliant jalapeno strands. I devour the best five-dollar green chile burrito north of the border, cross the river, and ascend US 84 along red rock cliffs to Abiquiú. I climb to the top of the mesa, an arid plain overlooking the cottonwoods of La Chama River valley. Highway 84 undulates in grand swales; tall buttes rise along side. The last mile to Ghost Ranch is a dusty drive that leads to a cluster of buildings surrounded by towering cliffs.

The history of Ghost Ranch is vivid as any frontier lore, rich in feuding brothers, cattle rustlers, bandit hangings, hard scrapple widows, poker swapped deeds, and eerie haunting. "It's the mystique of the West," explains Linda Seebantz, the director of communication, as we sit in rockers on a wooden porch, warm in the late day sun. The ranch's fate changed when a wealthy Easterner, Arthur Peck, purchased the spread and lured even bigger barons, like the Rockefellers, to his dude ranch. The stunning landscape also attracted artists. Georgia O'Keeffe had a house here; many of her most famous images are the rugged profiles that surround Ghost Ranch. In 1955, Peck donated the 21,000-acre property to the Presbyterian Church USA, which turned it into an education and retreat center. Today, Ghost Ranch hosts over 300 events a year; people come from all over the world to spend a day, a week, a season, rejuvenating their spirit in this place of myth and mystery.

I wake early in my simple Ghost Ranch room and climb the mesa before breakfast. I track the sunrise in the wide blue sky. The landforms on the west side of the hollow burst into color. The air is ambrosia. I want to fix myself to this spot, to be drenched in the sun's warmth, to imprint this ethereal light, which has captivated so many, into my psyche. Santa Fe is today's destination. It's been around for over 400 years. Surely it will still be there tomorrow.

For the first time in my entire trip I am inclined to linger. But my journey is dedicated to rolling, to seeking out variety among the folks who call themselves American. So, I descend Cliffside Trail, eat a satisfying breakfast sautéed with engaging conversations with striving poets and plein air painters. I like everyone I meet. Which is no surprise. After all, these middle-aged people of means exploring their creative impulses after a life of material success are, basically, variations of me.

As I pedal back out the dirt road, one thing is certain. I want to return to Ghost Ranch. Not just because it has invigorating air and sublime light. But because of the people: studying, exploring, turning old but still reaching out. In this high desert ravine, I find my tribe.

I believe the electro frequency of the heart is 4,000 times greater than our neural capacity. We have the capability of 7.3 billion people to reach out to other creatures in the cosmos. We are light beams stuck in this carbon-based moment.
—Matthew Rhodes, artist, Santa Fe, NM

Taiban, NM—October 13, 2016, 10:00 a.m.

The Plains are my favorite place to ride. Austere. Easy when the wind's at my back, tough when it's in my face. Mile upon mile of raw land and wide sky that meet at the taut horizon. The most elementary landscape. Climbing a dizzy mountain peak is thrilling, but I prefer rolling over a vast expanse—simultaneously grounded and on top of the world.

There's an empty church in Taiban, a near ruin without windows or doors. Earth and sky throb through the wooden structure's voids. I pull off US 60. I stand still and absorb the silence. I envision a past life, a time when Taiban was a real place, with people; when prayers rose from these hollow walls, beseeching God for bounty, for rain, for mere sustenance.

I pedal on. This is my fourth foray across the Plains. My final crossing. The rhythm of the grassy sea induces deep meditation.

There's a derivative within root cause analysis known as the "five whys": describe any problem or situation, ask "why" it is so, take that response, and ask "why." Drill down each "why" five times to reach the issue's essence. Cycling the plains liberates my mind so wide it triggers exploration of my own five ways. The regular pedal strokes, the unwavering land, spin me all the way back to childhood, to moments my rational brain considers better left unvisited, to the bristly recesses that swaddle my fundamental nature.

I am seven. My parents are in bed. My mother holds my baby brother in her arms, we four older children stand around the foot: a morning-after family meeting. I don't remember what precipitated this one. Maybe my father struck my mother the night before, or punched the wall, or clenched the front lawn howling at the moon. He was a sweet drunk, until he wasn't. Morning is mea culpa time; reassurance that it will never happen again. My father glosses over the facts by enumerating all the fun things he has planned, my mother nods in support. The children's task is to replace what we witnessed with this benevolent intention.

I stand. I listen. I watch. I conclude that these two people are in way over their heads, beautiful creatures whose attraction led to a slew of kids and bourbon frustration. I harbor no anger, no fear. Nor do I swallow their platitudes. They are neither bad nor good: they are simply overwhelmed. I am their child, but I don't feel dependent.

There's something chilling about a seven-year-old who analyzes his personal situation with such objective precision. I am supposed to be upset; I am supposed to find relief in the emotional plea for redemption. But observing my handsome father curry favor and plead from beyond the bedpost anchors me to reason before my time. The nun's assume that the age of reason will brand my tongue at the communion rail, but it knights me here, first, with a complicated venial sin. I refuse to suffer rage, then cathartic release, just to be wounded again in the next inevitable episode.

I understand, in that moment, my role in life. I will not contribute to the drama that swirls around me. I exist to watch and listen, detached. I can engage in life with my hands and my head, but I keep a distant heart. I travel alone, though I never feel lonely.

Perhaps this is why I love the plains. No highs and lows, no intention, no lofty peaks or looming shadows. The plains are not the result of explosion. They are simply layers upon layers of sediment
rolled out under the baking sun. They are boring, until you look
close at how the light strikes each quivering blade, and listen carefully to the slithering snakes and blackbirds rustling in the sage.

Geography will bless me with another week of this mental delight.
By the time I reach Fort Worth, gentler landscape and more frequent people will curb my reverie. Some satisfactions can only by
fulfilled by vast expanses of nothing.

Our country is like a very large family. Not everyone comes out quite right,
not everyone heeds to the guidelines and rules, lots of competitive fighting for control and voice.
There will always be the bully, the quiet one, the one with the brains,
and the one that just wants us all to get along.
　　　—Adela Taylor, nurse, Newark, DE

Dover, DE—July 24, 2016, 8:00 p.m.

A place like Taiban—empty, forgotten—may offer leisurely tonic for clearing my head, but such Zen is too fragile for the hubbub humans have created beyond desolate plains. People flock to cities to chase money, fame, and each other. The closer we rub, the more friction we generate, the thicker our shells become, the more difficult it is reveal our authentic selves. Today, we have so many modes of communication we cannot understand each other. The same devices that connect us over great distances, partition us into narrow silos.

Incivility abounds. Since I am too insignificant to generate true ire, I'm rarely its target. But I observe the inpatient drivers, impertinent clerks, and entitled customers. We are so ugly to each other. I figure it's a matter of respect. If we can glimpse our neighbor's point of view, maybe even find it credible, perhaps we can get along.

Then I meet Tanya Hall in Austin, Texas. She teaches me three little words that move me beyond respect. "Assume best intent." Tanya is CEO of Greenleaf Book Group, a publishing company with an innovative author/publisher strategy. She explains, "When you unravel issues from the perspective of each person's best intent, the resolution acknowledges everyone."

I adopt Tanya's mantra as I ride around the country. "Assume best intent" doesn't seem all that difficult, until I try to do it. It somersaults my experience of the road, where our default reaction to every other vehicle is annoyance. That irritating SUV, inching up my behind, that won't pass. Turns out, the driver is being polite; she turns at the next drive.

"Assume best intent" digs deeper. When a pickup slows and a flannel-shirted cowboy shouts "get a horse," I don't raise my middle finger. I treat his comment as an opportunity rather than a heckle, "I am my own horse," I shout back. We both laugh and move on, feeling connected rather than victimized or vindicated.

We live in a world that magnifies our differences. That's the drama, that's the news. That's what the media craves. Shielded by our ton of steel, road rage rules. Protected by the anonymity of our computer screen, we lash out on the net. It's so easy to find fault and think everyone is wrong. But when we "assume best intent" we step beyond respect. We acknowledge what's right.

Then I meet another wise woman, who invites even loftier aspiration.

The State of Delaware takes me by surprise; it's bicycle heaven. There are bike lanes everywhere, even left turn lanes. The drivers are respectful. I love the place; I only wish it were bigger. After three days I've run out of places to ride.

Delaware makes it easy for a guy on a bike to "assume best intent." Until Sara Haltunnen raises the bar. I arrive at Sara's apartment on one of the hottest days of my journey. She hands me a glass of water. "Don't worry about a coaster. All my stuff is from Goodwill." I take a drink and squat on the sofa. Sara sprawls across the largest beanbag chair I've ever seen. Two hours pass in non-stop conversation before I even change out of my cycling clothes.

"I am having a moment in life to figure out what I stand for." That moment proves long, deep, and all encompassing. "I'm a Christian. I'm a creationist. I don't accept the 'gay lifestyle.'" Then Sara relates a two-hour phone conversation with a guy she met online, who is grappling with his sexuality. For Sara, human struggle supersedes ideological purity. She is tuned to life's ambiguities, a woman steep in empathy. She cannot muster blanket condemnation because "we all matter to God."

Sara's moral exploration centers on issues of sexual violence. "The two things that are closest to me are sexual assault and abortion. They are not black and white issues; they are beyond grey. They are giant bundles of frayed nerves.

"Abortion is more complex than we acknowledge. If you're a woman, you are exalted for your ability to create life. If you terminate a life in you, the emotional residue is devastating.

"I was a rape crisis advocate. At our core, what we protect is our body. But how can we address the balance of what the perpetrator should suffer? I am trying to work out the limits of what we should forgive."

After talking, literally non-stop for 90 minutes, Sara says, "The divisiveness of our nation makes me not want to talk." Then she keeps on.

"Look at 9/11. Awful as that was, I never experienced such unity among Americans. Fifteen years later, we are so divisive. All these different kinds of people matter but they give no ground to anyone else. The oppression that people experience is real, but it is nothing compared to the oppression borne on the shoulders of the people they've stood upon. When people today are intolerant, there is no room for 'us.'

"There has to be a unified moral code within this country or we will wind up having civil war, because, and this sounds crazy, we have too much freedom. We don't understand that there is something bigger than you, your neighbor, even your government. There is something bigger than all of us. There is true right and wrong. It starts with the small things—a guy threw a pretzel in my car the other day—and extends to the big things, like Nice and Sandy Hook.

"People can't do everything that people want to do all the time. We're such a self-saturated people. Social media makes us self-absorbed. The thing that's spreading right now is panic and fear. Until we quench that, gay rights, abortion rights, black lives, blue lives won't matter.

"I had a very organic experience the other day. I met someone, a black woman, and we talked. Simple as that. It's not our job, as humans, to live our lives for other humans. It's our job to love other humans."

And then Sara says something that strikes me to the core. That takes me beyond respect or "assume best intent." "I want to get to the point that if I say something that offends someone, they can tell me, I can apologize, and they will believe me. Then we can move on."

Can we even imagine how good, how nurturing, that would be for all of us?

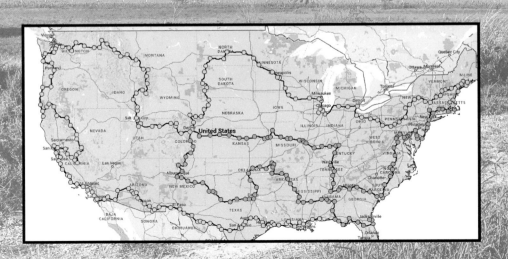

PART THREE
DIRECTION

*I had a foorball coach who said,
'Today you're either going to be
better or worse than yesterday.
You can't stay the same.
Which do you want?*

Pearson, student, Florence, SC

That's a fantastic question and I have no idea.
When you're voting against your self interest you have nowhere to go but down.
    —Michael, employee/owner of Homeland grocery, Oklahoma City, OK

Hulbert, OK—November 16, 2016, 7:00 p.m.

Sometimes, circumstance shakes out better than best laid plans. When I begin my pilgrimage, I don't anticipate that it will coincide with one of the most divisive presidential elections in history. My original itinerary deposits me back in Massachusetts before any ballots are cast, but a broken back slips that timeframe. Then my army captain nephew gets deployed to Afghanistan. I offer to spend a week with my niece and their boys, who could use a diversion during six-months without Dad. They suggest I visit in early November, so I park Tom in Oklahoma City and jet away. November 8 turns out to be a good day to lay off tomorrow: so many people are freaked out by today.

These two cycling breaks divide my journey into three tidy political segments: primary season before my accident, a two-candidate duel post-healing, and my final push under President-elect Trump.

Since I contacted all the presidential candidates way back in Postville, Iowa—to no avail—politics has been peripheral to my endeavor. During primary season, the first eight months of my journey, few people talk politics. There are too many candidates, and none look good. Actually, people scarcely mention government at all, unless to denounce it or discount its influence on a better tomorrow. The people in our government and the policies they enact seem irrelevant to the hum of our daily lives. Those talking heads mounted on the monitors in every McDonald's and Super 8 breakfast buffet are nothing but annoying bits of static from a pesky parallel universe.

No one mouths support for Donald Trump. If you're politically correct, Trump is politically incorrect; if you're politically incorrect, you know better than to let on. He is candidate *non gratis*. Yet in state after primary state, Republicans enter the booth and pull The Donald's lever.

Sometimes I cycle for a week or more in ignorant bliss of campaign bile. Until I stay with a news-junkie host and the whole mess floods his living room. The first debate I watch in full is the Republicans in Detroit on March 3, 2016, laid up in my Pensacola hospital room. When Trump and Rubio compare their privates as credentials for the most powerful office on earth, I come to appreciate Darwin's theory in a very literal way.

During my four months of rehab, the Republican's unthinkable becomes inevitable, while the Democrat's inevitable becomes, well, inevitable. When I mount my saddle and pedal again, it's a two-horse race. Still, all discussion centers on one man. Trump signs pop up on lawns 10 miles beyond every big city's limits; there are as many in southeast Massachusetts as in Kansas. I watch Trump accept the Republican nomination at a party in New Jersey with supporters in campaign shirts and hats. I'm hard-pressed to understand how Trump's message aligns with their interests: every one of them works in the public sector. Like most, I am slow to comprehend that content is no longer important; it's the anger and the fear that sways.

In October, when I ask New Mexicans, 'How will we live tomorrow?' and the response, "Hopefully without Trump," follows immediately upon "It will be a Trump world," I smile that Newton's third law is unshakable: the good old U S of A is bifurcated as ever.

On the Saturday night after Donald Trump is elected our 45th president, friends in blue blue Massachusetts beg me to Skype into their postmortem dinner party. Apparently my continental meanderings connote wisdom, as if being so slow and close to the ground during the entire election season enables me to grasp what others missed. I did not predict Trump's election, but I'm not surprised either. And I take obtuse pleasure in observing the pundits crash. Trump supporters, covert operatives who distrust everyone and everything at the most elemental level, delight in misleading information and spooking the political elite. That includes pollsters. Angry people blister all over our nation; folks so fed up we vote for the devil we don't know over the one we know all too well.

Post election, I resume my ride in Oklahoma, Trump's deep red strength. Yet it seems as if everyone's lost. Democrats are shell-shocked, women feel bruised, immigrants sliver their eyes, a transgender couple requests I remove their profile from my blog. Fear is palpable, if not yet justified. Yet the Republican victors don't gloat. Acting tough and ranting "lock her up" was such great fun; they looked forward to doing it for four more years. Now they have to govern. What a bummer.

There's a clear shift in responses to my question. People are more thoughtful; they choose their words more carefully. During dinner on a farm in Hurlbert, Denise Bell speaks in a cautious cadence. She calls for acceptance, not merely tolerance, of others in our society. Acceptance requires a deeper level of connection; it sets us on a path to sympathy, possibly empathy.

In the days following Trump's election, tolerance appears fleeting; acceptance downright alien. Denise Bell's hopes feel harder to achieve than a mere week ago. She is wise to couch her hopes with care.

I'm here to share love.
　　　　　—Delca Viva, patient advocate, Atlanta, GA

Bryant, AR—November 29, 2016, 10:00 a.m.

A guy on a bike needs more than Clif bars and reflectors to successfully navigate the Deep South: he needs vivacious blonde women with connections unavailable to a wizened Yankee, and big, soft, black mamas who draw me into their breasts and smother me in warm goodness. I am blessed to find two remarkable pair of these Dixie phenomenon.

In Houston, Patrice "Pete" Parsons, Governor Anne Richard's energy conservation guru in the 1990s, connects me to fascinating folks all over the Lone Star State, while Ella Russell folds me into her pretzel arms the moment I walk into her popup cupcake store at Project Rowhouse. "I don't do handshakes, I believe in hugs!" When Ella releases me, and I fall full into her thrall, I swear that whatever disease we infection-obsessed, cold-shouldered, fist-pumping Northerners fear, is completely vanquished by this joyful woman's solid embrace.

What's good in Texas only gets better in Arkansas.

After a year of gracious hospitality wherever I go, Terrie Turner, a marketing specialist in Little Rock, summits a new standard. Terrie is four degrees of separation removed from me, a friend of a friend of Pete Parsons. I reach out to her a week before I land in Little Rock; within days our email string runs pages long. She offers so many opportunities; we strategize by phone. I simply must meet Matthew Cleveland and Erica Swallow and Starla Gresham. Miles before Terrie and I greet face-to-face, we are already friends.

Terrie arranges overnight hosts and daytime interviews. Since I go where I'm invited and hang around as long as I'm engaged, I spend four days around Little Rock: more time than in New York or Chicago. The Arkansas capital proves to be a fertile place to talk about tomorrow.

Terrie hails from McGehee, down in the Delta. She honed her marketing skills in Dallas and Florida, though her ability to connect humans is innate. When Terrie and her husband returned to Arkansas to care for Dean's aging mother, Terrie decided to direct 30 years of marketing savvy toward educational, hunger, and children's organizations rather than corporations. Within four years, Terrie knows everyone in Little Rock's world of philanthropy. She not only builds their financial profile, she rolls up her sleeves and donates time. I am welcome all over Little Rock, thanks to Terrie's good word.

Terrie and Dean take me to Doe's, a Little Rock (and Greenville, Mississippi) institution where I enjoy the best steak of my journey. But we don't stay out too late. Dean has to rise at five a.m. for his prison ministry before work. In a world of good and generous people, Terrie and Dean Turner are extraordinary gems.

One of Terrie's referrals, June Hardin, is an enveloping black woman who suggests we meet at the Waffle House in Bryant. Based on her suggested venue alone, I fall hard.

Waffle House is a Southern institution. The first time I indulge is after a long morning of red clay roads in Thomson, Georgia. I'm taken aback when, the moment I walk in, the entire staff stops and shouts, "Good Morning" with the choreographed perfection of an MGM musical. My waitress shuffles up, "What'll you have?" and tosses a bewildering frown when I ask for a menu. She retrieves a laminated sheet. I grasp immediately that people don't need a

menu at Waffle House. When I decide on the All Star Breakfast, her expression conveys, "Duh, I could have told you that." The All-Star Breakfast lives up to its name.

It would be so easy for Waffle House to become my go-to routine; the food is tasty and fast, and there's one on every other Southern corner. Some interstate intersections boast two. But I hold Waffle House in reserve for special treats, since ubiquitous does not correlate with healthy, even for calorie-craving cyclists. Meeting June Hardin at Waffle House qualifies as a special treat in so many ways. I arrive early, order without a menu, and anticipate meeting this woman of the velvet phone voice and sublime YouTube poems amidst Waffle House's fluorescent clatter.

Three weeks after the election, Trump's win is still primary in people's minds. Among supporters, stunned disbelief has turned to strident rhetoric. Some foes settle into resignation. Others glue "Not My President" stickers on their cars, which is nothing more than petty and divisive intolerance from a different point on the political spectrum. Denise Bell's words still ring in my head. How can we move toward tolerance, toward acceptance, in a world that grows more polarized every moment? How do we hold on to convictions so easily smothered by shouts?

June Hardin is a solemn, expansive woman, the perfect foil to our garish setting. A Louisville, Kentucky, native, 1 of 17 children, June endured insult and physical injury during desegregation. She recounts trauma enough to cripple, but June transcends her past and leverages it as insight into the human condition. "The pain of the past is always present. You have to decide whether that can help you in the present. If you own the past in front of you,

you own it. If you bury the past pain, it is still there. It owns you." At age 50, June graduated college with a degree in psychology. "You have to find the balance—through education, or drugs, or talk. I love being in my 50s because I've pistol-whipped my demons. I own them."

June fills our booth with her flesh and her mountaintop view of our world. She savors every crisp fold of her pecan waffle, every smoldering drop of her coffee. She cautions me on limits to openness, even as she suggests hope and guidance as a path forward.

"America is a great nation and things get righted over time. But we will never right things by flames and stoking. Since when do we all have to agree anyway? We live in the age of dissension. If you only love whom you agree with, that's not love. Love transcends dissension.

"The toxicity that has gripped this nation will have a long effect, but the roots of decency that underpin this country will win out. The folks making the noise are not the majority; the majority will win out in the end.

"Material desires are fleeting. My hope for tomorrow is that people will learn that material things cannot bring contentment. We are far from that understanding.

"How will we live tomorrow? A lot more guarded, a lot more uncertain.

"The only way to change is to shut down certain communications. We are phonetical creatures. We learn what we hear repeated. But preserving decency and honor by stopping to listen to messages that are harmful, that's not intolerant, it's protecting certain truths."

I see tomorrow as one hundred million years from now. We will still be here. We are infants.
Don't get me wrong, there will be great suffering along the way, The US will disappear.
We will move toward a one-world government. That will be painful; it will only happen through war.
But we will survive. We will flourish.
—Tom Black, Zen practitioner, San Luis Obispo, CA

Little Rock, AR—November 28, 2016, 10:00 a.m.

The longer I travel, the less I worry about the major catastrophes that can swallow us whole tomorrow: thirst and flood and famine sprawled across an overheated planet. It's the little things that will do us in, cumulatively. Darwin theorized we evolved from apes, social creatures that groom each other, mutually extracting mud and lice from places beyond reach. I begin to think we're also akin to angry birds, hell-bent on pecking out each other's eyes under the false belief that a blind neighbor will enhance our view.

Every issue confronting our society incorporates four components: technical, political, economic, and social. The technical are the most entertaining to explore. We love conjuring how climate-change scenarios, drone dominance, and artificial intelligence will liberate or enslave us. Yet technical challenges are the easiest to address; their projections are mere distraction. The political, economic, and social adaptations of innovation will define tomorrow more than technology itself. Whether drones facilitate connectivity or enable isolation is not fundamental to the drone: their impact lies in how we use them.

The soft issues will define the quality of our tomorrow, and they are the hardest to answer. Will we live with open honesty? Will we live in caring community?

By the time I've profiled over 400 individuals and organizations I've learned a bit about candor, sharing, and fear. Few military people talk with me, none on the record. The military is a closed society where power is derived in concealing knowledge as much as having it. The same culture permeates our energy industry. Several energy mavens in Texas and Louisiana are eager to voice frustration about their environmentally destructive industry, and then just as eager to recoil once they see their words in print. Venting is cathartic, but public ink triggers anxiety.

When Megan Parks, a former environmental compliance advisor for BP, reads my profile of our conversation, she requests that I remove it. I comply. After all, I'm not an investigative journalist; I'm not trying to make people look bad. But the moment I hit "Trash" I realize my mistake. Ms. Parks is a well-educated person; she agreed to an interview; I did not misquote her. If she suffers interview regret, I need not accommodate her.

I take a much gentler position with hosts I profile because, even though folks see me taking notes and know I will write about them, our connection is primarily social. I will delete a comment they regret, or remove the entire post, but I won't "pretty up" a response after the fact. I may not be a credentialed journalist, but I'm not a PR agent either.

After I post a person's profile, I send him or her the web link. Most are happy with their portrayal. A few are discomforted. Yet no one, not a single person, cites a direct misquote. I'm proud of that accuracy.

It's teeming rain the morning I arrive at the Arkansas Food Bank to interview Rhonda Sanders, another friend of Terrie Turner. Rhonda's a lovely person who must be having a bad day. After touring me around and explaining the food bank's terrific work, Rhonda's response to "How will we live tomorrow?" strikes a bleak chord of downward spiral. "That's how society evolves. When you get to the point of more comfort than discomfort, then it starts to disintegrate. It's the cycle of life." Then Rhonda extends her perspective on human selfishness to the volunteers who work at the food bank. I stir in my seat to draw attention to the fact that I'm writing down her words. I know that Rhonda will not like to see them in print. But she continues, and I report her words accurately.

Sure enough, when I send her the profile link, Rhonda responds immediately. She doesn't ask me to retract. Instead, she offers clarification, which I am happy to append to the post. Her original statement stands, plus more. I like to think that, in the sprit of Darwin, we groomed each other's purpose rather than pecking out any eyes.

Rolling Fork, MS—December 2, 2016, 7:00 a.m.

Rolling Fork Motel is interchangeable with dozens of places I stay, owned and operated by Indian immigrants named Patel, a merchant caste surname more common in India than Smith is here. Patels have cornered the market on independent motels throughout our great land, except for the upper Midwest and Dakotas, where flat-accent Protestants still change sheets and tend the desk. Most Patel motels are located on pavement bypassed by Interstate highways. Some have as few as eight rooms. Others are extensive motor courts where two generations ago families pulled their station wagons right up to the door of the room, swam in the pool, and enjoyed Salisbury steak in the vinyl-boothed restaurant. Today, the polyester bedspreads may still date from that era, but the pool is filled with concrete, and the dining room is empty save a few metal tables and chairs that sit before a meager breakfast spread of tired coffee, Frosted Flakes scrolled from a plastic bin, and saccharine pastries whose sticky white icing clings to their plastic packages.

It's easy to think of immigrants as a monolithic group, much despised in these post-election days. It's just as easy to think all Patel motels are alike. They are not.

The Gateway Inn in Marion, Alabama, is set far off the road, amidst tall trees; so quiet I sleep for 10 hours.

The grim-faced owner of the Country Club Drive Motel in Colby, Kansas, cheats my credit card five bucks. I don't make a fuss; let the overcharge weigh on her conscience.

Sanderson, Texas, a near ghost town with a convenience store and a Budget Inn, offers the only services along US 90's 140-mile stretch between Marathon and Comstock, yet the place is famous among cycle tourists. Manager "Danny" offers me energy bars at check-in; he escorts me to a generous room with a sweeping mountain view. About seven, he knocks on my door with a silver tray of hot potato soup, curried rice with vegetables, and delicious papadum. We chat while I eat. Danny explains how he mail-orders vegan ingredients from Houston. For 45 bucks, this man offers a lot of hospitality.

On the other hand, 80 dollars seems a steep price to pay for the honor of being the only Saturday night guest at the Cameron Motel in Cameron, Louisiana, until I cross the threshold of the dazzling gold chamber with mirrored ceiling I claim as my throne room for the night.

The Red Roof Inn in Walterboro, South Carolina is one of the nicest places I stay on my entire trip; so clean and quiet, with such an ample breakfast (fresh fruit!) that I give it a thumbs up online review.

In our world of endless hierarchy and constant rivalry, there's a pecking order even among Patel motels. Unaffiliated places, like Sleepy Time Motel in Auburn, Maine, or the Villa West Motel in Florence, Oregon, are the most basic. Bottom-barrel franchises like the Budget Inn in Selma, Alabama are only a micro-step up. Big-time Patels own Super 8s, Econo Lodges and Red Roof Inns. I never meet a Patel proprietor of a La Quinta or a Hampton Inn. Then again, I don't frequent such swanky lodgings.

Like immigrants everywhere, the Patels fill an economic niche well beneath their capabilities. Motel offices feature framed diplomas from engineering schools back in India, even medical degrees. This seems doubly ironic considering how many Patel motel owners appear ill suited to hospitality. Many are curt by nature, transactional to the brink of unfriendly, and clueless to American standards of cleanliness. The beds may be made and the shower wiped down, but the lobbies are cluttered, there are dust-mites in the corner of the carpet, the bathroom floor scrim is near as thick as the grime on the windows. Still, Patel motels provide good value and tech-savvy Indians provide reliable Wi-Fi for a weary cyclist who craves nothing more than a warm and dry cocoon.

Rolling Fork Motel, lacking even the most rudimentary franchise designation, is not a promising place. The wind whips up the dusty parking lot. A pile of mattresses obstructs the front door. It sits too far out of town for me to walk to a restaurant: even with bicycle lights, I am disinclined to navigate narrow US 61 in the dark. There's a Dollar General across the highway in case I crave a buck's worth of fructose corn syrup. Since I've already passed the only other option in town—and deemed it decidedly worse—Rolling Fork Motel will do.

I enter the outer lobby; five-feet square, at most. I stand before the glass and ring the bell. A gaunt man appears, face wrinkled with more folds than the meandering Mississippi. At $45, the price reflects no delusions. "Bob" slides my credit card through his machine. The tape spins and sticks. He fiddles with it. He slides my card a second time. The register tape sticks. He opens the machine, extracts the tape, and inserts a new roll. He doesn't chat during his maneuvers; they take all his focus. He slides my card

a third time. The machine churns out a fresh-inked slip, which I sign. He apologizes in broken English. Tells me there is a coffee maker in my room. An unexpected treat. Though I doubt Bob's English can comprehend my question, I ask "How will we live tomorrow?" He responds, "Mahatma Gandhi and Martin Luther King, two great men." A second unexpected treat.

At 7:15 the next morning a loud knock shakes my door. In battered phrases and hand gestures, Bob explains that my credit card's been charged three times. He asks me to stop by the office for my refund before I leave. Half an hour later, even more impatient, he returns and asks for my card. I give it to him and he disappears. Only after he's gone with my credit card in his fist do I wonder if I'm too trusting, but the man's honest alarm is so palpable he seems incapable of deceit. Bob returns with a new receipt: three debits and two credits. I thank him and figure we're finished. Until he knocks again, tablet in hand, with an elaborate explanation about the charges. It seems very important to him that I understand the error. I gesture that everything is good between us, several times, until he sighs genuine relief.

Immigrants are everywhere. A cursory media view confirms they're ruining our country. The president-elect vows to build a wall against our neighbor to the south to keep these illegals out. Maybe Donald needs to get on a bike and ride the 800 miles between San Diego and El Paso to see that the vast majority of that border already has a wall.

Maybe he needs to meet E. T. Collinsworth in Portal, Arizona, an EMT who explains that the wall has a ditch on the American side, so when people scale from Mexico and drop down here, they fall further than they expect and often break their ankle or leg. Since whoever discovers an injured illegal is responsible for their medical costs in the United States until they are healthy enough to ship back, the Border Patrol is often slow to respond.

Maybe he needs to meet Surge Leposi, the son of illegal immigrants in Fresno, California, who teaches middle school in Madera. Surge explains how our tightened border forces illegals, who used to work the harvest and then return to Mexico, to remain north of the border year round. Locals complain that the illegals use our hospitals, our schools, our services, but it's no longer safe to return to their homeland.

Maybe he needs to meet Jesse Tillotson, an Anadarko Energy meter reader from Uvalde, Texas, who works along the border. "If we want to get rid of illegal immigration, go after the employers, not the people seeking a better life."

That's not likely to happen anytime soon because, though it is *verboten* to say out loud, we don't want to end illegal immigration. It's too profitable, both economically and politically. We want immigrants around, not just to do the jobs too demeaning to the rest of us, but also to be our political punching bags. They're such easy targets: so foreign; so vulnerable. They can't even vote.

Whether we go back 16 generations to the Mayflower, or 5 generation to the potato famine (as in my case), or 1 generation to Merced, California, and the Laotian Hmong who supported our war in Southeast Asia—unless we're Native Americans, we're immigrants. Yet within one generation, maybe two, we assimilate enough to look down on whoever knocks at our border's door.

I pedal away from the Rolling Fork Motel and ponder an immigrant's hardship: to run such a marginal business in such a strange land, to live in constant apology for all that you cannot comprehend. Yet on top of all 'Bob's' immigrant burdens, we shovel animosity.

Fort Smith, AR—November 25, 2016, 4:00 p.m.

Pretty much everyone I meet thinks I'm a liberal. They're wrong. I possess many of the usual blue trappings: college-town hometown, alternative transport, a trio of degrees from a fancy university, cerebral and skinny, materially comfortable (enough money to buy what I want, not so much that money owns me). If I ever wore the liberal label, I shucked it one starry night in Haiti, when I looked around a compound of volunteers after the 2010 earthquake and realized everyone else was evangelical Christian. The missionaries all had conversion agendas beyond erecting new homes. But so what? At least they were there, on the ground. The liberals extended their hand no further than writing a check.

Which is not to say I'm a conservative; a label that isn't even logical anymore. Conservatives today don't conserve; they impose. One set of values for all. Theirs.

Pretty much everyone thinks my hosts are all liberal as well. Wrong again. I stay with a disproportionate number of bicycle-wonks, vegans, and left-leaning college professors, but a culture of hospitality runs through Mormons and gun-loving libertarians as well. People from all quadrants of the economic and political spectrum appreciate a free spirit spinning outside of it.

Gary Palmer is the most idiosyncratic person I meet; a crusty guy who literally gives me a pallet on the floor in the garage he rents in Jackson, Wyoming. Gary, age 60, has to walk next door to heat up supper or use a bathroom. He's never owned a car; never works more than a month straight; never feels any compunction to "contribute" to society. Yet he has no expectations from that society either. I squat on my pallet in looming twilight in anticipation of a long, strange night. Gary disappears without explanation. Fif-teen minutes later he returns with a saucepan of chili. He drapes his long legs over his chaise and eats his dinner. He doesn't offer me any. He bends my ear against government of all kinds, at all levels. He chuckles that in two years, Social Security will give him $200 per month. "That's more money than I need. I'll never work again."

Gary and I are men of the same age with very different outlooks. "Tomorrow I will do what I am doing today until I keel over on the side of the road or die in my bed." I don't choose to live like Gary. I do, however, find him a refreshing anecdote to our society, where the majority of people inflate their perceived input against anticipated entitlements according to equations that inevitably leave them feeling gypped. There's integrity in a man who drops out so completely. Nothing added, nothing expected.

A good friend's sister-in-law, a widow in Fort Smith, Arkansas, invites me for Thanksgiving. I appreciate the gesture. My friend warns that Jean is very conservative and we might not get along. I don't refute him out loud, though I dismiss his comment. I may not be Will Rogers, who famously said he never met a man he didn't like, but by this time in my journey, I never meet a person I can't get along with, and find some value within.

I roll up to Jean's huge house with the same equanimity I bring to every garden apartment, every trailer, ever garage I enter. Jean and I share a common bond—as humans—that's more fundamental than any liberal/conservative dichotomy.

A Thanksgiving feast is a ritual meal. It takes time to eat so much food. Time enough to discuss all manner of problems in this world. Jean and I do not balance the relative weight of how we agree or disagree; we do not try to change each other's mind. We speak from our experience, our truth, and respect each other's positions. We are humans first. We give thanks for that.

Vertical integration will increase.
Warren Buffet bought CRX and is vertically integrating transportation.
Walmart is the largest employer in 20 states. Colgate is tied into how many bars of soap
are sold at Walmart and they adjust production accordingly.
    —Martin Siegenthaler, reluctant consumer, San Francisco, CA

Bentonville, AR—November 19, 2016, 7:00 p.m.

I spend more time in California, 50 days, than in any other state. I figure California is the place to get a handle on tomorrow. Isn't that where trends bloom? Though I absorb all kinds of opinion across the Golden State, nothing feels like direction.

Direction I find in Arkansas. Perhaps because Arkansas is my 47th state; perhaps because it's post-election; perhaps because enough people say, "we're a small town of three million people," I figure Arkansas represents an expanding tribe. Arkansas' thrust toward tomorrow is powered by three massive corporations that have transformed what used to be the state's poor, remote quadrant into a global center of influence and wealth: J. B. Hunt, Tyson, and Walmart. I've encountered plenty of evidence that, for better or worse, tomorrow will spring from the places we least expect it, favor large corporations, and increase inequality: a trio of conditions that thrives in Bentonville.

Walmart, the largest corporation in the world, with 2.3 million employees, is run out of a handful of long-slung grey buildings in this Ozark town where "Low Prices Every Day" is a way of life. Two generations ago, we chased a suburban ideal of fresh air and private transport under the guise that what was good for GM was good for America. Today, what's good for Walmart shapes the way we live, whether it's good for us or not. For product manufacturers, landing on Walmart shelves is like an actor landing a part on Broadway: if you can make it there, you'll get distributed everywhere. Walmart influences what gets made, how it is packaged, priced, and sold. Walmart's business model of large stores, often located beyond city limits, is vilified for destroying mom and pop commerce and turning so many downtowns into ghost towns. All true. But Sam Walton didn't force us to patronize his mammoth stores and buy his inexpensive stuff. We choose to do that every time we drive to his giant parking lot and stroll beneath the sea of fluorescent lights to save a few bucks. Problem is, in many areas Walmart is so successful that there's no other place to shop. This isn't a problem for Walmart; it's a problem for people who want a range of commercial options.

Downtown Bentonville is a picturesque courthouse square flanked by well-preserved commercial fronts. Locals laugh, nervously, how the merchant who destroyed so many downtowns preserves theirs. Bentonville's cultural heart includes the Walton Family Foundation, a sedate three-story brick building, and the Walmart Museum, located in Sam's first Bentonville location, complete with a street-front penny candy store and a vintage soda fountain—romantic shopping experiences absent from any actual Walmart. The museum's exhibits chronicle Walmart's inevitable march to dominance across our retail nation and the world. I love the huge maps that plot every Walmart location per decade. The dots grow closer; they merge. Like a community; like a cancer.

The dots also reinforce that my personal experience with Walmart is very recent. I've never been to a Walmart in Massachusetts, one of the last states the chain infiltrated. The nearest one to my home is 10 miles away; a short drive in rural Texas but well beyond the regular sphere of a city dweller who travels by subway and bicycle. On this odyssey, however, I've been to dozens of Walmarts. Energy bars and bicycle tubes are located in the same place in every one. When I ride 50 miles before discovering I left my pricy Marmot shell back in Alabama, I buy a new one at a Walmart in Tennessee for a quarter the price. It's not as nice as my Marmot, but it keeps me dry enough for the rest of my trip.

Walmarts are bright and cheery, as are the staff and the customers. Sometimes I take writing breaks at an in-house Subway. Free Wi-Fi. But after an hour I'm antsy for daylight. People talk with me at Walmart. Their complaints and contentments are about the same as anywhere else. If McDonald's is America's family room, and libraries are our collective parlor, then Walmart is America's community center.

Walmart is a savvy organization, keen to the bifurcated pulse of our nation, that sometimes leads where our elected officials fear to tread.

When Walmart raised its minimum wage to $10 per hour, it established the de facto minimum wage despite our government's inability to boost the official minimum.

When the Arkansas legislature passed a "religious freedom" bill allowing businesses to withhold service on moral grounds, Walmart opposed it, forcing Republican governor Hutchinson's signature on a watered-down version. Walmart doesn't want the option of discriminating among customers. They want to sell to everybody and avoid boycotts by insisting the government requires them to do so.

Walmart knows there's good press, and good money, to be made in recycling. They've established all kinds of net-zero targets. Their environmental corporate speak is slick. Don't be misled—the company it is still a net contributor to our ecological imbalance—but Walmart's track record on environmental practices is deeper than that of Congress.

There is a power shift in our nation away from government. People don't trust elected officials to act in our best interest, a doubt reinforced by legislative logjam. Corporations are the new power centers. They influence large swaths of our private and public sectors. The Waltons, the Bill Gateses, the Mark Zuckermans, the Warren Buffets; these people and their companies determine our available goods and services. Their non-profit arms, their foundations, essentially provide foreign aid, guide public health, and dictate education, endeavors once considered public.

We've seen this before, in the Gilded Age. But the Great Depression inspired us to dial back corporate influence and institute a greater role for government, a role that expanded even more during World War II, and eventually led a huge expansion of the middle class, perhaps the most unappreciated blessing of the twentieth century. For the past generation we've swung the pendulum back toward corporate privilege. Not because we love corporations so much. Rather, because we dislike our government even more.

Kyle Templeton, Walmart's global design director, sees an upside to corporations taking on roles traditionally reserved for government. "Walmart serves 160 million customers. Forty million could stop shopping there next week; they have other options. All of Amazon's customers can walk. Can you imagine having a four-to-six-year contract with your grocery? That's what we have with our politicians. Business is much more responsive."

But his wife Kyla warns about the limits of corporate responsiveness. "What about Halliburton? They have a huge business but not in consumer products. What influence do we have over what they do?"

Jackson, MS—December 3, 2016, 6:00 p.m.

I wake in my cabin outside of Vicksburg to the sound of rain. Nothing's more dispiriting than clipping my panniers onto Tom first thing in the morning, flying my right leg over his frame, and landing my bum on a wet seat. But the forecast is rain all day and the early morning splatters are light, so there's nothing to be gained in delay. I stiffen my spine, squish into the damp saddle, and pedal on.

Things start well. Jackson is only 50 miles away. Eain is light along Warrior Trail, there's few hills, no wind, and thick trees glisten. Until I descend into a ravine and the pavement gives out, sure sign I'm off track. I dismount and walk Tom through a gravelly stream. I suck in a deep breath to counter mounting unease. I taste the thick Southern atmosphere. It blunts the reality that I'm sort of lost.

I find Old US 80. There's no shoulder, but no Saturday morning traffic either. I cross Interstate 20 in Bolton and continue along Northside Road. The rain is heavy now, but the wind's negligible. I feel stable. I come over a summit and roll beneath a promenade of trees so grand I imagine entering an ethereal Tara. By now, I'm too wet to even feel the rain.

Rural Mississippi is light on road signs, but my directions are good. I'm confident of my track, until, whoa, I am back in Bolton, 12 miles later than my first visit. Suddenly, Jackson seems so far away. The rain drives, the wind picks up, my spirits dive. I consider climbing on the I-20 shoulder and muscling my way to the capital. Instead, I find cover in an empty car wash bay, eat an energy bar, check my directions, and discover how one wrong turn spun into a giant detour. I recalibrate to a simpler route.

I pedal, consciously. I run through my status checklist. Am I cold? Is the pavement solid? Am I wet? Do I have a safe shoulder? Am I hungry? Can drivers see me? Am I climbing? Is the wind my ally or my foe?

I recite these mantras whenever conditions turn harsh, until recitation turns into mediation, my mind calms, and progress steadies. Reiterating these parameters reminds me of all the glorious days when everything is right: smooth pavement and wide shoulder, the wind at my back, and the sun on my hands. They also remind me how rare it is that all obstacles multiply against me: the mere handful of times I reckon conditions so unsafe I seek refuge.

Enumerating and evaluating my circumstances doesn't change them. It alters my perspective on them. It sharpens my acuity and soothes my worry. The first step in addressing any problem—physical, mental, social—is to acknowledge it. After that, appreciate all that's good. Be aware of problems, respond to their threat, but don't let them vanquish you.

This is not a day for sightseeing and my hosts live on the north side. I avoid downtown and the Capitol. I stay rural along Clinton-Tinnon Road and then turn right on Kickapoo. I am past caring how wet I am, past kicking myself for so many wrong turns. I am where I am, and no amount of second-guessing will put me any closer to my destination. Besides, that allée of trees, cresting in the silvery mist, has imprinted on me. A vision I never would have absorbed, had I not been lost.

I cross US 49; Kickapoo turns into County Line. Traffic picks up, as does the rain, and the wind. By the time I reach the I-55 intersection, traffic is heavy. I brace against gusts. Saturday afternoon is peak shopping time for this major retail area. Signs and driveways and left turn lanes. Cars pull in and out in all directions. Everyone is in a rush. Except me. I hold my own; stay visible, stay calm. Look and listen in all directions.

Despite the rain and wrong turns, it's too early to arrive at my host's home. I pull my sopping carcass into a nearby McDonald's. For a few moments, I simply breathe. I never ruminate about the effort it takes to navigate a world scaled for cars—a world in which I am virtually invisible—while I'm surrounded by their mass and power. Only afterward, thankful to be safe, do I fully exhale.

A few hours later, showered and dry and laughing about my adventure, my host Dixon pulls out his phone and scrolls to a pic, a photo taken through a rain-dropped windshield of a yellow cyclist in a swarm of vehicles, angled against the wind. "I knew it had to be you. How many crazy cyclists would be in Jackson on such a rainy day?"

The guy in the photo is me, for sure. But I am not the guy in the photo. He looks precarious and fragile. I never feel that way, even in the rain and wind and traffic; even after I pedaled more of Mississippi than I bargained to see. I don't feel vulnerable on my bike. I feel confident and strong. Which is a good thing, because the drowned rat in that photo doesn't look like he could ever go the distance I've achieved.

I will live like I'm dying. Nothing more to it.
> —Waitress note on my check, Dakota Family Restaurant, Mandan, ND

Demopolis, AL—December 5, 2016, 6:00 p.m.

What am I doing in Alabama for the third time on this trip? The last time I was in the Heart of Dixie I got chased by pit bulls and lost my fancy raincoat. The first time a Porsche made me kiss the pavement. I must be crazy to be here again, on a grey afternoon, my third day of cold rain. Cars bank left into the Walmart Supercenter on US 80. Windshields glisten in the rain. The eyes behind that glass don't see me: they're focused on Low Prices Every Day. I can feel where I am not wanted, and it is here.

I ride with hyper caution through the turnoff to downtown. No shoulder in this inhospitable place. I reach the Greenwood Motel with no injury more serious than a quickened pulse. I lean Tom under the faded porte-cochère and set off a tinkle when I nudge the lobby door. A middle aged blonde woman sits at the far side of an ample reception desk, rifling through paper with her back to me. A big-bellied man sprawls on a sofa; his features betray his surname: Patel. I stand at the obvious spot and await service. The man looks straight at me with disinterest veering upon disdain. The woman keeps sorting. I shuffle to make some noise. No response from either. I clear my throat. Minutes pass. Finally, I say, "May I check in please?" The woman swivels to me, annoyed. The first and only nasty female I meet in the entire South. I give her my name. She claims I have no reservation. I show her the confirmation on my phone. "That's nothing to me. You need to call booking.com." Whatever snafu exists is between the website and the motel. Besides, I have an approved reservation and there are plenty of empty rooms. No matter. This woman's pettiness is steadfast. Light is fading. The evening is cold and rainy. I have history in Alabama. A room with a grudge is better than none at all.

I call the website. A very pleasant customer service representative, undoubtedly Indian, apologizes for an ugly woman she's never met. After 20 minutes I get a room.

The next morning I shake the dust of Demopolis from my feet. I harbor revenge. Not just that the Greenwood Motel will go out of business—that's inevitable. Rather, that no good comes to the nasty woman and opaque man who fill that lobby with their ill humor. It only takes a few miles of spinning for my ugly fantasies to dissipate. Clouds part. A streak of sun strikes my face. Cattle fix their knowing gaze on me. They preach patience. The rural roads of Alabama's Black Belt, one of the poorest and most picturesque places I've seen, testify to fortitude. Meanness is its own special hell. I can't lay anything worse on those unhappy people.

The urgent answer is, can we all get along?
—Gerald Black Elk, member of the Sioux Tribe, Rapid City, SD

Montgomery, AL—December 8, 2016, 2:00 p.m.

In 1964, on the steps of the Alabama State Capitol where segregationist George Wallace reigned as governor, four months before President Johnson signed the Voting Rights Act, Martin Luther King Jr. made a speech at the close of the five-day march from Selma to Montgomery. He paraphrased the Unitarian minister Theodore Parker in a quote now largely attributed to MLK. I never knew this phrase before this trip. It has become my mantra, my lens, for understanding all that I hear and see across our land.

The arc of the moral universe is long, but it bends towards justice.

Our nation is gripped by racial tension. It throbs everywhere I go. I have come to see it as a good thing. Not the tension, but what it represents. The third wave. The Emancipation Proclamation freed the slaves. The civil rights movement provided equal protection under the law. But today, people demand more than loose shackles and legal equality. They want to be treated as equals. They want respect.

Society doesn't always move, or always move forward. We do not stride in a singular, optimal direction. Some days, some years, we backtrack. But over decades, over generations, we inch toward equality, we crawl toward peace, we incline our faces toward love.

I pedal the route of the historic march from Selma to Montgomery. My legs spin in accord with those marchers more than 50 years ago, demanding their right to vote. But my mind also considers the white supremacists who bullied them along the way, who still bully today.

Segregationists do not construe their actions as hate; they couch bigotry as heritage, they camouflage fear as honor. Yet surely they know, in their hearts, their case is unjust.

We are all bound by the limits of our perspective. The more our perspective is tainted by power and fear, the more distorted it becomes. The world's evolution away from slavery and toward equality threatens supremacist power. It heightens his fear. It leads to maiming unarmed people and denying fellow citizens basic rights. Actions beyond the bounds of tolerance that are wrong, wrong, wrong.

The march from Selma to Montgomery might have never taken place if the eyes of the wider nation had not peered into Selma's soul and found it rotten. But the rest of us have no cause to be smug. Circumstances that propel us towards justice are never so pure as history pretends. We did not respond in horror when black men were killed for demanding their rights; we only acted after James Reeb, a white minister, was murdered and inhuman violence upset the quiet comfort of our living room TVs.

Still, we make progress. The progress is too slow; slower than this aging man's legs can pedal; slower even than thousands of marchers can walk. It is littered with sidesteps and missteps. But, nevertheless, over time, we make progress.

There is a meme about the wisdom of the old man that plants a tree
whose shade he will never sit under. The real wisdom of this meme is that the old man
is planting a tree that will provide shade for a future incarnation of himself.
We are the children that will inherit the earth we leave behind. This is the irony of tomorrow.
—Ed Barron, model, Boston, MA

Tallahassee, FL—December 13, 2016, 9:00 p.m.

I come upon the following couchsurfing profile and feel a moral duty to verify the third-party assessment it contains.

A bit about me: +-1m71, +-71 kg. Clear brown complexion. Dark hair. Brown eyes. Big rounded nose. Beautiful ears. The most handsome man in the world according to my mom.

Call me a fact checker. Or call me shallow. Regardless of my motives, the mom only got it half-right. Amre is indeed a handsome man, easily among the most handsome in the world. But his perfectly proportioned shell supports an equally handsome soul, rich in curiosity and insight.

Amre is a citizen of the world, though officially French of Syrian refugee parents. He lived in India ("my right opposite, my rebirth"), married a Venezuelan woman, and settled in Miami. Then, in one weekend, everything fell apart. "Within 48 hours we decided to divorce, I found a job in Tallahassee, packed up, drove here, and started a completely new life." Amre is circumspect on the details, but I gather it was not entirely his idea.

I arrive at Amre's apartment with a question on tap. Yet this young man, half my age, pressing his own search after life tossed him into a maelstrom, asks even more questions of me. What provoked my trip? How has it changed me? What advice would I give my younger self? We sit on his sofa deep into the night, mining singular and shared strains of experience and aspiration.

I recall myself at Amre's age, married, with a baby on the way: hell-bent on becoming the man I concocted in my head, denying the beat of my heart, ignoring every pulse below the waist. "So-and-so makes me nervous" was my code for "I'm attracted to that man." Once I caught that inkling, I steered clear. Self-deceit piled up until it loomed too large to ignore. I navigated divorce and coming-out, raising children and losing preconceptions. I landed over-the-hill with less stature than my fantasies envisioned, but with dignity intact. Twenty-odd years later, the life I worked so hard to determine has withered into diffuse memory. In its place, a life I never imagined, the one I actually lead, suits me so well.

What can I tell this young man whose life was on such a pleasant, steady course until its underpinnings collapsed? Only that we learn nothing from a life that unfurls according to plan. Challenges, defeats, reversals, these are the seeds of contentment, of satisfaction, of triumph.

People sometimes preface their thoughts on tomorrow with the phrase, "Until we have a revolution …" This qualifier encapsulates complementary perspectives: the future will unfold as a continuity, except for the catastrophes. We will either establish environmental balance or we will burn; robots will enhance our lives or they will become our masters; we will share economic bounty or we will incite revolution. Life is both continuous and episodic. We remember big events, whether cataclysms or celebrations. We do not recall every inhale, despite the fact that each breath is critical. Stop breathing and we die.

Amre is marking time in Tallahassee, licking his wounds from a marriage gone sour, coming off the excitement of a gorgeous wife and their Miami life, marking time, conscious of his breath. Perhaps something will happen here to quicken his pulse, perhaps he will move on. Either way, Tallahassee's a good place for him, for now.

Our conversation turns broad; the handsomest man in the world does not wallow. We explore a tomorrow when people don't need to work. The economics of this are less daunting than the cultural transformation required of a nation that equates work with worth.

"I am a big believer in universal income. In purest form, you're given a basic income to cover your expense just for inhabiting the earth. I do not believe this will make people lazy; they will be energized. Look at you, on your bike. If everyone who makes a non-economic choice can be happier, then universal income will lead to greater creativity and happiness."

Amre transcends the conventional notion that people are only motivated by money. If we can move beyond that concept, will people pursue higher, purer, forms of motivation? Amre's ideas reflect his French upbringing; a nation with a wider social net, a culture less focused on what people "do" than ours. Yet, like every immigrant I meet, Amre hopes to stay in the United States. "I believe America still has the idea of freedom. It still has more opportunity than most of the world, much more than Old Europe."

Universal income may come to pass, either through societal evolution or dramatic action: continuity or catastrophe. But it won't happen in any near-term tomorrow so long as engaging people from countries with socialist traditions prefer to come to the United States: the nation where opportunity is still synonymous with work.

Montgomery, AL—December 8, 2016, 8:00 p.m.

20,000 miles!

For a nanosecond I take satisfaction that I roll over my odometer along the marcher's route from Selma to Montgomery. Until I realize it's demeaning—and wrong—to pretend any equivalence between people struggling for justice and a guy struggling against a headwind. I focus on their achievement all the way to the steps of the Alabama State Capitol. Only after I honor their contribution to humankind do I consider my personal milestone.

Celebrations call for kindred spirits. I search warmshowers for a long-distance cyclist host and spend the night with Bethany and Dave Garth, a fun couple who spent two years riding 22,000 miles over four continents. Their experience—more camping, cross-cultural hijinks, and lingering periods in favorite places—favored different parameters than my journey's continuous movement, intentional interactions, and creature comfort. We share good food, good beer, and great stories of frozen chains in rural China, eternal up climbs in the Andes, and Turkish delights. Every long-distance cyclist has his own style and preferences, but the fundamental joys of bicycle touring are the same. As Dave surmises, "There's something profound about showing up in a place on a bicycle."

I wonder how many people on this planet have bicycled over 20,000 miles. I would love to share dinner with any of them.

It's all going to come down in the next few weeks.
It will either be all bad or all horrible.

　　　　—Lisa, Native American, Oklahoma City, OK

Gainesville, FL—December 17, 2016, 7:00 p.m.

What is wrong with this country?

We install a media room and a backyard pool and then wonder why we're isolated and alone.

We expect our schools to feed, educate, exercise, integrate, and socialize our children and blame the teachers for failing what we don't practice at home.

We are wary of the elite. Not the rich or the powerful; we idolize them. The educated are the elite.

We only value what we can monetize. Bee transporters shuffle hives all over the land, for a fee, after monoculture farming ruins the pollination nature once provided for free.

We value beliefs over facts. We elevate beliefs into truths and denigrate objective reality, leaving us no common ground.

———————

Gainesville, Florida, is a blue-bubble college town bobbing in a red-state sea. My host, Bonne, takes me to the 30th Annual Veterans for Peace Solstice Concert, a gathering of activists and musicians at the Unitarian-Universalist Fellowship. It's a variety show of left-leaning entertainers playing to a packed house of kindred spirits: part concert, part revival, part reunion. The energy in the space ricochets off the walls, an energy of release, of relaxation, of strength; an energy that can only come from being among one's own. This is a family, a tribe, under siege. Less than six weeks since Donald Trump is elected, these folks need to affirm each other in this long dark night. They come together to be one.

What is wrong with this country?

We have elevated money beyond a medium of exchange. It is our objective, our purpose, our value, our morality, our worth.

We will have peace only when peace makes more money than war.

We will have health only when wellness makes more money than drugs.

We will have good food only when fruits of the earth make more money than the processes of man, when the lobbying power of the potato exceeds that of the potato chip, when there is more subsidy in broccoli than beef.

———————

The emcee tells funny Trump-isms. His patter is less caustic than Saturday Night Live or liberal comics from the coasts. Gainesville may be less than 75 miles from the Atlantic Ocean, but it's still in the South. Certain crudities are best left unsaid, even among friends. One between-the-acts story includes a reference to bankers and the Rothschilds: a reference that apparently offends. Before the next act, the emcee apologizes for any disrespect toward Jews. Even among friends, we bruise so easily.

What is wrong with this country?

We have lost our proportion and balance.

The advertising mantra of insufficiency makes us insatiably hungry.

The media drumbeat of fear masks our relative safety.

We cannot differentiate petty annoyances, micro aggressions, and first-world problems from true threats.

We cannot acknowledge that although everyone's problems are real; not everyone's problems are critical. My problems—however defined, however felt—are always critical.

We cannot yield to another. Deference is a sign of weakness rather than politeness or concern.

———

The house band retakes the stage. They riff mean Crosby, Stills & Nash covers. Grey-haired ex-hippies flood into the aisles and rock out to "Carry On." For a fleeting moment, the Unitarian Church is Fillmore South, bright and hot. Ladies and gents shake down like it's 1968, like they hold the answer of peace and love in their hands. They jive on an elevated plane; post-election, post-hunger, post-race, post-strife, post-division. They boogie-down to a heightened consciousness. An alternative lyric rises in my own head, less easy to dance, more poetic, a riff off Paul Simon's "American Tune." Of all the roads I've been traveling on, I can't help but wonder, what went wrong.

What is wrong with this country?

We live better than any 18th-century king.

We have more comforts than our founders could imagine.

We hoard our abundance rather than share; fear devours our goodness

We are fat cats starving.

If we all learned to listen before we spoke,
that would take us in a good direction.
I can't say I always do that myself, but I try.
—Andy Archer, Charleston Preservation Society, Charleston, SC

Vicksburg, MS—December 2, 2016, 7:00 p.m.

"When was the last time you changed your mind on a major issue?"

Kelle Barfield's question, in the middle of our chili supper—the supper where I learn that the key to perfect cornbread (moist interior with thin-crisp crust) is to preheat the cast iron skillet sizzling hot—stops me mid-bite. Kelle's been a writer for decades, from *Southern Living* to the International Atomic Energy Commission. Her son Waid is a recent graduate of UT Austin, taking a gap year before law school. We share food around the large kitchen table in the impressive house that the Barfield family built themselves. I describe my tour of Vicksburg National Military Park, graced by so many Southern spirits. Kelle explains Vicksburg's civil engineering tradition owing to its key navigational position on the Mississippi River. Waid bemoans the tenor of our political discourse. "Ideally, debate is an effort to shape opinions and find common ground. If the future is 'my opinion versus your opinion' and one is right, we are not going in a good direction."

Kelle recommends Rachel Botsan's TED talk about the demise of institutional trust and the rise of trusting strangers; why we're wary of bankers and politicians but invite itinerant cyclists into our home for dinner. She wants to explore speech's complement. "I am interested in studying listening. People are not trained to listen." She describes how we become entrenched in our ideas, often formed by incomplete or inaccurate information; how we stop accepting new input. By any standard, it's a rich dinner conversation. But when Kelle asks, "When was the last time you changed your mind on a major issue?" our discussion notches up.

For over a year, I have been listening, absorbing what I see and hear, consciously trying to withhold judgment. I'm not fully objective—I am human—though I strive to find value in every point of view. But if we're ever going to slow the centrifugal forces pulling our nation apart and reverse them toward centripetal unity, some of us, all of us, are going to have to shift our opinions, to change our minds. This will require psychological evolution, to move beyond confirmation bias and other tribal-think tactics to embrace a wider realm of the possible. It will also require compromise. We'll have to reframe our best interest, to yield ground in the here and now in exchange for greater long-term progress.

Kelle's question challenges me, the guy accustomed to asking. Have I've changed my mind? I realize that I have. My attitude about state's rights has bent; they need to be both stronger and more clearly articulated. My ideas about immigration have congealed; we ought to institute a guest worker program. I used to consider loans as fixed obligations to be repaid; now I see how debt strengthens the heavy hand of power. I used to crave a society rooted in meritocracy; now I believe we need to define ourselves and distribute our prosperity according to who we are, not what we do. That's a particularly hard nut for a guy whose upward mobility sprouted from higher education and professional status. Kelle's question floods my brain with ideas. No sooner does one fly into my head than I peck at its faults and inconsistencies. Still, each amorphous concept shelters a kernel of direction, realization that my previous position was either too narrow or too vague. By the time dinner is over I'm unsure what I believe. Yet I'm buoyed by the prospect that if I can evolve and change as an individual, so too can our society.

Which is not to say that we will walk off, hand in hand, in peace and love anytime soon. Having just elected a man of many attributes, of which reconciliation is not one, we Americans are going to inflict new rancor upon ourselves before we redirect toward consensus.

Americans want cures, not healing.
—Grandmother Korn, Mormon settler to California, Santa Maria, CA

Bentonville, AR—November 18, 2016, 7:00 p.m.

The further I travel the more I marvel that these United States are still cobbled together as one country. Any map illustrates conflict in all directions; the political map of two blue coasts slashed by a red middle; the economic map that mirrors these same contours; the land-use map of government-owned property that the West wants to log and mine and graze, that the East wants to preserve; the water-wars map that differentiates the hydrated haves from the thirsty have-nots; the geological map of shrinking coastlines and rising tides. Yet of all the different ways we map our divided nation, the granddaddy of divisions, the Mason-Dixon line, is still the most-hard felt.

Before I begin my journey, I know little about the South. More than a year later, I know the South is beautiful; the people engaging and hospitable; the food superior to any other region. I appreciate the South, though I don't come anywhere near understanding it.

My third foray into Dixie begins in Bentonville, Arkansas, a place I barely consider the South. But there he stands, in the center of the downtown square, a Rebel soldier, rifle proud, on a granite pedestal grounded by the word "CONFEDERATE" in block letters.

The math behind this memorial is instructive. Arkansas became a state on June 15, 1836. Less than 25 years later, May 6, 1861, Arkansas seceded. It was readmitted to the Union on June 22, 1868; 40 years after that, in 1908, the citizens of Bentonville erected the confederate statue, where it has stood for over 100 years: a tribute to a way of life that lasted a mere generation, more than a 150 years ago.

Actually, the statue doesn't commemorate a way of life. Benton County was never a stronghold of slavery. At its apex, fewer than 400 slaves resided here, less than a single plantation's worth along the Mississippi delta, far fewer than the over 1,000 Benton County men who lost their lives defending it. The statue doesn't represent any reality. It represents a romantic vision of a lost cause and a time gone. The statue isn't really about the Civil War at all. By 1908 it's about the emergence of Jim Crow, about making sure Negroes know their place in this poor Ozark town long before it became the seat of the world's largest corporation.

I appreciate the statue as a piece of art and history, but I cannot understand the point of honoring an ignoble heritage that never even existed. I'm a Yankee. We are too practical. We move on.

Branford, FL—December 16, 2016, 10:00 a.m.

The Florida panhandle is an unexpected delight: needle thin pines and weeping cypress; mythic morning fog on the sleepy Gulf; bright midday sun; crystalline sand beaches. Still, I am tired. Not from cycling. Five hours a day on the bike remains the most rejuvenating activity in the world. I am weary of my question; the accumulated overload of more than a year's responses. I stop on the Suwannee River Bridge at Branford and stare into the lethargic water. Though I have no mammy or pappy, I miss my own folks at home.

I've been trying to keep conclusions at bay, to pretend that as long as I keep cycling, keep gathering new data, I don't have to think about what I've learned, to ponder what comes next. But I am only four tomorrows away from dismounting Tom for the train ride north. My mind cannot compartmentalize itself from what I'll carry into the tomorrows after that.

As I pedal on to Gainesville I let my mind spin over what I've learned, both mundane and profound. I concoct this list of 11 lessons learned: the standard 10 plus a bonus.

1. People in the United States are nicer, and happier, than the media reports. Happiness is not dramatic. It doesn't sell.

2. People who chase a dream other than the almighty dollar are happy: every one of them.

3. Sustainability ends at the bathroom door. Everyone's bathroom is full of plastic bottles of weird colored liquids.

4. People who don't have a TV are happier than people who do.

5. People who leave on their TVs 24/7 either channel Fox News or HGTV. Depends whether they're motivated by fear or possessions.

6. Everyone says "yes" in Saint Louis. I request interviews at four institutions, and make three host requests. Every one of them invites me in.

7. People in the Midwest want to be liked. They tell you they are the nicest people in the world. People in the Mountain States don't give a damn if you like them. They know their land is beautiful; they just want you to move on.

8. Only Southerners use the word "honor." They say it with grace and focus. "It is an honor to meet you." Makes my head swirl.

9. The oddest region of our country is New England. Since I am from there, how was I to know? Terrible weather, somber people, many more college graduates than veterans, and hardly any Walmarts.

10. Asking for something is not a weakness; it is an opportunity.

11. The slower a person travels, the more patient he becomes. Time shifts. Expectations ease. Anger abates. Sleep rejuvenates. Food satisfies. Living slow nourishes the mind, the body, and the soul.

People were surprised that we overturned the death penalty in this state.
We just focused on three basic issues: the death penalty is unfair, expensive,
and rooted in vengeance rather than justice.
    —Byron Peterson, Nebraskans for Alternatives to the Death Penalty, Scottsbluff, NE

Tallahassee, FL—December 14, 2016, 7:00 p.m.

Five years ago I began a list of interesting names and stories in case I ever rode my bike to the 48 states. Those stories became pushpins on the map that established my route. I have only one left: Kate Grosmaire, Tallahassee, Florida. I don't know Kate; I don't have a phone number or email address. I send a message to her Facebook profile. The morning I wake in Amre's apartment, Kate replies. I lay over a day in Florida's capital so we can meet. Best layover all trip.

The movie trailer of the plot goes something like this. Conor McBride, a 19-year-old college student, shoots his girlfriend, Ann Grosmaire, in the face at close range on Palm Sunday. He leaves her for dead, drives around in a daze, turns himself in to police, and is taken into custody. Ann is found, alive. She survives on life support in the ICU. Her parents, Kate and Andy, hold vigil at the hospital. Julie and Michael McBride, Conor's parents, visit and express their grief. Ann deteriorates. On Good Friday the Grosmaires pull the plug. Ann dies. Conor is charged with first-degree murder. Kate Grosmaire visits Conor in jail. And she forgives him.

That's the hook that elevates this story above its CSI cousins. Kate Grosmaire forgives Conor McBride after he kills her daughter. Thus begins the story of how one family bends the arc of our judicial system from revenge and punishment to redemption and restitution.

"Forgiveness is not a pardon. Forgiveness is not reconciliation. You owe me a debt you cannot pay, but I'm not collecting the debt." Six years after the crime and the forgiveness, after interviews, television spots, and a memoir, Kate is well practiced in speaking about forgiveness.

Kate invites me for an evening. "We'll meet at our house because Andy has a deacon meeting at church and won't be home until late." Julie and Michael bring the food. "These look sweet, but are actually savory," Julie explains as she passes a platter of toast points. We discuss the changing pattern of deer sightings in their wooded neighborhood; Kate shows off her blue ribbon–winning wax block. I struggle to fathom the domestic warmth these two couples share.

Supper is hearty soup with crusty bread and crisp salad. When Andy arrives we pull another chair up to the table. Conor calls during dinner; everyone chimes in on the events of his day and prospects for a new job. That he's calling from prison doesn't even warrant mention.

As I listen to anecdotes of rescue dogs and honeybees between these longtime good friends, the sordid event that binds them doesn't lurk beneath the surface. They have brought it into the light, acknowledged it, addressed it, and forgiven it. Which enables the Grosmaires and the McBrides to move beyond it.

When Kate and Andy found forgiveness in their hearts and interceded on behalf of a troubled young man, they championed the first case of restorative justice in the state of Florida, a concept that turns our legal system on its head. Traditional criminal procedures freeze relationships at the point of the crime; they isolate victims from perpetrators under the guise of protection. This hardens all parties. Restorative justice brings perpetrators and victims together in structured settings to negotiate punishment and restitution. This does not mean that punishment will be lighter. Rather, punishment can be more appropriate. Perpetrators are forced to confront their actions; victims have the opportunity to move beyond powerlessness.

"Anger is the easiest emotion to be in touch with, but we seek more. We understand that we need turmoil in order to bring us to the point we have to change. We cannot keep turning people away. We have to change."

Restorative justice provided an avenue for the Grosmaires to forgive—not pardon—Conor. Although Florida's penal system contains no mechanism to do this, a creative interpretation of the pre-plea conference allowed the Grosmaires, McBrides, Conor, and a collection of attorneys and restorative justice advocates to meet face to face and discuss the young man's fate. The result—a 20-year sentence without probation plus stipulations on community service and speaking about teen dating violence—is less creative than restorative justice in other jurisdictions might allow, yet is far different than any doled out to a murderer in Florida.

Conor is not the only person who's benefitted from restorative justice. Kate and Andy are lifted above being collateral victims of his violence; Julie and Michael's isolating burden as parents of a murderer is ameliorated. Conor's crime does not just affect one young woman and one young man. It reflects our culture and affects the entire community.

Kate explains, "If enough people start to think in a certain way, it spreads beyond them. If six million people believe something, it can spread to the collective conscientiousness. We had never heard of restorative justice, but we have learned and we are spreading the word. Andy and I are not yet the snowball at the top of the hill, but we're one of the people who are going to understand forgiveness in a way we cannot understand now.

"The core of what I believe is 'God is love.' If you are good with that, I am good with you. I feel like forgiveness has allowed me to transcend most of humanity. I reflected on that for a very long time. You become a teacher, you share your story, but you occupy a place that few other people do."

I have never been challenged as Kate Grosmaire has; I do not know if I could rise to forgiveness. I can only pray for such grace. But I find solace and strength in her example. I have traversed this glorious land in search of a positive path toward tomorrow. I am fortunate to find it in Tallahassee.

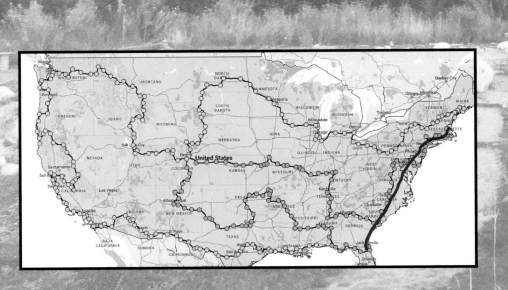

PART FOUR
BALANCE

Cycling puts us in a
fundamental rhythm and connection
to the natural environment.
We need more of that.

Nicolas Kazan, writer, Reno, NV

219

There is always another tomorrow. It never ends.
—Naomi Holloway, motel clerk, Brewster, WA

Jacksonville, FL—December 20, 2016, 9:00 p.m.

I bicycle 20,733 miles over 397 days, bunk with 267 different hosts, post 464 individual profiles and document thousands of responses to "How will we live tomorrow" My pedaling ends at the Amtrak Station in Jacksonville, Florida, a squat building in a downtrodden industrial district five miles west of downtown's gleam. Two trains a day each way: Miami or DC.

I arrive early, well before dark. Kendall, the counter clerk who doubles as custodian and baggage handler, is a friendly, handsome guy, a Navy vet who circled our world from danger point to danger point and then returned to his hometown. When I present my query, the fresh-creased man stands for a moment beside his housekeeping cart. "We need to respect each other." I figure Kendall's given more respect than he's gotten. Likely he's stronger for that.

For hours, I'm the only passenger in the waiting area. I type away, unaware of when the trickle begins. Two hours before train time I look up to a quiet assembly of women slumped with shopping bags and young mothers dragging shy children. Few male passengers. Suddenly, sirens roar. Flashing lights pierce the dark glass facing the parking lot. A pair of police cars blocks the entrance. Four officers descend upon two scrawny teenagers. It's impossible not to eavesdrop. The girls are runaways. No, worse than that. Human traffic. They mumble replies to the officers' questions in a halting jumble of fear and relief. The female officer mentions grandparents, no word of a mother or a father. The police escort the waifs away, gentle, with respect.

Passengers pull shopping bags of wrapped presents closer to their seats. We sit still, in profound hush. Until a few fresh folks amble in, unaware of what transpired, and the quiet buzz of people weary even before their travel begins once again vibrates through the space.

About 10:00 p.m. the train arrives. I stroll Tom to the baggage car. Amtrak charges $10 to check a bicycle, no packing required if the passenger delivers and retrieves it himself. Five days before Christmas, I anticipate a packed train. I'm wrong. Few people ride the rails anymore. A handful of stout black women place food baskets on the seats beside them. My seatmate is a tiny grandmother from Waldo; a farmwoman with a voice so soft and an accent so thick I have to cup my ear to catch the utterances that whistle between her three teeth. Then I must pause to decipher their meaning. She's bound for North Carolina to visit her son and tend her disabled granddaughter. It's a slow conversation, but we have plenty of time. Around midnight I wish her well and shuffle across the aisle to an empty seat. I curl my knees to my chest and close my eyes. South Carolina is a dream.

When I wake, my neighbor's gone. A cold sun stretches its rays between stark trees. The train parallels a stretch of North Carolina I pedaled, which floods me with memory. I'm destined to become one of those old codgers who moistens his lips before launching into a story, "When I was on my bike trip ..." I will be such a bore.

The train slows through Cary. Main Street had been under construction when I cycled through here. I had sat in the sun and called my children before spending an afternoon in the library. The librarian suggested I visit the Paige-Walker mansion, a beautiful restoration. My country has become an idiosyncratic collage of handlebar impressions I recall with crystal clarity.

Rolling through the countryside, in full daylight, I log onto the web. I receive a new response to my question, from an army officer. He requests anonymity, of course. He is deployed, fighting ISIS, confronting terrorism, confident we are making that region more secure. Midway through his response, an essay, really, he states, "I will return home soon and will love my wife and my sons fiercely."

That single word, "fiercely" turns me off like a switch. I no longer ride my bicycle; I no longer have to chronicle people's ideas of tomorrow. The rules of the journey, to post every response I receive without edit, no longer apply. I send the serviceman an appreciative note of thanks, but his words never reach my blog. I don't ask my question of another soul. My project is complete.

From this moment I am allowed my own opinion. And I distrust the tenderness of any love described as fierce.

222

Washington, DC—December 21, 2016, 5:00 p.m.

Capital cities suffer a superiority complex. I retrieve Tom from the baggage car and we stroll through our nation's capital. I could lock him up, but then I'd have to carry or stow my panniers. Alternatively, I could take him for a ride. That doesn't appeal on a raw afternoon in the busy city. So we walk, an aimless couple meandering amidst so much limestone, granite, and pompous purpose.

Our nation's capital is unlike any other place in the United States. It's not a real city, with commerce at its core, though the former swamp is no longer countryside. Perhaps there was a time when the District of Columbia existed in balance with the rest of our nation, providing an overarching structure of stability, security, and guidance in exchange for collected tax revenues. Perhaps it will provide that role again, someday. But right now DC is a distasteful collection of aggressive suits dining on sushi and vintage wine leeched from our collective wallet. The extravagant architecture, the inflated postures struck by our elected representatives, their minions, and the legions of lobbyists who curry and preen, have more in common with the court of Louis XIV than any democracy our forefathers envisioned. No wonder most everyone beyond the Beltway deplores the place.

The real tragedy, of course, is that our form of government was devised to avoid this excess, to promote man's fairest, highest sensibility. Democracy is a wonderful concept, maybe even a viable governing model for a small community of civic-minded folks. Unfortunately, as contorted and scaled to 300 million diverse agendas, our democratic republic is simply not strong enough to ennoble our baser motives. We vote these guys into office and almost never turn an incumbent out. We pay for the fancy facades they dance behind. Washington, DC, has become the Rome of our times, except that neither Obama nor Trump can fiddle like Nero, and a city built of quarried stone cannot burn. We have no one but ourselves to blame.

My red eye train to Boston is also near empty, although riders in the Northeast are different from their southern counterparts. No picnics, no chattering about visiting relatives. Trim women in ear buds thumb smartphones and pluck yogurt raisins from neat bags. Everyone ignores each other. I rouse at Penn Station, and then sleep sound through Connecticut. The train pulls into Boston's South Station right on time. I retrieve Tom from the baggage car and we ride home: simple as that.

We do not get up in the morning and go to work.
We get up in the morning and we live.
—Chip Spencer, farmer, Marion Junction, AL

Cambridge, MA—March 8, 2017, 2:00 p.m.

One year to the day after I fly home in a back brace, I swim 36 laps in the Boston Sports Club pool. Swimming is the best exercise for my back. For 60 years my back was so sturdy I never even gave it a thought. It's not really in pain any more, just the throb of steady awareness. I channel the dull ache positively, as a memory trigger. My bicycle journey is history, but the peak experience lingers, as a soldier relives her glory, as a father cradles his firstborn. For over a year I pedaled early each day to avoid travelling in the dark. Now, I take to bed in the bleak New England winter and enjoy cycling dreams. I ascend mountains and traverse plains all night long. I wake refreshed.

My seventh grade English teacher gave us a class assignment: write a paragraph beginning with the phrase, "I am a _____." She collected our responses and read them aloud. "I am a guitar player." "I am a Catholic." "I am a helpful daughter." The class enjoyed guessing each author. The more she read, the more I squirmed. Clearly, I had misunderstood.

"I am an inpatient person." Mrs. Werner read with a quizzical voice. Mine was the only essay couched in criticism, laced with judgment. Read aloud, the words winced. I identified and renounced my perceived fault with clever superiority, a perfect kernel of my bifurcated self. Yes, I was uncoordinated, fat, and lonely—an unloved kid with skin so riddled with discomfort that I wanted out of it. But book smarts pumped me with pride that sometimes punctured through my shame. I could not wait patiently for this awkward time to pass.

Fifty years later that boy is gone. I have become a patient person. Perhaps it would have happened in due course, the inevitable wearing of time and age. But I credit Surly and Tom for helping me appreciate the moment. Automobiles take us other places; bicycles immerse us in our present.

The United States of America reminds me of my seventh grade self, oscillating between boast and loathing, so uncomfortable in our collective skin we keep moving impatiently rather than finding any comfort in where we stand. We are a continental centrifuge, ever accelerating, spinning ourselves to extremes: drug addicts craving that new high in order to feel we're alive. More and more news, more and more social media, more and more outrageous positions that fuel our differences and stomp on our commonalities. That's what centrifuges do: whirl homogenous fluid to extremities in order to break it into constituent parts. We have to stop spinning so fast. We have to slow down, congeal, come to the center. Unfortunately, there's little excitement in that.

My life has returned to its pre-bicycle rhythm. Swimming is my movement of choice, though it's claustrophobic compared to spinning the open road. Two days ago I posted my final profile, a personal response gleaned from birds on wires. Upcoming writing will require more editing and less invention. Reunions with local family and friends are grand, though they lack the adrenaline rush of knocking on an unknown door and dipping into some completely new life. Although a body cannot sustain excitement forever, the rhythms that nourished me before I cycled the lower 48 fall flat.

Just as Haiti gave me a fresh, critical perspective on my own country, traveling throughout the United States gives me a new perspective on New England. Not a flattering one. Most Americans think New England is a harsh, uppity place. By and large, they're right. People here are cold, colder than the weather, quick tempered and irritable. This was hard to recognize before, since Massachusetts is my home and I can be as big a prig as anybody. But after so many more temperate, hospitable experiences, I acknowledge that our rigid caricature, like all stereotypes, is rooted in some fact.

Consider heckling. Across our country I got heckled every few hundred miles, maybe once a week. Now I'm harassed simply riding errands. It's not just the frequency that's bothersome; it's the ugliness. Spritzing a cyclist with a water bottle is unwelcome, but there's a cleverness, a joy to the act. When a pickup driver bothers to slow down and then gas pedal a cloud of exhaust in my face, at least he's acknowledging my presence. Here, drivers simply curse me out when I extend my arm and slide left to claim dry pavement on a snow-clogged street; joggers berate my polite request to shift to the adjacent sidewalk so I can pass in the bike lane. Cambridge prides itself on bicycle infrastructure, but no amount of designated pavement can compensate naked incivility. This all stings deeper because of where it occurs: we want to think the best of our hometown.

Fortunately, the patience and courtesy I found in my travel have sunk so deep that these abrasions don't ruffle me for long. I am simply not in a rush anymore. I strive to be pleasant to everyone I meet, to give respect without measuring whether it's returned. A patient smile may be worth zilch in a kingdom whose currency is college degrees and technology, but contentment and balance are what our maddening world needs, and so that's what I practice. I balance my bicycle; I balance my consumption; I balance my contribution. Perhaps others observe my nurturing balance. Perhaps it inspires a shift in their behavior. We cannot know whom we influence, whom we enrich. We are not supposed to know.

Maybe, when I was young, I hoped that big programs, big policies, big change would makeover our world in goodness and light. I don't believe that now. We are remarkable, wounded, fallible, noble, erratic, exasperating creatures. We are evolving in a positive direction, albeit so slowly we might flame out before we achieve a higher level. We are better than our ancestors; our society is ever so modestly more equitable and just. Yet we are so much less than we ought to be. We are human.

How will we live tomorrow?

We will live like birds on a wire,
tethered to the technology that holds us above and apart
from the rest of our world.
We will balance our tenuous perch
scanning a horizon that appears ours alone,
despite sitting shoulder to shoulder with our brothers.

Thermal delights will lift us in joyous dance.
Harsh winds will drive us to sheltering roots.
We will move in concert with one another,
some leading, others lagging, clumped tight,
more afraid than we ever admit.

When the sun returns and the breeze grows calm
we will return to our wire.
Precarious balance is the price of dominion.
We will stare out on the vast expense
and imagine that we are free.
　　　　　—Paul E. Fallon, cyclist, Cambridge, MA

Images

All photos by the author unless otherwise indicated

Cover: Logo, courtesy of Chris Marston,
      Stonefish Graphics—Portland, ME
      Beach—Rye, NH
      Skyline—New York, NY
      Wabash River—Mt. Vernon, IN
      Refinery, Norco, LA
      Misty morning—Chicago, IL
      Bike sculpture—Oerlich, SD
      Cotton fields—Slaton, TX
      Grand Teton National Park—Jackson, WY
      Big Sur—CA

3: Logo, courtesy of Chris Marston,
      Stonefish Graphics—Portland, ME
      Bike sculpture—Oerlich, SD
      Cotton fields—Slaton, TX
      Grand Teton National Park—Jackson, WY
      Big Sur—CA

4: The author, courtesy of Carol Kallmeyer
      —Tulsa, OK

5: Charleston Strong—Charleston, SC

6: Subdivision—Rio Medina, TX
7: Subdivision—Rio Medina, TX
7: Route map, courtesy of Chris Marston,
      Stonefish Graphics—Portland, ME
8: Storm clouds—Chadron, NE
10: Subway—Wellington, OH
12: Yurt—Union, ME
14: Freeway—Dallas, TX

16: Pickup truck—Abington, MA
18: State Line Road—Bessemer, PA
19: Ribbon route map—Cambridge, MA
20: House, Dearborn, MI
22: Grocery store, Dearborn, MI
23: Field—Postville, IA
24: Prairie—Fargo, ND
26: Pacific coast—Florence, OR
28: Lady Bird Johnson Grove,
      Redwood National Park—Orick, CA
29: Big Tree, Redwood National Park—Orick, CA
30: Eagle Lake—Susanville, CA
32: Raisins—Fresno, CA
33: Hmong farmers—Merced, CA
34: Chicago, IL
36: West 18 St—Chicago, IL
38: McDonald's Sign—Breckenridge, TX
39: D Acres Farm—Dartmouth, NH
40: Oil Wells—Post, TX
42: Skyline, Houston, TX
45: Silver Plume, CO
46: Western slope—Loveland Pass, CO
47: Nutcrackers—Leavenworth, WA
48: Galaxy image, NASA Goddard Visitor Center
      —Greenbelt, MD
50: Interior, Boston Avenue Methodist Church
      —Tulsa, OK
51: Twelve Tribes Community—Cambridge, NY
52: Church of Jesus Christ of Latter-day Saints
      —Orem, UT
53: Catskills—Knox, NY
54: Saguaro—Stone Cabin, AZ
56: US 95—Quartzite, AZ
57: Kiko Auction—Edinburg, OH
59: Scrap truck—Carson City, NV
60: Roadside attraction—Albion, ME
62: Scrapyard—Santa Ana, CA
63: Scrapyard—Santa Ana, CA
64: Bicycle boneyard—Missoula, MT
66: Simply Bulk, Longmont, CO
67: Oneida lanyard—Williamsport, PA

CPSIA information can be obtained at www.ICGtesting.com
Printed in the USA
LVIW01n0815130218
566386LV00019B/212